LEADERSHIP

TEXAS HOLD'EM STYLE

ANDREW J. HARVEY, Ed.D.
RAYMOND E. FOSTER, MPA

ISBN: 1-4196-7438-2
ISBN-13: 978-1419674389

Visit www.booksurge.com to order additional copies.

ACKNOWLEDGEMENTS

No one works alone or accomplishes anything without the significant support of others. Both Andrew and Raymond would like to thank a number of people who directly, or indirectly, assisted with this work. First, we would like to thank Dr. James Rocheleau and Dr. Elizabeth Pastores-Palffy of the Union Institute and University. Before Dr. Rocheleau as the dean of California hired us, neither knew the other. His involvement goes well beyond the simple act of hiring two faculty members. Dr. Rocheleau engenders the spirit of innovation. It was his leadership that brought Andrew and Raymond to talk about leadership, leading to this work. We sincerely thank him for his continued leadership at the university. As the Assistant Dean in the Los Angeles Center of the Union Institute and University, Dr. Palffy has been key in creating a supportive environment for faculty growth. While they both have distinct styles of leadership, both inspired portions of this work.

Finally, we would like to thank Raymond's wife, Maria Elena Foster, for editing the first draft.

ANDREW J. HARVEY

Andrew J. Harvey served in law enforcement for 25 years, the last 12 as a captain with a Southern California police agency. He holds bachelor's and master's degrees from Cal State Los Angeles, and an educational doctorate in the field of organizational leadership from Pepperdine University. He is a graduate of the FBI National Academy, the California POST Command College, the West Point Leadership Program, and is recognized in California as a master instructor.

Dr. Harvey is an experienced college educator, currently serving as a professor at the University of Phoenix, and as a faculty advisor at the Union Institute and University. He has been published numerous times in national and international publications. He is a recognized expert in leadership and career development, and has served as an instructor in command leadership at the Los Angeles Police Department Academy. He has appeared as a leadership authority on television and radio, including the internationally-broadcast Bloomberg Business Television Show, and the nationally syndicated Joey Reynolds Radio Show.

His first book, *The Call to Lead: How Ordinary People Become Extraordinary Leaders*, received national attention. The book shows the way for leaders toward ethical and competent leadership. Through his company, Andrew Harvey Seminars, he provides leadership training and consulting to individuals and organizations throughout the nation.

Dr. Harvey can be reached through his website at www.thecalltolead.com or via e-mail at aharvey6@earthlink.net.

RAYMOND E. FOSTER

Raymond E. Foster was a sworn member of the Los Angeles Police Department for 24 years. He retired in 2003 at the rank of Lieutenant. He holds a bachelor's from the Union Institute and University in Criminal Justice Management and a Master's Degree in Public Financial Management from California State University, Fullerton. He has completed his doctoral course work. Raymond is a graduate of the West Point Leadership program and has attended law enforcement, technology and leadership programs such as the National Institute for Justice, Technology Institute, Washington, DC.

Raymond is currently a part-time lecturer at California State University, Fullerton and the Union Institute and University. He has experience teaching upper division courses in law enforcement, public policy, technology and leadership. Raymond is an experienced author who has published numerous articles in a wide range of venues including magazines such as Government Technology, Mobile Government, Airborne Law Enforcement Magazine, and Police One. He has appeared on the History Channel and radio programs in the United States and Europe as subject matter expert in technological applications in law enforcement.

His first book, "Police Technology (Prentice Hall, July 2004)" is used in over 100 colleges and universities nationwide. Raymond has two additional contracts with Prentice Hall to publish works on global terrorism and an introduction to policing. As an outgrowth of his writing, Raymond maintains two websites and acts as the editor of a monthly newsletter with a growing subscriber base.

Raymond can be reached through the Criminal Justice Forum at www.criminaljustice-online.com or by email at raymond@hitechcj.com.

DEDICATION

Andrew J. Harvey dedicates this to his wife Davida
and daughter Rachel.

Raymond E. Foster dedicates this to his children,
the next generation of leadership.
(in order of appearance)
Raymond E. Foster, Jr.
Dorothy J. Delaney
Grace E. Foster
Zachary J. Foster
Antonia (Ise) Foster

TABLE OF CONTENTS

SPADES

HEARTS

CLUBS

SPADES

Industry executives and analysts often mistakenly talk about strategy as if it were some kind of chess match. But in chess, you have just two opponents; each with identical resources, and with luck playing a minimal role. The real world is much more like a poker game, with multiple players trying to make the best of whatever hand fortune has dealt them. In our industry, Bill Gates owns the table until someone proves otherwise.

David Moschella, "Computerworld"

CHAPTER ONE
Two of Spades
Introduction and the Goal of Leadership

Gets down to what it's all about, doesn't it? Making the wrong move at the right time.

Lacy Howard, in the *Cincinnati Kid*

Just a desire to play and win never got anyone a seat at a poker table. A poker player needs chips to enter the game-a stake. When a new pastor is called to a church, a pile of chips is normally stacked up for use as the pastor chooses. They represent the good favor and support of the church people. They may be saved for a rainy day or risked in the first hand of play.

Lieth Anderson, How to Win at Parish Poker

Leaders today are facing daunting challenges in the new workplace and beyond. As Robert Tannenbaum and Warren H. Schmidr said:

[Societal changes] make effective leadership in the future a more challenging task, requiring even greater sensitivity and flexibility than was ever needed before. Today's manager is more likely to deal with employees who resent being treated as subordinates, who may be highly critical of any organizational system, who expect to be consulted and to exert influence, and who often stand on the edge of alienation from the institution that needs their loyalty and commitment. In addition, he is frequently confronted by a highly turbulent, unpredictable environment.

Most experienced leaders immediately identify with this statement. However, if you think that these are only recent problems, that is not the case. This quotation was taken from an article written over 30 years ago, in 1973.

Have leaders risen to today's challenges? Not necessarily, if you rely upon these sample evaluations of officers reputedly taken from the files of the British Royal Navy:

- His men would follow him anywhere but only out of curiosity;
- This officer reminds me of a gyroscope — always spinning at a frantic pace but not really going anywhere;

- Since my last report, he has reached rock bottom and started to dig;
- He sets low standards and then consistently fails to achieve them;
- This pilot should not be allowed to fly below 250 feet;
- Works well when under constant supervision and cornered like a rat in a trap; and,
- This man is depriving a village somewhere of an idiot.

These extreme examples of military officers showcase how leaders may not have learned how to lead, but then it is difficult to become a good leader without first having mastered the art of following. Good leaders are invariably good followers first. Leading requires sensitivity to the follower's position and the knowledge, based on experience, of what motivates a person to follow a good leader.

Leaders are faced with a myriad of challenges, many times under stressful and paradoxical conditions. These challenges include managing multiple priorities, balancing competing concerns, and the demand to accomplish more with fewer resources.

In seemingly simpler times, President Dwight Eisenhower demonstrated the art of leadership with a short piece of string. He would put it on a table and say, "pull it, and it'll follow wherever you wish; push it, and it will go nowhere at all." This illustration showed the importance of "leading from the front."

Through experience, a leader learns which techniques are successful and which are not. Using pure positional authority, you can get people to do things to a certain point. There are techniques, such as fear or negative reinforcement, which make the use of positional authority work – usually in the short-run. A good leader may use any of these techniques, depending on the situation and the people involved. However, if this is the only way that you can gain compliance, you will likely never reach the top mantle of leadership.

Through such techniques, you may be able to control people's bodies and even their minds to some degree. To win their hearts, you must go much further. No amount of authority, coercion, or fear will make people follow, invest with their heart or strive for excellence. Leadership is indeed the art of demonstrating to people that it is in their best interests to follow you, oftentimes in directions and to places they might not ordinarily be inclined to go. You must be willing to coach, mentor, support, and gently guide people toward the path you want them to follow.

Andrew lives near the route of the world-famous Rose Parade. Each New Year's Day, should he so choose, he can watch the parade on television then walk a couple of miles up the street and see…the arrival of the Rose Parade. This is so because that is how long it takes for the parade to make it over to his side of town. Should he be so inclined, he could run out in the street in front of the lead pace car and begin marching. He wouldn't be out there long before security gave him the boot, but he would always be able to talk about the time he "led the Rose Parade." But did he lead it, or did he merely get out in front of a group of people who were already traveling in a predetermined direction? Jumping to the front and claiming to be a leader does not make it so. Persuading and influencing people to voluntarily change their direction based upon your skills and their trust in you is leadership.

We have chosen poker and its many variations, as well as card play in general, as a means to demonstrate the art of leadership in action. The cards, the suits, the games and strategy are metaphors with which we paint a picture of leadership. Like all art, there is an underlying element of science – a painter chooses colors, the musician notes, and the leader chooses actions. Moreover, we have worked to weave current academic research, theories, models and practical experience into the art and science of leadership. For instance, in poker, each player draws from the same 52-card deck. Yet, some players are extraordinary in their application of those randomly chosen cards. Often times leaders find themselves thrust into a new unit or given a new mission. The poker player and the leader share the same dilemma – they can't choose the resources they were given, they have to play those cards. Poker and card play are the rich metaphor from which we draw lessons about leadership.

> **The companion website for this book is – www.pokerleadership.com**

As you journey through this book will you find a few chapters wherein we do not provide a metaphor to poker or card play. Frankly, there were concepts that were important in developing leadership skills for which we could find no clear poker or card play analogy. In truth, in the two or three spots where the analogy wasn't clear, we could have stretched it. We could have forced it into place, but we knew you would know. Perhaps, that is the first lesson of leadership with an actual poker analogy – you can only bluff so many times before your followers begin to think you are bluffing all the time. Just as you don't want to lose credibility as a leader, we don't want to risk our credibility as leaders, educators and authors.

As we prepared this book we realized there was a lot of material we would like to include, or at the least make available to you. But our space was limited. As a solution, we have developed a companion website to this book. As you progress through the book you will see that it is completely integrated with the website. For instance, when we look at team building we will refer you to the website where we have outlined a number of valuable team building exercises. Moreover, we are committed to continually updating the website and providing it to you as an additional forum for leadership and discussion about leadership issues. You can visit the site at any time – www.pokerleadership.com.

Leadership is foremost about working with people, and as such, it is perhaps more art than science. The difference between management and leadership will be traversed throughout this book. For now though, a good reference point may be as follows: Management is the development of work through people; and, leadership is the development of people through work.

The goal of leadership is to get people to work willingly toward accomplishing the goals of the organization. It is only through the pulling of Eisenhower's string that people will follow with their greatest effort, but you must first convince them through your actions that you truly do have their best interests at heart. If you are able to do this, they will tend to follow you anywhere.

It is toward that end this book is written: to provide current and aspiring leaders with the knowledge and skills necessary to effectively ply the craft of leadership. We want to demonstrate that you may not always be dealt the best hand, but you can learn to play that hand quite well.

Leadership involves remembering past mistakes, an analysis of today's achievements, and a well-grounded imagination in visualizing the problems of the future.

Stanley Allyn

CHAPTER TWO
Three of Spades
Vision

*Poker is the game closest to the western conception of life, where life and thought
are recognized as intimately combined, where free will prevails over philosophies of
fate or of chance, where men are considered moral agents and where - at least in the
short run - the important thing is not what happens but what people think happens.*

John Luckacs, *Poker and the American Character* (1963)

The first and foremost responsibility of leaders is to have a vision of where
they want to take their organizations. You certainly wouldn't sit at a poker table
without the vision of winning the game. This is not something one can find in a
book, be it this one or any other. It must emanate naturally from the heart and
mind. A skillful poker player without the vision of winning will miss the "tells"
or subtle clues in the other "player's actions. The player will miss opportunities
and ultimately succumb to his or her lack of vision by losing. In an organization,
if the leader does not possess this vision, the company will quickly become a head-
less horse, galloping in all different directions but not really getting anywhere.
Although it is fine to seek out as much information about the organization as
possible, the leader must intrinsically have a firm sense of direction.

Wild Card A tell is any habit or behavior that gives other players
more information about your hand than they would
have simply from your play. For instance, you might unconsciously play
with your chips when you have a strong hand. Or, perhaps you notice
that another player blinks a lot whenever he has a strong hand.

If leaders cannot create a compelling vision for the organization, their
leadership is seriously impaired. Your vision does not have to be too grand or
lofty, but you must be clear, at least in your own mind, of where you perceive the
destiny of the corporation to lie. Your vision should be meaningful and concrete

7

so that it is easy for people to rally behind. It must also be credible in the sense that people believe it is possible to achieve.

A vision statement expresses the aspirations of the organization. It identifies the direction of the organization, what it hopes to become, and the principles it will follow to achieve its goals. It should encompass the core beliefs and values of the organization.

Within this vision, you should create a type of guide as to how your organization will conduct itself: how customers will be served; how employees will be treated; how the organization will carry out its social or environmental responsibilities; and, how the company will be structured. The vision reflects the reason for the formation of the organization and possibly even the industry.

Formulating a corporate vision requires an assessment of the organization's history and culture: the expectations of the stockholders, employees, customers and suppliers; and, an appreciation of the place the organization occupies in the context of greater society. These factors, plus the societal imperatives, should guide the formulation of a corporate vision. Increasingly, leaders are incorporating faith-based concepts into their vision. Issues of corporate responsibilities to preserve and protect the environment, enhance the communities they occupy, fulfill social responsibilities to the disadvantaged, and provide a family-oriented work environment reflect the increasingly important aspects of social accountability and influence.

Envisioning your organization's future begins by combining your mind and heart. It is what you know and what you believe expressed concretely. It is a supremely creative, yet somewhat simple process. Think of a box. The box in your mind is different from the box in Andrew's or Raymond's mind. Before you describe the box, turn it over in your mind. Move it around, upside down, open it, and change the color. This is the mind part of the process. The heart process involves creating a future history for your box. Where will it go? What will it be used for? How will other people see it? The mind creates the state, but your heart creates the action.

One of your authors, Andrew, has worked for many years helping people with career development and promotional opportunities. One of the exercises he typically has people engage in is the development of a first-rate resume. This doesn't sound particularly innovative, but here's the twist: he has them create a resume that represents their career five years into the future! This exercise is often difficult to complete but very productive in the sense that, when people complete their future resume, they are creating somewhat of a vision for themselves. There are many creative ways in which people or organizations can create their visions. This example is but one way of approaching such an endeavor.

A vision serves to unify the organization with a shared direction. This gives a sense of commitment and focus to every member of an organization and encourages them to fulfill the aspirations of the vision. A purposeful direction also gives individuals confidence because they know where they are headed. A strong vision statement can be used for planning and problem solving by both employees and leaders. It lets every member know what the priorities of the organization are and what principles guide all decisions. When conflicts arise, the vision statement can be looked upon as a "true north" reference point; a guide that shows the destination of the company and the means it employs in order to reach that ideal.

A wise leader incorporates multiple aspects into the vision. It becomes a guiding force to incorporate societal concerns, the well-being of employees, and sustainable growth in a long-term plan. Often, leaders spend weeks wrestling with the sometimes contradictory demands of various corporate and societal imperatives. In the end, the leader may make a choice that results in compromise. Intense meditation often facilitates this arduous process. A focus group of key employees, officers, directors, and advisors can be used as a sounding board for the evolving vision.

At some point, the formulation phase must transition into the adoption phase. The leader must become the foremost advocate of the vision; it must be definite, defined, and delineated. The mind and soul of the leader must be fully committed and it becomes his or her "mantra" to the organization.

Leadership begins when the executive can "own" the corporate vision, articulate it clearly, and passionately advocate for it.

A leader must personally "own" the vision before attempting to incorporate it into the organization. A leader must also be passionate about this vision, for it is not likely that it will sustain itself. Without a vision, an organization may become rudderless and end up following the personal whims and quirks of the leader.

Once you have a clear vision, the hard part begins: communicating it to the organization so that everyone understands it. In this aspect, vision in poker is exactly the opposite of vision in organizations. In poker, you vision is personal; not to be communicated. No advantage is given to the other players because, if they know your vision, they see your tell, they deduce your play and block your vision. In organizations, visions must be strongly communicated.

Andrew worked for someone who he thought had an organizational vision, although the leader was not able to effectively articulate the vision. Over time, it became evident that articulation was not the problem. Rather, the problem was that the vision never existed! This individual did his best to fake it, but like the player who bluffs at the wrong time or too often, his effort was ultimately futile. People will follow such a leader until they realize the real lack of vision, at which point disillusionment sets in. In poker, when you bluff too often and are unable to follow through on your play people sense your lack of coherent strategy, or a lack of vision and will begin to bet against you.

> **In discussions of great leaders, Abraham Lincoln's name invariably comes up. Leaders would do well to emulate his approach to creating and communicating a vision. Lincoln's approach to vision is interpreted in Donald T. Phillips' book, *Lincoln on Leadership*:**
> - **Provide a clear, concise statement of the direction of your organization and justify the actions you take.**
> - **Everywhere you go, at every conceivable opportunity, reaffirm, reassert, and remind everyone of the basic principles upon which your organization was founded.**
> - **Effective visions can't be forced on the masses. Rather, you must set them in motion by means of persuasion.**
> - **Harness your vision through implementation of your own personal leadership style.**

Many people have worked for bosses who did not have clear visions for the organization. As a result, the employees end up trying to please the boss on a day-to-day basis without an idea of the larger goals or long-term direction of the organization. This creates a "fire department" group where the most important thing is the current task. Workers are not directing their actions to serve a long-term direction or higher purpose. If a leader cannot effectively articulate a compelling vision, the result is the same as not having one at all. Being able to effectively communicate ideas is as important as having them.

In their superb book, *The Leadership Challenge*, Jim Kouzes and Barry Posner address the importance of leaders sharing their vision with an organization:

> "Leadership vision is necessary but insufficient for an organization to move forward with purpose toward a common destination. As important, if not more so, is the ability to communicate that vision so that others come to see what the leader sees. Followers, in fact, have no idea what a leader's vision is until the leader describes it."

The vision needs to be effectively communicated to the organization in a variety of ways and repeated frequently. The idea is to use multiple and rich mediums to communicate your vision. A simple memo of what the vision is may be a good start, but it doesn't end there. Personal communication of the vision by the leader is mandatory, both in groups and individually. Examples should be used to provide further illustration. Metaphors, analogies, models, or even humor can all be used to make the vision understandable. Part of the responsibility of management is to constantly be aware of the vision; leaders must restate, refresh, remind, and repeat the vision often. The vision must become as clear in the follower's heart and mind as it is in the leader's.

Repeating the vision so many times should not be boring for the leader who truly believes the message. At this point, remember that there will still be people in the organization who have not heard the message, have forgotten it, or don't understand how it applies to them. You must be passionate in your communication of the vision. Just when you can hardly stand to say it again, there will be someone in the organization who is hearing it for the first time. Just like a good teacher, leaders tell and retell their lesson; they emphasize and persuade, convince and illuminate everyone in the organization. Each repetition of the vision is like a new hand in a long game. You must play each hand skillfully. You must communicate your vision each and every time as if it is the first and most important time.

Once you feel you have effectively articulated your vision, then missions, values, goals, and objectives must be identified and communicated in order to support the vision. This is hard work, but it produces results and will serve as the organization's emotional and practical foundation for further work efforts.

In *The Secret of a Winning Culture*, Larry E. Senn and John Childress make an astute observation about vision. They state, "A compelling vision consists of two elements: a future-state that captures our imagination and a passionate desire to reach it."

This point is illustrated in a story about Walt Disney's approach to building Disneyland. His highly competent planners and engineers had laid out a precise plan for what would be built and in what order. There was a logical progression so that one area's completion would flow naturally into the next. Within this plan, the centerpiece castle was to be built last.

Walt Disney changed this plan and had the castle built first, over the objection of his staff. His reason can be found in his vision. He wanted the castle to be built first so that everyone working on the remainder of the project would be able to see it. In his view, the castle was the tangible example of the magic kingdom he had in mind; it was the bricks-and-mortar realization of his vision. What a great example of communicating one's vision in a most unique way.

In his book, *Managing People is like Herding Cats*, Warren Bennis takes note of the importance of vision and the necessary follow-up once the vision is identified:

"Executives must not just articulate a simple and compelling vision, but they must take this vision into account when doing everything that they do – when thinking about recruiting and reward systems, when considering empowerment, when changing the structure, when pursuing new markets, and when making decisions. The only way a leader is going to translate vision into reality – an ability that is the essence of leadership – is to anchor policies, practices, procedures, and systems that will bring in people and empower them to implement the vision."

Developing a persuasive vision, articulating it perpetually, and incorporating it into the organizational culture are not easy tasks. However, if accomplished correctly, each person will know what needs to be done. Most of those who are working in contradiction to the vision will stand out. Then, these individuals can be coached and counseled to work toward the vision. If this is ineffective, other measures may become necessary including letting go of those who are impediments to the realization of the vision.

VISION CHECKLIST

It is imperative that a leader has a strong vision in order to successfully guide an organization. Here is a list of the most essential elements of a fully developed corporate vision:

- It can be expressed in simple terms;
- Everyone in the organization can understand it;
- It is concrete, and its achievement can be measured;
- It is credible and feasible;
- It considers the "bigger picture" or how the organization fits into society; and,
- It is capable of pervading into every policy, procedure, and action the organization takes.

On the companion website at www.pokerleadership.com, you can find a page listing stellar examples of visions from a variety of organizations.

If you don't know where you're going, any road will get you there.
Cheshire Cat in Alice's Adventures in Wonderland

The very essence of leadership is that you have to have a vision. It's got to be a vision you can articulate clearly and forcefully on every occasion. You can't blow an uncertain trumpet.

Father Theodore Hesburgh, University of Notre Dame

CHAPTER THREE
Four of Spades
Clear Direction

The entire table can't help but hear him say, "I'd just like to know one thing - what is the biggest difference between playing 100-200 and 10-20?" I look at him and say, "The limit - this is a different limit," and he gives me an uncomprehending look and then smiles because he thinks I'm joking and says again, "No, really, I mean what's the major difference in play in these games?" And I say, "The chips are different - these chips are worth more money." And I say it completely deadpan and now he thinks I'm taking the piss out of him and he wipes the smile off his face. I see Johnny trying hard not to laugh. "You see if we were playing 10-20 we would be using red chips, but we're not." Everybody thinks I'm trying to make a fool out this guy, but I'm just saying the only completely honest thing that I can. But it's not what this guy wants to hear. I want to shake him. I want to shout, "Look at me! Listen to me! There is no difference in play!!" But I don't say that, I just repeat in a small voice, "This is a higher limit. The game is exactly the same as 10-20 but we use different chips.

Jesse May from *Shut Up and Deal*

Not providing clear direction is one of the most common mistakes a leader can make. Followers want to know what is expected of them and when the task in question must be completed. They also want to know any restrictions or parameters up front so they do not go in the wrong direction and waste valuable time. Simply put, followers, like players, want to know the rules of the game.

Many followers have shared stories in which they finished a long-term project only to be told by their leader, "Well, that's not exactly what I was looking for." The leader did not bother to clearly articulate what was wanted so the followers were left without guidelines.

Another version of this is the leader who fails to keep people informed. As an example, years ago Andrew was given a major project to complete. The project involved statistical research and developing a variety of charts and graphs. After working on the assignment for several weeks, Andrew submitted the project. Without the least hint of remorse or regret, the leader advised Andrew that the direction had changed and the project was no longer needed. Not communicating that changes in projects or policies have occurred wastes time. Far worse, it demonstrates a lack of respect for your followers.

Leaders should be as clear as possible about what is desired from a follower when a task is assigned. If a leader is not clear on the goals of a project, it should not be assigned. It is unproductive and disrespectful to have people making frantic efforts to please you, when you, the leader, don't even know what you want. The "I'll know it when I see it" philosophy just doesn't work. This is not a window-shopping excursion where you can browse around until something catches your eye. Sometimes it seems that the delegation of projects is an effort to keep people busy. This is a symptom of a larger problem of human-resource planning. Leaders have a responsibility to not waste people's time or corporate resources.

Once the task is clear in your mind, you should identify when you need the project accomplished. Don't set meaningless or false deadlines. Give your follower a fair and realistic goal for completion. Once you receive the project, don't let it sit on your desk for six months. There are countless complaints from people about such actions. It usually sounds like this: "I busted my butt to get this thing done on time and then it sits on his desk for six months with no action! That's the last time I'm going to do that." One of the greatest ways to show respect for people is to respect their time. If you impose a deadline, make sure you do your part when the person meets that deadline. Let the person know in the beginning if there are restrictions on how the task is to be accomplished. This saves time and gives people additional confidence in the job they are performing.

A leader must be clear on how the goals of an organization are to be accomplished. Some leaders are intentionally unclear in their direction. At times, being unclear has a purpose. Some individuals believe that unclear direction is a means of mentoring. They figure the less direction they give, the more people will have to fend for themselves and figure it out on their own. They feel this will help develop the follower more quickly than if the leader gave precise instructions.

This "sink-or-swim" approach has its merits but it is greatly limited. You should always make it clear what you want accomplished. If the task has a mentoring component then you obviously believe this is a new frontier for the follower. Think about the poker story at the beginning of this chapter. Should the players let the "new guy" find out the difference in the game by playing? Perhaps the new player would understand the difference between a ten dollar chip and a hundred dollar chip around the time he lost his house. There are a variety of ways to use delegation or task assignment as a means for mentoring and allowing followers the freedom to express their talents.

As an example, you can create unambiguous, definite goals for the follower. A simple method is to provide you with a briefing at regular intervals. You are setting the table limit, defining the game that will be played and then letting the follower play their hand. Of course, by having them check in every once in a while, you ensure that you can take them off the table before they lose their house.

While talking about giving direction, let's look at the purposes of delegation. In reality, you should only delegate a project to followers for three reasons. First, and perhaps foremost, is use of delegation as a development tool. A good leader is constantly growing his or her followers to take over the leader's job. This concept is one of paramount reasons the United States Marine Corp is a successful combat organization. In the Marine Corp, every leader is responsible for teaching their job to their subordinates. In combat, a secondary leader can find that they are suddenly thrust into a position of great responsibility. If the next level of leadership is unprepared, the mission fails. Of course, your organization probably isn't going into combat. Or is it?

 A primary rule in leadership is that you can delegate authority to act, but not responsibility for the outcome.

The survival and growth of any organization depends on all members. Indeed, while you may not be going into combat, how many times has a secondary level of leadership been placed in a position of making a critical decision with customers, suppliers or other stakeholders? When you delegate tasks as a method of preparing you ensure your people are ready at critical times.

The second reason for delegation involves expertise. You may not have the expertise to do the best job. In fact, if you are a good leader you have selected and groomed first class people from diverse backgrounds and with diverse talents. Often, we give projects to people because they are the best equipped to handle them. Unlike delegation as mentoring, with this type of delegation, if you give up your seat to a better player, you let them play the hand.

A third reason involves the use of your time. Often leaders are charged with a duty that can be easily accomplished by a secondary level of leader and your time is better spent performing some other task. So, we pass the project down the chain of command. This is probably the biggest reason people tend to delegate; and, yet, considering the importance of the first two, somewhat surprising.

Wild Card **What is the difference between the chips?**
Somebody once said "There are no stupid questions,
only stupid mistakes." Perhaps for the well-rounded leader, "There
are no stupid questions, there are only teaching moments."

People have their own style of working and should be free to follow it. This approach of delegating and monitoring creates clear direction while still allowing people to figure out the process they would use on their own. Some people like to have explicit instructions and follow a plan.

Occasionally, an ambiguous leader can have more devious or strange motives. Andrew relates that he had a leader who never clarified his directions. Goals were always stated in uncertain terms. Even when aggressively pressed, this person would not come forward with more precise instructions and this was frustrating to his followers. They could not understand why a leader would not want to give clear direction.

Soon the followers noticed that when a project was successful, the leader would take the credit making sure to inform his superior of the success. On the other hand, when a project failed, the leader would claim that his subordinates had not carried out his orders properly. If reminded exactly what his directions were, he would deny ever having given such orders. Of course, he would inform his boss that his instructions had not been properly followed. This left his reputation with his superior somewhat intact as successes were attributable to his efforts and failures were blamed on incompetent subordinates who could not properly follow orders. Although he was able to temporarily gain favor with his leader, he lost all the respect and support of his people.

A leader who loses follower confidence can survive for a short period of time but eventually the followers will rebel. Leaders must have the conviction to give clear direction to their people and stand behind them regardless of resultant success or failure. Indeed, this may be one of the major reasons that some leaders are poor at communicating direction. Moreover, it is just as important to understand why you want your followers to do something, exactly what you want them to do, and making sure you communicated to them clearly.

If we don't change our direction, we're likely to end up where we're headed.

Chinese proverb

Air power is like poker. A second-best hand is like none at all - it will cost you dough and win you nothing.

Lieutenant General George Kenney,
Commanding General of the 5th Air Force

CHAPTER FOUR
Five of Spades
The Use of Power

In poker, money is power.
Alvin Clarence "Titanic" Thomson, A legend of hustles & cons, 1892-1974

Before retiring and becoming an educator and author, Andrew Harvey's previous role was as a command-level law enforcement officer, and people often asked him about the best part of his job. Without hesitation, he always answered "power." Some people were shocked by the response. At first blush, you might think that Andrew is power mad, but he explains, "Power can be used either positively or negatively. I always try my best to use power for good purposes. When power is backed with a conscience, it can have a very beneficial impact on the organization."

People have a difficult time with the word "power" because it carries potentially negative connotations. However, in the leader realm, power is the amount and type of influence the leader possesses. At the poker table, there are several different types of power. Some cards are more powerful than others. As one anonymous card player observed, "A king can do no wrong ... unless it runs into an ace." Of course, different combinations of cards, the amount of money a player possesses, his or her cards in relation to the other players, or simply the player's skill are power bases. For the leader, there are also different types or bases of power. It is important to understand the types of power and, their strengths and their weaknesses.

Let's define five of the power bases before we move further into our discussion on the use of leader power.

- **Compensatory Power** – The ability to reward team members. Rewards can be praise, cash, a corner office, a title, control over schedule and priorities, recommendations, choice of the next assignment, promotion, or any number of things. In the government service, compensatory rewards are usually recognition and special assignments.
- **Expert Power** – Knowing the task, especially when you know the task better than the followers.
- **Referent Power** – Respect of your followers. Usually developed when you have a track record of making successful decisions and you develop bonds with your followers.
- **Positional Power** – Authority based solely on your organizational ranking.
- **Connective Power** – Possession of high-level connections within the organization.

Although power can be used to impact major issues in an organization, it can also be used for the little things. Seemingly minor gestures often leave lasting and meaningful impressions. You may often have the opportunity to use your authority in positive ways to help employees do their jobs more productively. This type of support is easily recognized and valued.

For example, one day, as Andrew was walking through his organization's Records section, one of the clerks mentioned they needed an industrial-size three-hole punch for the large reams of paper they process. The one they had been using was old and in a state of disrepair. Requests had been made for a new one, but somehow these requests had been lost in the bureaucracy. Andrew left and drove to the local office supply store where he purchased a new punch, an action that due to his position needed no further approval.

When he walked into Records and presented them with it, they were stunned but very happy. He personally purchased the punch for two reasons. On a practical level, they really needed the new hole punch. More personally though, by handling their request, the Record's personnel knew that top management really did care. In the long run, this meant much more than just acquiring a new hole punch for the staff. It had an immediate effect and demonstrated a number of dimensions of power.

First, Andrew was building referent power. In the scheme of a large organization the condition of the hole punch was a minor matter. Of course, the hapless person using the punch damns the organization for their shoddy equipment and probably the treatment of staff. Andrew was building his referent power by showing he cared, using his expert power by showing he understood the importance of working equipment, and demonstrating his positional power by going out and getting the equipment. However, Andrew was not demonstrating compensatory power or connective power. Providing people with the necessary tools for their job is not a reward, nor should such action be based solely on who is involved.

Wild Card People know what can be changed and what cannot. In Texas Hold 'Em, the first two cards are about luck. They are what they are and cannot be changed. People know this. But, it is how those cards (what cannot be changed) are played against everything that is a variable. Your followers know you are playing with certain cards that cannot be changed, but they also know what you as the leader can do. The clerks knew that Andrew could not authorize a pay raise, but they also knew he had some authority over the purchase of simple, yet critical equipment.

Kouzes and Posner stated their position on the use of power in eloquent terms in *The Leadership Challenge*, noting the irony that the higher up you go in an organization, the more dependent you become on others:

"Managers who focus on themselves and are insensitive to others fail. They fail because there is a limit to what they can do by themselves. Leaders succeed when they realize that the limits to what can be accomplished are minimal if people feel strong and capable. In fact, what leaders do, as paradoxical as it may seem, is make followers into leaders. They do this by using their own power in service of others rather than in service of self."

Along with any type of power comes responsibility. The use of power is one of the biggest responsibilities of a leader. Most everyone has worked for a boss who abused power. The use of power by a leader often demonstrates the morals, ethics, and principles of the organization. Far too often, power is seen as a "perk" to provide extravagant benefits on behalf of those holding power. Sometimes, it is used to consolidate influence and stop opposition within the company. When power is abused in these ways, it can affect the integrity of the leader and the organization as a whole.

Thus, a leader must be aware of the intoxicating effects power can have. We have all seen those people whose inability to deal with power led to abuses of discretion. Power can blind some people and lead to errors in judgment. Good leaders are certainly not afraid to use their power, but they use it to make a positive difference in their organization.

The misuse of power is probably more common in organizations than the abuse of power. While we all recognize the abuse of power, the misuse of power is a much more subtle leader pitfall. Simply put, the misuse of power is the application of the wrong type of power in a situation calling for the use of a particular type of power. During some situations, clear and concise direction is called for. You are supposed to use your positional authority or power. For example, at a four-alarm fire, deputy chiefs from surrounding fire stations may respond. However, only one of the fire chiefs is the incident commander. This person is the leader based on his or her position within the overall organization. Conversely, positional authority is probably the most misused, or perhaps, over-used power.

POKER TERMS

- **American Airlines refers to a pair of Aces**
- **The hole is the first two cards dealt down; only the player knows.**
- **The "flop" is the name for the first three cards dealt face-up on the board**
- **A bullet is a single Ace.**
  This would be a very good hand, at a minimum, three of a kind.

Someday, watch a Texas Hold 'Em tournament. You will see that the ultimate power is the use of chips. At the end, it is financial position. Building your bank in poker is like building your referent power base. You don't get to the strongest position without building each hand. You certainly don't build a bank without expert power; without understanding the game and the people. Leaders who don't know their follower's jobs are like poker players who don't know the nuances of the game – losers. Sometimes you build with positional authority like an "American Airlines in the hole and a bullet in the flop."

At other times you are skillfully building power by giving it away. Yes, maybe you lose a hand, or perhaps you don't win as big. That is because the ultimate aim is to build your bank responsibly and then spend your power.

Power intoxicates men. When a man is intoxicated by alcohol he can recover, but when intoxicated by power, he seldom recovers.

James Byrnes

Nearly all men can stand adversity, but if you want to test a man's character, give him power.

Abraham Lincoln

CHAPTER FIVE
Six of Spades
Pick Your Battles

"Poker is really about reading people. What happens when you bluff? What does it look like when the other guy bluffs? Does he look right, does he look left? Under what circumstances does he fold or call? Poker is about understanding human behavior and managing emotions--yours and the other guy's. That's huge in poker, and it's huge in business"

Phil Hellmuth Jr., Nine Time World Champion

Don Schiltz wrote a song about a gambler which was popularized by Kenny Rodgers. In the song we are told that every hand can win and every hand can lose. The gambler also tells us that the goal is not to win every hand, but to win the game. Leadership is like that, sometimes you just don't have the resources (chips) to risk battling out the hand. Other times, you might lose a little now to change your opponent's mindset and set him up for when it really counts. In the worst case, you don't have the cards to even continue with the hand, you take the minor loss and plan ahead for the next hand. Whatever the reason, every hand is not meant to be won.

In an organizational setting, battling can be defined as the sharp use of leader resources to take a definitive course of action. Now, an organizational battle is not when you see or perceive your organization is doing something illegal, immoral or unsafe. Situations that are illegal, immoral or unsafe are times that leaders go "all in." Picking your battles means husbanding your resources as a leader so you can focus your time and efforts to be effective. For a leader, resources are your time, energy, your staff and, most importantly your reputation. One of the most effective bases of leadership power is referent power. More often than not, leadership battles are going to involve your peers, other organizational units and in the worst case, your supervisor. By leadership battle we are referring to those occasions that you decide to sharply exercise your power horizontally or upward in your organization. Rarely does a leadership battle take place down your chain of command. Indeed, if you are battling down the chain of command you likely have a serious problem.

Sometimes it is beneficial to stave off a battle or at least defer it for a time. At other times, you need to recognize what is crucially important and fiercely fight for it. This is the crux of knowing when to play the hand you've been dealt or to bow out and wait for the next time. Raymond related an occasion where members of his staff came to him and complained that a leader in another organizational unit and a peer was going to Raymond's and the peer's boss and sowing seeds of dissension. The peer was relating information to the boss that was half-true and the perspective was skewed. The staff wanted Raymond to march into the boss's office and set the record straight. The staff wanted an immediate leadership battle. Raymond asked his staff a few questions. Was the information true? Of course not. Did the boss have other sources of information that would ultimately show the information was untrue? Yes. Was the boss informed enough to realize a "bill of goods?" Yes. Would inaction cause harm to the organization, the unit or the mission? No.

The situation was somewhat like a card game with one player who is bluffing. You know they're bluffing. You know what cards they likely hold or you have figured out their personal "tells," but the other players don't know. Sometimes it is just better to wait, and let the irrational hands, the unimportant office politics pass, and pick the right moment and win the game. In less than two weeks, the boss figured out that he was getting skewed information. He figured out the peer was bluffing; he didn't hold any cards. The peer lost referent power (chips if you will) with the boss.

A colleague of Andrew's working at the executive level had a deserved reputation for battling on every issue. This individual was very intelligent, creative, and hardworking, but his inability to pick his battles was his downfall as a leader. Having the capacity to be ferocious when necessary is a good thing, but like anything else, it can be taken to an extreme. If you challenge every issue regardless of its relative importance, people will begin to ignore you when you go on the offensive. You will become a "chicken little" leader. This is a sure way to render yourself ineffective.

There are times you "pull out all the stops." When you see your organization headed in the wrong direction you have a duty to take action. Often, this means going to your boss and calling it as you see it. Pulling out the stops refers to the times you believe that your organization is headed in the wrong direction. You want to make a change or correction. But, you might lose the battle. Your direction may not be the one the decision maker decides to go. This highlights the need to understand the dual sides of leader battles – rights and responsibility.

> ## POKER TERM
>
> In no-limit Texas holdem, a player may declare himself "all in" and bet all of his chips into the pot. You either win or you're out of the game. And, perhaps another simile with leadership is that when you go "all in" you don't necessarily win the pot, only an amount equal to what you bet.

As a leader, your organization has entrusted you with a special position. You attained your position as a leader because of your abilities, your expertise, and your character. You were hired because your opinion was trusted and desired by the organization. As an organizational leader, your organization gave you the right to appropriately express your opinion, even when it is counter to current thinking. However, if you pull out all the stops and lose the battle, you now have the responsibility to lead in the direction decided by your boss. Again, if it is not illegal, immoral or unsafe, if you've battled and lost, you have the responsibility to implement the decision as if it were your own. There is no room in leadership for sour grapes.

We suggest a two-fold approach to picking battles. First, you should evaluate the overall importance of the issue. Obviously, the more important the issue, the more reason you have to take it on. Secondly, you should evaluate your chance for success. Some battles you can be reasonably confident that you will win. Others, it may appear that you have little or no chance to succeed. Using this approach, combine the importance of the battle with the chance for success. Only then should you make your decision on whether or not to take up the fight. It's only common sense to choose important issues in which you have a high probability of succeeding.

The two by two matrix above is a powerful, yet simple tool to analyze your situation when you are faced with a battle. Obviously, if it is of high importance

Figure 5.1

Success

	High	Low
Importance	Do Battle	Defer, if possible
	No Battle	No Battle

Low

and your chances of success are high, you should ride into battle. If you have a situation that is important but your chance of success is low, you may still want to take on the battle simply because the issue at hand is of paramount significance. Vocalizing and taking action for your core beliefs is an attribute expected of a strong leader. History is full of examples of people who took the lead to champion causes that seemed hopeless. Standing up for others in need and adhering to your sense of justice and morality should not be viewed as a liability, regardless of whether or not you foresee a "victory." Instead of an immediate, somewhat hopeless battle perhaps you can fallback, regroup and approach the situation from a stronger position. You might marshal further resources and support for the issue.

If the issue is not important and you don't have much of chance at success, what is the point? If you are battling just to battle, you are exercising poor leadership. On the other hand, what about those times you could win, but it's not important. That is like betting $10 to win an $8 pot. Yes, you might win and you would be up $8. But, you would have given your opponents valuable information about your style, resources and ability and it has cost them nearly nothing. You expended resources for a very short-term gain and have risked the entire game.

Taking a firm stance on an issue should not be a way to showcase your position of authority within an organization. People do not like being dominated simply for the feeling of power it gives the leader. This only alienates them. Battling on inconsequential issues reduces your referent power with your staff, your peers and your boss. Choosing battles that improve or benefit the organization is what you should be focusing on. Being proven "right" is not the most important issue. Creating divisions or rifts within the group out of arrogance is not a healthy approach to leadership. You must seek to bring unity and consensus to your organization.

Two by two matrixes are helpful analytical tools, but there will be many times when it is a close call on which action to take. Leaders are called upon to make just these types of difficult decisions. That is why it is so important to have a congruent personal vision, a strong sense of morality, and a view of the situation that encompasses all significant aspects. In deciding upon the right choice, outstanding leaders often consult others, gather all the facts, weigh the relative merits, and then carefully reflect before acting.

A final note on battles comes from former Secretary of State Colin Powell. His philosophy on the use of military force has been referred to as the "Powell Doctrine." Its essence is that force should be used as a last resort. If, however, it becomes clear that force must be used, then it should be used in an overwhelming fashion. If you are taking on an issue for the overall good of the organization, then play to win and go all in. If you decide to take on a battle, don't do it with a half-hearted drive or energy.

You can no more win a war than you can an earthquake.

Jeannette Rankin

CHAPTER SIX
Seven of Spades
Accomplish More by Doing Less

Remember this: The house doesn't beat the player. It just gives him the opportunity to beat himself.

Nicholas (Nick the Greek) Dandalos

Andrew recalled an organization that had a leader with a major problem. This individual had great difficulty prioritizing organizational goals and objectives. When asked what the top priorities were, he would maintain that everything was equally important. This was a real problem because people need a leader who possesses a clear set of priorities. Taking the approach that everything is equally as important creates confusion. In reality, if everything is equally important, then nothing has any priority. A leader who fails to help employees prioritize assignments is creating a potentially dangerous situation. The resulting confusion can rapidly lead to fatigue and staff burnout.

We are reminded of a *Dilbert* comic strip in which the strip's namesake was asking his boss for clarification. He brought two separate projects to the boss and told him it was only possible to complete one within the designated time frame. That being the case, he asked which one was the priority. The boss of course replied that they were both important. Dilbert took another run at it and said he knew they were both important but he could only do one, so which one was the priority? The boss finally "compromised" by telling him to go ahead and combine the two into one and just do the one project!

Nobody can do two things at once. Multi-tasking is an over-worked idea in most organizational settings. Consider your computer. It appears to multi-task. It looks like it is doing many things at one time. The truth is your computer does things one at a time, but very fast. Of course, make too many demands on your computer, treat it improperly, and for no "apparent reason" – it crashes. The point is that even the computer we depend on to "multi-task" is simply an electronic device that is able to organize, prioritize and apply resources quickly thereby giving the appearance of multitasking. Our computers are demonstrating some valuable advice for leaders. You can do more if you organize the work; establish clear and sensible priorities and properly apply resources.

In any poker game, the ultimate goal is to walk away with more chips than when you started. In an organization, leaders, like poker players, have to keep their eye on the ultimate goal. For the poker player, each hand involves decisions about the level of resources (chips) and the strategy to be applied based on the situation (the cards dealt). The poker player evaluates the situation, organizes the information, develops priorities, and applies resources – he or she bets. Based on feedback from the table, the player re-evalutes the application of resources based on a change in the environment (somebody else raises or calls, perhaps). Although the player is constantly shifting priorities and resources based on the situation, he or she is doing so with the ultimate goal in mind – walking away a winner. A leader must be do the same thing for their staff and themselves.

The first step in doing more with less is to understand the concepts of efficiency and effectiveness. Effectiveness is goal attainment. Doing what your organization has set out to do. Efficiency is doing something with fewer inputs. It has also been expressed that effectiveness is doing the right things while efficiency is doing things right. You can certainly do something efficiently while not contributing to the overall effectiveness of your organization. This often happens when leaders fail at the second step of doing more with less – they don't have a clear understanding of their organization's overall goals.

If the leader does not understand the goals, and the priority of the goals within the overall mission of the organization, they will be ineffective. Interestingly enough, ineffective leaders are often very efficient. As Andrew points out at the beginning of this chapter, a leader that does not organize his resources and set priorities to achieve organizational goals will have his staff very efficiently running themselves into the ground. For the leader, the next step is to get personally organized. Not only to be effective and efficient as a leader, but more importantly to model for the follower.

There are habits you can form to help you prioritize tasks, such as making daily "to-do" lists. You may want to make a separate list of on-going, low-priority items and refer to it weekly. You can also make a list of your larger goals and then create a plan on how to achieve them. One technique is to place high-priority items at the top and mark them off when completed.

Alternatively, Raymond keeps a lengthy to-do list which is added to as things come up. For instance, Raymond was writing in his office when a fellow Rotarian called on the telephone about the next board meeting. Raymond wrote the Rotarian's request for the inclusion of an agenda item on his "to-do" list. Later, after finishing his thoughts on the writing project Raymond moved onto another item, eventually adding the agenda item. Like Radar O'Reilly on the old M*A*S*H television show, Raymond always carries a small notebook and pen. Humans simply forget. But, if you write it down, put it on the list, you will get back to it.

Andrew calls Raymond the King of multi-tasking – or some such part-complimentary part-derisive term. Raymond denies he multi-tasks and says he slices pizza. Large projects are like large pizzas. You don't eat a pizza all at once, you slice it up. And, you often give slices out to other people. By slicing the pizza, the project can be eaten up in small pieces and nobody gets heartburn. If it is a project you are solely responsible for (your own pizza) you still slice it up and eat it one piece at a time. And, you can always delegate your staff to eat a slice of pizza.

Visit the companion website at www.pokerleadership.com for more ideas and techniques on getting and staying organized.

Making some type of visual diagram or list of steps to accomplishing your goal may help you stay focused. These organizational tools help you see the "big picture" and prioritize objectives. Raymond has focus charts for different projects. They are large poster boards with the critical parts of the project outlined. Focus charts, white boards and bulletin boards help to organize information because if a random piece of information comes into your office you can look up at the focus charts and quickly decide which project the information belongs to, and its relative priority. Furthermore, white boards with due dates help to give task priorities. Whatever method you use, you simply need to find ways to stay organized and attuned to organizational priorities so that you can make good decisions about resource application.

Having clear goals and ideas on how to accomplish them lets you judge your priorities and when they can be adjusted. When prioritizing, there are a few things to keep in mind. First, you must decide when the task must be finished. Firm and clear due dates help you determine task priority and provide clues on breaking the tasks into smaller, initial steps. Secondly, you need to consider the importance of the task relative to overall organizational goals. It's at this point that you should consider whether or not this is a task that can be delegated. As we saw in Chapter Three, delegation can free some of your time and allow you to focus on the high-priority objectives.

Good employees are able to effectively manage multiple responsibilities but there is a breaking point. Good leaders almost instinctively feel when this is near and shift or alter priorities accordingly. This requires insight into your staff and your organization. Communicating with and getting to know followers can help you to identify where individual strengths and weaknesses lie. Indeed, as we look further at leadership in this book we will see how communication may be the most critical of leadership skills.

Even a very large corporation like General Electric never has more than five major initiatives going on at any one time. It is their belief that having more than a few chosen priorities will result in a house divided. Good leaders create top priorities and continually evaluate them. Like the poker play, the good leader is watching for a shift in the environment. A shift in the environment can be something as simple as a key employee off sick or as complex as a major goal shift by your organization. Your watchfulness and attention empowers your staff to stay focused on what is important. Simply put, your staff is more focused and less stressed when you clearly communicate goals and priorities.

There may be times when you cannot fully commit to accomplishing certain tasks or projects. When this occurs, you should hold off on them. Do not initiate a project when you cannot give your full attention to it. Priorities should only be established when there is a full organizational commitment to accomplishing them.

A scene from the movie, *The Karate Kid,* helps to illustrate this point:

Karate student Daniel arrives for his first lesson. The old master asks him if he is ready. Daniel says, "I guess so." His teacher explains to him that the proper answer is either karate yes or karate no. Never is it karate "I guess so." His teacher tells him that karate requires a full commitment. If you cannot make such a commitment, then do not pursue karate. Daniel understands the lesson and answers that he is ready.

Unfortunately, many leaders have failed to understand this lesson. They make many "I guess so" commitments on behalf of the organization. Leaders should make every effort to avoid this. If you cannot bring your full attention and energy to a project, you cannot expect your employees to do so. If you don't keep your eye on the goals, organize your work, establish priorities and apply the appropriate resources the house will beat you on a consistent basis.

A jack of all trades is king of none.

P.K. Thomajan

It is not enough to be busy; so are the ants. The question is: what are we busy about?
Henry David Thoreau

CHAPTER SEVEN
Eight of Spades
Determination and Adversity

Show me a good loser and I'll show you a loser.

Stu Ungar

One day a chump, the next day a champion. What a difference a day makes in a tournament poker.

Mike Sexton

The good news is that in every deck of fifty-two cards there are 2,598,960 possible hands. The bad news is that you are only going to be dealt one of them.

Anthony Holden, author of *Big Deal* (1990)

Determination is perhaps the key to success in any endeavor and the field of leadership like the game of poker, is no different. In order to achieve the greatest level of organizational success, leaders must display determination in everything they do. Most importantly, employees tend to take on the characteristics of their leaders. If leaders are determined to succeed despite all obstacles, employees will see this and learn that tenacity is an important ingredient of success. An organization full of determined leaders and employees is a formidable force indeed.

Poker can teach us a lot about adversity and determination. In poker, you are dealt a set of cards for each hand. In Texas Hold 'Em, those are the only cards you are going to get. This is very much like working in an organization. How often have you, as a leader, inherited a staff? Or, perhaps you work under rules and regulations, like many of us in the public sector, that make changing staff problematic. That's your hand. Your staff are the only cards you are going to get.

You might be lucky and be dealt the perfect staff. It is more likely though that, if you could, you would ask for different cards. Or, perhaps your staff is great but you are given a task that is, at best difficult. Again, if you could, you would turn the task down. But, that's not possible. Like leadership, the essence of poker is not the lucky draw of cards (or staff, or task), but the skillful playing of the hand you're dealt. The primary lesson in determination and adversity is to realize that any hand can win depending on the skill of the player.

POKER TERMS.

If the first two cards dealt down (so that only the individual player can see them) are a pair, it is often referred to as a "pocket pair." The "flop" is the first three community cards dealt up. Everyone can see them and uses them to fill out their five card hand.

In poker, we have the concept of the "bad beat." A bad beat is a loss in which the losing player had the better odds on the winning player earlier in the hand. In a bad beat play, after the first cards are dealt, odds on winning can be calculated. For instance, if you have a pair of Kings and the player across from you has a three and a four, your odds of winning the hand with a pair of Kings is much better than the player with the inkling of a straight. But, suppose the "flop" is five, six and seven. Even more dramatically, suppose the flop is King, five and seven. At this point the player with three Kings has fairly good odds of winning, but the other player could be dealt a five and win. There are only four fives in the deck to begin with! These are very long odds. Now, we are not suggesting that you bet long and hope to be on the winning end of a bad beat. What we are saying is that things change. What looks disastrous in the beginning can be skillfully played and won.

Colin Powell has thirteen rules for leadership. Several of these rules have direct bearing on a leader's attitude toward situations involving adversity and determination.

Indeed, the first rule, "It ain't as bad as you think. It will look better in the morning" directly relates to being dealt a rough hand. It is your skill as a leader (or player) that ultimately determines the outcome.

Employees need you to display determination even when you are uncertain. If you give up as soon as things look difficult, it sends the message that when the going gets tough, it is acceptable to give up. If your goals are not worth struggle and effort, what's the point? Why should anyone care if they are realized or not?

COLIN POWELL'S RULES FOR LEADERS

1. It ain't as bad as you think. It will look better in the morning.
2. Get mad, then get over it.
3. Avoid having your ego so close to your position that, when your position falls, your ego goes with it.
4. It can be done!
5. Be careful what you choose, you may get it.
6. Don't let adverse facts stand in the way of a good decision.
7. You can't make someone else's choices. You shouldn't let someone else make yours.
8. Check small things.
9. Share credit.
10. Remain calm. Be kind.
11. Have a vision. Be demanding.
12. Don't take counsel of your fears or naysayers.
13. Perpetual optimism is a force multiplier.

Your determination motivates employees to struggle for what is important even if it involves hardship. You will increase their enthusiasm and they will probably view you with more respect and admiration.

Modeling determination for employees is even more important in times of adversity. Leaders are closely watched at all times but particularly during stressful times. People want to see that their leaders are strong and determined in crisis situations. Leaders are nothing if not providers of hope, determination, and tenacity. Consider the player who is dealt a weak but potentially winning hand. If they communicate to the other players that they have a weak hand, the other players will change strategy to win. If you consistently project strength and confidence, people will believe you are confident and they will act accordingly. Your staff will follow your lead. If you demonstrate anything less than determination in the face of adversity, so will they.

Leaders should be very visible in the organization in times of adversity. This is certainly not the time to stay in the office behind the desk. People want assurance that everything will work out and it is the leader's job to provide that assurance. This is not to say that a leader is required to sugarcoat tough issues.

On the contrary; people appreciate a leader who is open and honest about the circumstances. Moreover, research and practical experience has shown that what people fear about situations are the unknown aspects of the situation. The more information you can provide your followers the better prepared they will be to handle the adversity. However, they also want a leader who has the ability to give them hope just when all seems hopeless.

> **Communicating during times of adversity is often referred to as Risk Communications. For more information on Risk Communications and leadership visit the companion website at www.pokerleadership.com.**

When there is an unusual noise or severe turbulence during an airplane flight, experienced fliers immediately look to the flight attendants for any clue of distress. If there is none, comfort levels increase. This is the calmness a leader can give an organization when crisis occurs. People watch their leaders. They want to see quiet confidence coupled with a good grasp of the facts. They want to see determination and they want to feel hope. Good leaders really earn their money during tough times.

Lieutenant General Lewis "Chesty" Puller is considered the quintessential Marine. More than being brave and heroic, he was always there with his people when things seemed at their worst. From the Island of Haiti with a few ill trained local gendarmes, to Guadalcanal where his Marines fought off massive enemy counter-attacks at the airfield, to the Chosen Reservoir in Korea he was there through three wars instilling confidence and displaying leadership and determination in the face of extreme adversity. When the First Marine Division was surrounded by eight divisions of Chinese Communists at the Chosen Reservoir, Lieutenant General Puller summed up his attitude saying, "We're surrounded. That simplifies the problem."

Perseverance may seem something inborn not something you can learn. However, we believe that you can develop your determination. History is replete with examples of people who failed repeatedly. The reasons they are noted by history is that they failed, but were not defeated. Failure is about experimentation and learning. Failure is about the idea that didn't quite work out. Defeat is not getting back into the fray. Defeat is not using failure as a learning experience. It takes confidence and a positive attitude to face uncertainty and possible failure and still be determined to push on. If you are genuine, have a strong vision, and are committed to your goals, it is easier to stay focused and not let doubts erode your confidence. It is at these times that a strong faith in yourself, your vision, the corporate vision, and your organization and people is crucial. Such faith will give you the confidence you need.

It is important to maintain a balance between determination and stubbornness. You should not give in at every obstacle. By the same token, you should not hold out when it is painfully obvious that nothing is going to be accomplished. You may be thinking of "saving face" by not admitting defeat or you may be worried that failure will expose you as incompetent, but it is important that you know "when to say when." There will be times when it is simply necessary to end a project because it is no longer productive or possible to continue. Betting that the last card is going to be the exact card you need to make a winning hand is the essence of a long shot. The great comedienne Lucille Ball once said in regard to her success that she didn't know anything about luck. What she knew about was hard work and determination and the ability to know what was, and was not opportunity. As a leader, you have to have the education, experience and judgment to know a long-shot from adversity that can be overcome. In these cases, it is better to quit gracefully than to drag everyone through a pointless and unpleasant situation. The art of leadership includes knowing when to advance despite the odds and realizing when a strategic retreat is the wisest course of action.

Some people succeed because they are destined to succeed, but most succeed because they are determined to succeed.

Winston Churchill

Adversity introduces a man to himself.

Anonymous

CHAPTER EIGHT
Nine of Spades
Lifelong Learning

"I've lost money so fast in these clubs it's left me reeling. I've read every poker book ever written, but the only way to get better at the game is to go out and play with people who are really good. The problem is, you stand to lose a lot of money doing it."

Matt Damon, who, along with "Rounders" co-star Edward Norton, was quickly eliminated from the $10,000 main event at the WSOP in 1998.

"Poker reveals to the frank observer something else of import—it will teach him about his own nature. Many bad players do not improve because they cannot bear self-knowledge."

David Mamet on Poker

"How long does it take to learn poker, Dad?" "All your life, son."

David Spanier, *"Total Poker"* (1977)

Education and learning are extremely important. Recall from the Chapter on Power that one of the leader power bases is "Expert Power." You only gain and maintain expert power by constantly learning about your field. Leaders are expected to have knowledge and expertise; your people look to you for answers. If you are going to be effective, you need to be involved in on-going learning. Things are changing at a breakneck pace, and it is difficult to stay completely current. Part of your responsibility as a leader is to strive constantly to keep your knowledge as up to date as possible.

Being a lifelong learner has gone from being an option to being a necessity. There are a variety of different ways leaders can do this. Formal education, training courses, independent reading, and networking with other leaders are all excellent methods. No matter what route you take, be sure that you pursue a path to stay versed in new developments, ideas, or technologies that may be beneficial to the organization. There are different types of learning and every leader should be aware of the different types and work to continually improve themselves across a broad spectrum of learning experiences.

One of the traits that poker and leadership clearly share is that they are about people. Anyone can learn the basic rules; they can calculate the odds and even get lucky. But the real champions are able to read people and they are able to interact with the other players in the most advantageous way. Leadership is about people. Unlike the poker table where the goal is to influence others for personal gain, the leader is striving to understand and influence people toward organizational goals. We suppose that the primary difference is that leaders are influencing people in a positive way whereas poker players are influencing people for their own gain.

You can only learn about people and how they work under varying conditions by seeking experiences with them. Major Brian Tribus, a leadership instructor at the West Point Military Academy puts it this way:

"We as leaders need to be attuned to the subtle signals that indicate what members of our organizations need or want. How do we acquire this ability? For starters, be with your soldiers as often as possible-you can't pick up subtle signals if you're not there. Next, walk a mile in their boots. In fact, walk as many miles as you can in their boots. Know what it is like to be a member of your own organization."

A solid leader looks for ways to interact and train with his staff so that he or she can learn how the staff will perform under varying conditions. Some leaders find experimenting with "near histories" a fulfilling means to develop their own talent and that of their staff.

A near history is something that almost happened or could have happened. Generally, the leader picks an event in the organization's past and then includes the current state of the organization and the environment into the equation. He or she then asks the question, "How would we handle this?" This form of "table top" exercise is used in the military and paramilitary (like police and fire services) around the globe. The idea is to use lessons from an organization's past as a guide to future actions. Most importantly, this technique of "near history" means that the event could "almost have happened" or "happened differently." By thinking in terms of "near history," leaders are given a larger playing field from which to learn.

Alternatively, "de-briefing" any major event is always a good idea. The difference between "near history" and "de-briefing" is: with near history it didn't happen or it didn't happen to you; with de-briefing it did. An internal de-briefing involves the leader and the staff going over what happened and looking at what they did right and what they could have done better. Notice the phrase "What could have been done better." Both Andrew and Raymond find that people are more apt to open up and share their experiences when they are asked, "What could have been done better." It helps remove some of the natural defensiveness and blame passing when you avoid looking at what went wrong. By working with your staff on near histories and de-briefings you will learn about your staff's capabilities, problems in your organization and your own skills.

Another technique that can be used for increasing chance for success in major projects is called a "pre-mortem". This approach is used to discover the hidden flaws and minefields that may exist in any project. As described in their book *The Leadership Challenge*, Kouzes and Posner state it works like this:

"When a team gathers to kick off a new project, people conclude that meeting by looking six-months into the future, with an assumption the project has failed. A brainstorming session ensues that tries to identify both the probable and improbable reasons why the project would have failed. Based on this information, the plan is revised or enhanced in whatever ways are possible to create the greatest chance for success. In essence, they try and attack possible reasons for failure before they actually launch the project. Although it is always conceivable the project will still fail, this process seems to enhance the overall chance of success."

Formal education is another method of life-long learning. Whenever we discuss education with a leader who lacks higher education or graduate work, the leader always says that they learned everything they need to know about their organization by doing the job. This is extraordinarily limiting. First, when you learn as a practitioner you generally concentrate on how things get done. A good university education can open a leader to exploring why things are done a certain way. Often, it is learning the theory behind the model that enables the leader to see outside of the box. Essentially, it is the people who question why who can facilitate extraordinary leaps for their organizations.

Sit back and think through your day. Think about the questions you answered, the decisions you made and the people with which you interacted. Can you think of any theories that might support your actions? Have you explored why people are motivated one way or another? How does your organization tend to learn? How will technology impact your organization? These are the types of questions a good university education should help you frame. If you don't know why you do what you do, you need to consider further education.

In addition to the experiential-based learning found in near histories and debriefings, and the theoretical and analytical frameworks learned in the classroom, leaders must be constantly learning about their environment. Constantly scanning your environment is critical to the success of your staff and organization. You must see the pitfalls, minefields and opportunities.

In 1943, the United States Army was defeated at the Battle of the Kasserine pass by the German Afrika Corps. Subsequent to this, George S. Patton was promoted to Lieutenant General and placed in command of the Second Corp. A hard trainer and constant student of military history, Patton helped to defeat the Germans in North Africa. After one battle where American forces routed the Germans, Patton has been credited with remarking, "Rommel, you magnificent bastard. I read your book." Patton was constantly learning, constantly scanning his environment so that he could give his troops the advantage in battle.

There are several ways you can be a good scanner of the environment. For instance, through the magazines, newsletters and conferences sponsored by professional organizations, you will receive filtered updates on what is current in your field. If you are the least bit tech savvy, you can find any number of Internet based ListServs or email services that will scan, filter, condense and forward information to you. As an example, Raymond has other writing projects dealing with Homeland Security and Terrorism. Through the State Department, the National Institute for Justice, several universities and a variety of other organizations Raymond receives daily digests. By scanning these digests, Raymond is able to spot information appropriate to his tasks and then undertake a more in-depth reading.

A second method of scanning the environment involves belonging to professional and community organizations. Professional organizations open the door to best practices within your industry. From newsletters to conferences, you can receive current information on the future of your organization's environment.

Moreover, conferences give you the opportunity to meet other leaders exposing you to people with different expertise. When a member of your staff asks you a question, if you don't know and can say, "I don't know. But, I know someone who does," you receive as much expert power as if you knew the answer. While you can't know everything, you should know who does know.

Community organizations tend to give you a well-rounded view of what is happening in your organization's community. This is part of your local environment. Someday, you may find yourself before a city council arguing a change in zoning. It would be nice if one of the council persons was a member of the service organization to which you also belonged.

Learning about your people is more than learning about their skill set. A good leader seeks opportunities to learn about their followers as human beings. Sometimes this can be accomplished by walking around and talking with your staff. You might want to consider a somewhat more formal method of exploring your people. Raymond has started "Breakfast Clubs," "Brown Bag Conferences" and "Coffee Chats." These are meetings were you eat and talk. There is no agenda. A good meeting starter is often having each person give brief updates on their interests. You lead off – set the tone. You can start by talking about your family, your interests, or the future of your organization. You are looking for something to open people up in an informal setting.

Most organizations want their employees to be lifelong learners as well. Again, it starts with the leader. If the leader is constantly striving to learn, this will encourage people; they will see it as part of what the organization expects. The benefits of having knowledgeable team members who continue to learn is immense and the effects will continue to ripple throughout the organization.

A person is not old until regrets take the place of dreams.

John Barrymore

The man who graduates today and stops learning tomorrow is uneducated the day after.

Newton Baker

CHAPTER NINE
Ten of Spades
Dependability

"If you know what he does with certain hand types, you have a significant advantage"
Michaeil Cappellettie, "Betting Archetypes," *Card Player Magazine*

Dependability is one of the United States Marine Corps' (USMC) primary leadership traits. For the USMC, dependability is a primary trait because it says so much about your leadership ability and can have a huge effect on your followers. Dependability is saying what you will do and doing what you say. Leaders must have an impeccable reputation for dependability. It is critical that your bosses, peers, customers, and subordinates all feel that you can be relied on to follow up your words with actions. One of the best ways to explore dependability is to look at how the different points of view of bosses, peers, customers and subordinates interpret dependability.

Everyone answers to someone. As a leader in your organization you receive instructions from your superior. From your boss's point of view, dependability means you can be trusted to complete a task. It also means that you can be trusted to make decisions consistent with the goals, policies and procedures of your organization. The more dependable you are the more latitude you are likely to be given as a leader. As a dependable leader, your boss knows you are going to consistently perform to the highest possible standards; you can be trusted.

Raymond recalled one of his first meetings with a new captain. At the time, Raymond was a sergeant working an administrative assignment within the police department. The captain said that he had been reviewing the schedule and noted that Raymond had been given permission by the previous commanding officer to use telecommuting as a means to complete his assignments. The captain said, "I don't think the department is fully behind the concept of telecommuting."

Raymond thought for a second. He had a few options; he could argue the merits of telecommuting, fall back on the previous boss's arrangement, or adjust his schedule and complete his tasks at his duty station. Raymond took the latter course because he felt the captain simply didn't have any experience with Raymond's level of competence and dependability. A month later the captain walked into Raymond's office. By this time, the captain knew Raymond's level of competence and dependability. He handed Raymond a project and said, "I know this is unusual, but I am certain you can figure it out." He paused and then added with a smile, "I appreciate being able to depend on you. And, by the way, if telecommuting will help you complete your work go ahead and schedule the time." From the boss' point of view dependability built trust. Again, the more dependable and trustworthy you are, the more latitude you are given.

> **Telecommuting is a term used in the United States, coined by Jack Nilles, to describe a work arrangement in which employees enjoy flexibility of working in one location (often, at home) and communicating with a main office in a different location through a personal computer equipped with modem and communications software.**

Telecommuting requires a leap of faith on the part of an employer. Initially, the size of this leap was too great for the Raymond's captain. The gap was closed through Raymond's actions, which, in turn, built a relationship of trust. Although the captain was still making a leap of faith when he authorized the telecommuting, Raymond's actions created a situation where it was more of a step than a leap, thus fitting into the captain's comfort zone and benefiting all concerned.

The follower's point of view is somewhat different, yet, the outcome can be very similar. Andrew once faced an awkward situation when a boss instructed him to enter into a negotiation with another public agency and reach an arrangement agreeable to all. Through some hard work and a little bit of finesse, Andrew was able to reach a good agreement in which both parties got what they wanted. After he had drafted the agreement for his superior's signature, the boss stated that he no longer wanted to participate. Worse yet, the boss gave no reason for the change of heart. As you can imagine, a very frank discussion between the two ensued. Andrew was forced to contact the other party and tell them that there would be no deal. What an uncomfortable position to be put in, especially since there was no identifiable reason for the reversed decision. It was as if the leader had changed his mind on a whim.

From that point on, Andrew was very cautious when dealing with him, and always held his integrity suspect. Andrew never again believed this person to be dependable and his interactions with him reflected this. As a leader, when you make a commitment, you must live up to it.

If circumstances change and you cannot complete the commitment, at the very least explain in detail to those involved why the change occurred. Even if they are upset about the situation, they will be more understanding and retain their respect for you. Needless to say, you should only break obligations under very pressing circumstances. This is why it is so important to think through the situation before you commit. Too many leaders find themselves over-committing and then scrambling to get out of their obligations later.

Undependable leadership can have devastating effects on followers. One of the most common follower responses to unreliable leadership and unreliable organizations is the "hunker down effect." If a leader or organization pursues goals, issues policies or makes promises that it does not follow through on, followers learn to ignore what is said. They simply "hunker down," or lay low until the newest "idea" passes into the museum of fads. A dependable leader engenders just the opposite. Raymond related a recent incident where his car was burglarized causing him to miss teaching a seven AM class at a university. Twenty of 37 students went to the department secretary because it was unlike him to not be there. The students were convinced that Raymond must have been in a horrible accident because it was not like him not to be where he said he was going to be. When people can take the leader's word for something, they will believe it, carry it out and do the best job possible.

Being dependable is critical to your organization's success with customers. Typically, we think of customers as external to the organization. The reality is that many of us work in organizations where the customers are internal. Anyone who relies on you or your staff is a customer. Much of customer dissatisfaction is rooted in dependability. Organizationally, they are peers, but practically speaking they are customers. Perhaps your unit didn't produce it on time. Or, the quality was inferior. Or, it didn't perform as your unit stated it would. Consider the number of advertising campaigns centered on the concept of dependability. Shippers to auto makers tout dependability. People want it on time and they want it to work. We, as customers, leaders, peers and subordinates simply want dependability.

You should be cautious and conservative in making commitments. Think it through and do not act based solely on your first reaction or your desire to please. People will remember for a long time the commitments you keep. More lasting, however, will be the impressions left by the commitments you failed to meet. If you have over-committed and don't have the time or resources to do a job well, you will disappoint everyone involved – including yourself. Good leaders also recognize when they can't make a commitment. You should never write checks you can't cash.

Although you are striving to be dependable, there are going to be situations wherein you let someone down. Stuff happens. The best leader course of action is to acknowledge your mistake, apologize and do what you can to make the person whole. On the other hand, perhaps you promised some action and then circumstances changed. Perhaps permission is outside of your control. You are always better off acknowledging to the follower that you are not the decision maker. Typically, we are talking about a promise you made to a follower that you were unable to keep. If the change is due to something you can share with the follower, then you should spend time explaining why you can't keep the promise. On the other hand, there are some circumstances that involve a changing environment that cannot be shared with the follower. Perhaps, your organization is going to launch a new product, go in a different direction, or you just simply deal with secret stuff. No matter the reasons, you can't share it with the follower. This is where you may have to spend a little referent power. Again, acknowledge to the follower that the initial agreement has changed. Apologize for the inconvenience and tell them that you simply aren't able to explain all of the circumstance involved in changing your mind. Hopefully, you've built up enough goodwill to be able to spend some with this individual.

It has been said that actions speak louder than words. Dependability is about more than keeping your promises. It is about modeling the behavior you expect from your followers. If you expect them to be on time, you should be on time. If you expect them to be honest, you should be honest and open. Always demonstrate more than you expect. There is an old saying in customer service circles: "Under promise and over deliver". This seems also to have application for those in leadership positions.

Okay, so you read the chapter and missed the poker analogy. That's because it is very subtle to tease out. In poker, dependability is a strategy you can use in betting. Raymond's favorite game is California Black. A seven card game somewhat similar to Texas Hold Em in that the best five-card hand wins. The cards are dealt differently causing a slightly different betting structure. More importantly, in this game, low Spade in the hole (the cards only the individual player sees) wins half the pot. One time Raymond's first two cards down were the Ace of Spades and the Ace of Diamonds. He knows he is going to get at least half the pot because the Ace of Spades is considered the lowest card. And, he has a very strong beginning hand. His betting strategy is to be dependable. Bet evenly and slowly, hoping to keep the other six players in the game. What Raymond was playing for is half the winnings and a little bit from everyone. When the fourth card is dealt up it was a ten. Raymond began to bet a little more aggressively, hoping to send the dependable message that he was betting on a pair of tens. People act on how dependable you are and the dependability of your message. They're watching you and won't they be surprised when you take half the winnings?

Being dependable is directly tied to your integrity. If your employees cannot depend on you, your reputation will evaporate. It becomes difficult to work for a leader whose word is essentially useless. Some workers will feel that they do not have to work as hard at objectives because an unreliable boss may just dismiss the task in the end. Others will suffer because the managerial support they need is lacking. Some will take their cues from the leader and feel content to be undependable themselves. An unreliable leader causes the cohesion, organization, and productivity of the organization to decline.

You can't build a reputation on what you are going to do.

Henry Ford

Magnificent promises are always to be suspected.

Theodore Parker

CHAPTER TEN
Jack of Spades
Decision Making

This was the first time he had seriously confronted what he was doing, and the force of that awareness came very abruptly - with a surging of his pulse and a frantic pounding in his head. He was about to gamble his life on that table, and the insanity of that risk filled him with a kind of awe.

Paul Auster, *The Music of Chance* (1990)

Bet, call, fold – you decide. Knowing absolute risk separates poker from leadership. With poker you know how much money you've bet; you know the risk. But in poker, like leadership, you don't know the absolute outcome. We know the intended consequences and we fear the unknown and unintended consequences. You still have to decide. Indeed, the concept of scarcity – limited resources and unlimited needs - forces us to choose at every turn.

Most people have worked for bosses who were indecisive. Andrew once worked for one who studied everything to death. No matter how much information he assembled, it was never enough for him to make the call – to decide. With this leader, if the building caught fire he would have formed a steering committee and developed an action plan on how to escape! This leader suffered from what is sometimes called "the paralysis of analysis." People involved in crisis situations (like police officers, doctors, firefighters and combat leaders) are called upon to make split-second decisions on a regular basis. Some of these decisions involve life-or-death.

Perhaps more importantly, as leaders we are called upon to evaluate the decisions made by our staffs. As part of Andrew's job, he continually evaluated the decisions made by police officers in the street. Andrew tried to evaluate the decision based upon the information that was available to the police officer at the time of the decision. Furthermore, he judged the decision against a standard of what was reasonable considering the totality of the circumstances. If the decision was reasonable, Andrew supported the decision even if it was not the same one that he would have made. It is critical for leaders to be empathetic and remember that there are many different ways to do the job correctly.

In his book *Further Up the Organization*, Robert Townsend makes some interesting observations about the decision-making process and perhaps provides us with some general leadership cues: According to Townsend, "There are two kinds of decisions: those that are expensive to change and those that are not. Common decisions – like when to have the cafeteria open for lunch or what brand of pencil to buy – should be made fast. No point in taking three weeks to make a decision that can be made in three seconds and corrected inexpensively later if wrong. The whole organization may be out of business while you oscillate between baby blue and buffalo brown coffee cups." General George S. Patton mirrored Townsend albeit in a more dramatic fashion. According to Patton, "A good plan violently executed now is better than a perfect plan executed next week.

Figure 10.1

Consequences

	High	**Low**
Time	Analyze, decide, monitor, adjust	Delegate
	Decide, monitor, adjust	Decide

Low

By combining time and consequences into a simple, yet powerful 2X2 Matrix, a leader may gain some insight into the decision making process. In figure 10.1, the amount of time available to make the decision is listed on the vertical axis as either high or low. High is having a lot of time, and low is having very little time. The reasonably known consequences are listed on the horizontal access also as high and low. If you have the luxury of taking time to make a high consequence decision you should do so. This would be a "high/high" decision. In this example a good leader might use formal decision making techniques to conduct an analysis. Use that extra time to research the issue and solicit input from the various stakeholders. Everyone understands the desire to carefully plan and check a decision. However, people usually can sense when time is up and they will look to the leader as the one to come forth with a decision. If leaders either cannot or will not do this, their credibility will suffer.

Wild Card **YOU'RE THE LEADER!**
As such, there is an implied agreement between you and the follower that you will continually learn your craft–leadership. Every leader should be familiar with decision making techniques such as:

- **Pareto Analysis**
- **Paired Comparison Analysis**
- **Grid Analysis**
- **Decision Tree Analysis**
- **Plus/Minus/Implications (PMI)**
- **Force Field Analysis**
- **Combinations**

You can find out more about these and other decision making techniques at the companion website for this book at www.pokerleadership.com

Many decisions are time sensitive. Time sensitive decisions are those in which you do not have an extended time period in which to make your decision. Low time decisions can be either high consequence or low consequence. For a low consequence decision a good leader will simply make the decision. For high consequence decisions you must decide, monitor and adjust. At the poker table, every decision is low time/high consequence. You have no time, you have no back-up, you can't pull out your calculator and figure the odds. In low/high decision making leaders do not rise to the occasion – they default to their level of education, training and experience. Poker players and stellar leaders are life-long learners who build a reservoir of instinct for making low/high decisions.

One of the primary functions of good leadership is developing the next generation of leaders. Decisions with high time and low consequences are good learning exercises. You can delegate high/low decisions and give your staff experience at making decisions. Truly, high/low decision making is the road to your staff developing the ability to make the low time/high consequence decisions. If your staff doesn't learn how to make decisions, your organization will ultimately suffer and you will find yourself in the position of having to make every decision. Having an indecisive person in a leadership position can have a very adverse impact not only on employee morale but also on the goals of the organization.

Good decision makers avoid procrastination. You see this at the card table: someone staring at their cards willing them to change. The facts aren't going to change. You have to decide – call, raise or fold! There are some key points to remember in order to bypass the problem of procrastination. First, you must be aware of your own style of reasoning and thinking. You may require some reflection and introspection to assess your decision-making style. Work with your style to arrive at sound, timely decisions. You may also want to inquire about other's thinking and reasoning processes. How do they differ from your own? Do they give you any new insight or perspectives?

A relative of the indecisive person is the "waffler." In many ways, the waffler is even harder to deal with than someone who is just plain indecisive. Now, waffling is the not the same as making a decision, monitoring the outcome and adjusting to the environment. The waffler will make a decision but will continually reverse it. Andrew recounted how dealing with a waffler can be an arduous experience. Andrew could never count on anything the leader would say and this, of course, made it difficult for Andrew to do his job. Sometimes, the decision would be changed within a few months, a few weeks, and even within days. There were even moments when the decision would be reversed several minutes after it was made! The waffler usually gave no reason to explain why the decision had to be changed. In the rare cases where a reason was given, it was often nonsensical. The waffler put Andrew in a tough spot; he was forcing Andrew to filter the decision making-process for the good of the organization. This is an extreme no-win situation for subordinate leaders.

On occasion, you may have to reverse your decision. It happens. As an example, suppose in a card game your first two cards look pretty good. But, the flop is no help. Your odds of winning the hand have seriously decreased. Do you continue to play? Do you throw good money after bad? Of course, the decision to stay and play or fold depends on more than just the cards; it depends on the entire situational environment on the table. Our point is that you do continually monitor the environment and occasionally reverse course. Maybe change and decide to lose a little and keep a lot.

In leadership, however, you keep these occurrences to a minimum. Make sure you have justifiable reasons and then explain to the appropriate people why you had to change your decision. If you have a rational reason for changing course, people will accept it, and your reputation will be enhanced. Remember that although you should acquire information and get input prior to making most decisions, too much intellectualizing can paralyze the decision-making process and lead to the proverbial "paralysis by analysis."

PLANNING FOR DECISION MAKING

When making a decision, whether it is involves a problem you face or a task you want completed, it is sometimes helpful to make a written plan of how you are going to proceed. Here are some steps to help you during the decision-making process:

- Identify the goal or problem;
- List potential negative consequences. Consider alternative solutions;
- Decide who will be involved. This includes employees working on the task and other departments or organizations;
- Determine what resources you will need, from equipment and training to funding;
- Create a timeline for when your decisions will be carried out and set deadlines for goal completion;
- Determine how you will monitor the outcome; and, adjust as necessary.

When you come to a fork in the road, take it.

Yogi Berra

The man who insists upon seeing with perfect clearness before he decides, never decides.

Henri-Frederic Amiel

CHAPTER ELEVEN
Queen of Spades
When You Don't Know

But when you're playing poker, you don't know the answer to that until after the cards are laid down, and then it's too late.

Fred Thompson

Despite a leader's best efforts to continually stay informed and educated, there will be many times where the right answer or right way to proceed is unknown. Nobody expects a leader to know everything all the time. As a leader, however, the responsibility to act under such circumstances belongs to you. At this point, there are two basic options. You can admit it and seek out the appropriate information or you can attempt to bluff your way through. We suppose that people attempt to bluff their way through because they don't know and don't think you'll figure it out. In poker, bluffing is good unless someone calls you on it. If you have bluffed badly, you probably didn't lose just the hand, but control of the game.

For leaders, losing control of the game equates to losing respect from your followers. There are leadership techniques that you can use to turn a situation in which you don't know something into a very positive growth experience for both you and your followers. Although there are certainly leaders who will disagree with us, we almost always recommend the first option; don't bluff in leadership. People want a confident and able leader. Workers want to feel that if they need guidance or help, he or she can always turn to their boss to find answers that he or she do not have. It is preferable to admit when you don't know the answer and we will demonstrate why.

First, we do not think that people expect their leaders to have all the answers. In fact, no one appreciates a "know it all" even at the managerial level. As a leader, you should maintain some degree of humility. While you do not want to be meek and controllable, you also do not want to be overbearing and arrogant. It is acceptable to have pride in your work and your accomplishments, but there needs to be a balance. You are not going to know everything, and you are not always going to be right. Being humble means you acknowledge this human frailty and allow the input and help of others when needed. Humility will also allow you to face suggestions gracefully when you do ask for help. If people are continually faced with arrogance each time they try to help, they will eventually stop sharing their ideas and creativity. Furthermore, admitting that you do not know the answer humbles you and lets your employees see that you are human as well. More than demonstrating your humanity, admitting you don't know demonstrates your courage and integrity. People want and need integrity from their leaders. They are more loyal and productive when they believe in the moral character of their leader. An integral part of demonstrating integrity is being honest, even if it means showing that you do not know something.

A second benefit from admitting you don't know is also a demonstration of moral courage. If you asked someone to define courage they might tell you that it is the absence of fear. Anyone who has acted courageously will tell you that courage is acting despite your fear. An overlooked aspect and critical component of personal courage is moral courage. Moral courage often manifests itself as candor, which is essentially full disclosure against your own self interest. When you admit you don't know, you are showing a small weakness. However, if you bluff, you may be demonstrating that your ego is larger than your integrity. It takes moral courage to admit a weakness in front of subordinates.

Thirdly, as leaders, we expect people to carry out our direction. Why would you, as a leader, consciously give your followers direction of which you are unsure? They are going to go out and apply your answer in some practical setting. Giving advice or an answer to a question when you are unsure of the answer is potentially dangerous for your followers. The danger might be minor; they make some organizational mistake. The danger could also be larger like they lose a valued customer, or, in the worst case they are injured. With three good reasons to admit you don't know, lets look at how you can handle things when you don't know.

You have to prepare for what you don't know. A good leader starts by collecting reference materials along their leadership path. Your library of reference materials, should build as you grow as a leader. There are going to be situations where you actually don't remember! You knew the answer at one time, but some other arcane piece of information has filled that memory slot in your brain. The second and probably best way to prepare is by building a network as you grow as a leader. Your personal leadership network should include all manner of experts.

If you don't know, you should know where to find the answer or know someone who does know.

Raymond related his early days as the Officer-in-Charge of fugitives. He had seventy-five detectives working for him, on cases all around the nation and in some foreign countries. For months he was asked almost daily about subjects for which he did not know the correct answer. Raymond used his library of references and leadership networks by employing two phrases with his followers: "I don't know, but I know where to look. Let's find out together." Or, "I don't know, but I know someone who does. Let's find out together."

You can communicate a lot about your personal expectations by demonstrating that you don't know. Your followers learn about your integrity, your courage, your emphasis on doing the right thing, the importance you place on their queries, and probably much more. We think it is pretty clear – when you don't know, you don't know.

Along these same lines, we encourage others to admit when they are wrong. Most people do not like to do this and leaders are no exception. The following story illustrates the type of stubborn behavior some employees have to deal with from their leaders:

There was a man who believed he was dead. Much to the dismay of his family and friends, they were unable to convince him that he was in fact alive. Out of desperation, they made an appointment for him to see a psychiatrist. The proficient doctor spent many painstaking hours with the client trying to convince him that he was alive. He used every angle he could think of, but nothing seemed to work. Finally, the doctor ran across one final approach. He spent a few sessions with the man talking about the physical impossibility of dead people bleeding. After hours of tedious convincing, the patient relented. "So you do agree that a dead person can't bleed?" asked the psychiatrist. "Yes, I do," the patient replied. With a sigh of relief, the doctor pulled out a pin and pricked the man's finger. Out came a squirt of blood. "Now," the doctor asked, "What does that show you?" Pausing briefly, the man got a startled look on his face and replied, "I would have never thought it so…dead men do bleed."

Everyone probably has a similar story about a boss who just could not admit to being wrong. As a leader, you have a responsibility to set aside your ego and admit if you have made a mistake or have been wrong. This allows the problem to be solved and helps everyone to move on as quickly as possible. Admitting error is difficult, especially when you are the leader and feel as though you are held to a higher standard. However, not acknowledging a mistake and postponing any needed corrections may cost your organization in tangible (money) or intangible (time, morale) ways. This is certainly not what a good leader is charged to do. In the long run, you will attain a higher level of respect if you take full responsibility for your actions and decisions.

Admitting you're wrong obviously takes integrity and moral courage. It is also a very powerful way to model behavior for your followers. If you admit your mistakes, your followers will be much more likely to admit their mistakes. By making honest admissions you can guide your team toward a work place where people seek the right thing to do, admit their mistakes, correct their errors and help to mitigate organizational losses.

Conversely, Andrew once worked for a boss who made all the wrong moves when he was uncertain about an issue. Of course, to hear the boss tell it, there was nothing he didn't know! The boss would never admit he was wrong, even though he was repeatedly wrong. Whenever in doubt, he would try to bluff his way through. Worse yet, when he finally asked a question and someone answered it, he would said, "I know that." Of course, people were tempted to ask him why he had asked the question at all if he already knew the answer. This type of boss can alienate people quickly with such arrogant behavior.

Regardless of what comes your way as a leader, work the problem out logically to come to a solution. The fact that you do not have an immediate answer is not a big deal. What's important is that you effectively handle the issue. Now, if as a leader you never seem to know the answer or how to effectively proceed, that is another situation entirely. At that point, perhaps another line of work is in order!

If you begin to recognize a pattern in the types of areas that challenge you, this is a good time to identify weakness and work to strengthen it. Initial lack of knowledge is acceptable but remaining ignorant to recognized problems is not. You may find that you have difficulty making decisions in a particular field because you lack the expertise in that field. Identify these areas and strive to become better educated in these subjects. This will make you a more effective leader. Simply put, bluffing is for poker, not leadership.

If man evolved from monkeys and apes, why do we still have monkeys and apes?
George Carlin

CHAPTER TWELVE
King of Spades
Leadership Approaches

"Sir, I really like poker. Every hand has its different problems."
Henry Fonda, playing Wyatt Earp in *My Darling Clementine*

The poker table changes constantly. If you played every hand exactly the same, you are assured of losing. Your cards change, your bank changes and even the people at the table can change. Indeed, not only is every hand different, every game is different. Each table you sit at is composed of players with different skills, different cards and different banks. Like a good leader, the poker player continually adapts to his or her environment and the situation.

There are many different approaches to leadership. Each leader has their individual personality and style that will affect how they manage their workers. However, good leaders also take into account the situation, people, organization and task when deciding how they will approach the leadership role. Simply using whatever style comes easiest for you is not always going to produce the best results. Moreover, using the same style in every situation will not be as successful as learning to adapt.

Some people are "hands-off" managers and others are "hands-on" leaders. Hands-on management sometimes turns into "micromanagement" where the boss must have control over virtually everything. Neither type is right or wrong; certain employees need certain things. Some need a great deal of structure and want to be guided every step of the way. Others resent this and want a more hands-off approach where they are allowed more individual liberty in their work. It is important to assess each employee for what they need from management; something that takes time. If you give employees the type of leadership they need rather than what comes naturally to you, they will be much more productive and happy.

In addition to your people having varying degrees of skill, the task also dictates what type of leadership style you might use. Some tasks require a high amount of direction while others don't necessarily require high leader involvement in providing direction. Just as a task sometimes dictates style, follower ability often dictates leadership style. For example, you wouldn't expect a new employee to know certain things about your organization. You may have to tell them or provide them with specific direction.

Authorities such as Paul Hersey and Ken Blanchard have articulated the concept of situational leadership. The Hersey and Blanchard model views the leadership approach in relation to the situation (task) and group involved. The basic notion is that leaders should have a toolbox filled with different approaches and resources for effective leadership. Depending on what factors are present in the situation (such as task) and who is being led, the leader selects the style of leadership that will most likely yield the best results. By choosing the appropriate approach based on these criteria, leaders can ensure a higher probability for success and development of their people.

> **Refer to the companion website, at www.pokerleadership.com, for fuller definitions and discussions on the different styles/types of leadership**

For example, if a leader in law enforcement is confronted with a hostage situation, that person will probably adopt an autocratic style of leadership with the recovery forces. This is simply because that type of situation requires orders to be given and followed immediately. There is no time to break into small groups and make lists on a flip chart. The situation has dictated the appropriate style of leadership.

The ability and skill of the people being led are also key factors in which leadership style a leader should select. You should assess your follower's abilities and skill levels in an effort to determine what will help them succeed. For example, if there is a well-trained, experienced, and motivated work group, the leader will probably allow them a great deal of freedom and autonomy. On the other hand, if it is a new group that has not shown much in the way of perfor-mance or motivation, the leader may be inclined to select a more authoritative and watchful style of leadership. Again, the style is dictated in part by the readiness and willingness of those being led.

It is difficult to be a situational leader. It forces you to evaluate constantly the present situation, including the skills and motivations of those working for you. In addition, everyone has a style that comes most naturally. Often, the leadership style most suited to the situation and people is not the style with which the leader personally feels most comfortable. Indeed, this is often a criticism of the Situational Leadership Model – the ability of a leader to overcome their natural tendencies and adapt their style to the task and followers. That being said, it may very well be the inability to adapt that separates good leaders from mediocre leaders and poor poker players from their money.

When Andrew first entered law enforcement employment 25 years ago, the different bosses in his organization would rotate on a regular basis. Each had an individual style and it was up to the officers to adapt to the bosses styles, not the other way around. This made it easy for the bosses, as they just had to do what came naturally. Conversely, this was often difficult for the followers who were the ones who had to alter their style to fit the boss. Although there are still some leaders like this, the concept of situational leadership has taken hold. Now, leaders are being asked to adapt, rather than the employees. It is much better for one person to change and adapt to the work group rather than the group adapting to one person. It is not easy, but leadership is not always supposed to be easy. It takes a lot of desire and practice to become a good situational leader. The results are likely worth the dedication required.

As you move further up in your organization you will also find an additional value in Situational Leadership. When you are in a position to select and train subordinate leaders, you would be well served to consider mixing dominant leader talents with task and group. This concept has a number of applications: You may want to use a high direction leader as a change agent; you may want to keep a well-motivated group working; or, you may want to expose your subordinate leaders to a variety of situations and groups so that they can grow. Raymond explained that he once had a subordinate leader who was very high direction orientated. The leader was very knowledgeable and had potential to move further up in the organization if he learned to work also with well-motivated and highly knowledgeable groups. Raymond explained to the subordinate leader that next month his assignment would change and he would be taking over a very well-oiled and performing group. This required the leader in training to shift from a more directive style of leadership to a more participative style. More importantly, Raymond explained the purpose of the assignment and provided the subordinate leader with high task direction.

Over the next several months Raymond worked closely with the leader and the group. It was important not to disturb the equilibrium of the group and at the same time teach the subordinate leader a different leadership style. As time passed, Raymond moved from providing the subordinate leader with high direction, to coaching and ultimately the subordinate leader and the group worked well together.

Another approach to leadership is described in Tannenbaum and Schmidt's decision-making model. It is a continuum that looks at how a leader exerts control over a group in order to manage them. Chris Loynes outlines the six positions of this model in the 1993-94 *Expedition Planners Handbook and Directory*.

Figure 12.1 (Decision Making Model)

Tannenbaum and Schmidt's decision-making model:

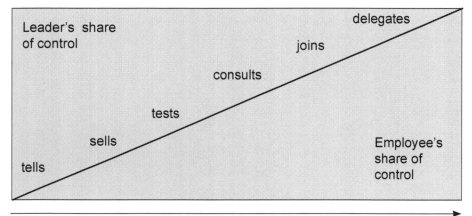

Degree of employee involvement in decision making

Degree of employee involvement in decision making

1. **Tells** Leaders make decisions based on their own evaluation. They decide what action will occur and then tells the group. The leaders do not give explanations, and employees are not involved in the process.
2. **Sells** Leaders again make the decision but give the group reasons for what they decided.
3. **Tests** Leaders evaluate the situation and offer a solution along with reasons. Before making a final decision, leaders allow questions and discussion from the group.

4. **Consults** Leaders present the situation and its background and ask for ideas on solutions. Leaders then make the decision.
5. **Joins** Leaders present the problem and begin a discussion with the group. The decision is made jointly by the group and the leaders.
6. **Delegates** Leaders or members of the group present the situation. The group is responsible for coming to a decision about what actions need to be taken. Leaders may participate in the discussion, and they support the decision once it is made.

From approach one to six as displayed in figure 12.1, the leader is gradually sharing more control with employees. The authors would like to add a seventh position to this model. Following delegation, there is an additional phase which is best described as "supervision." This phase is concerned with the level of follow-up and review that a leader exercises over tasks. If a leader does not supervise a delegated task, that is, in a sense, abdication of the leadership role. On the other hand, if a leader is "micromanaging" every step of the task, that is not true delegation. A crucial point to remember is that you delegate authority and not responsibility. Since you are still responsible to the organization for the outcomes it is incumbent upon a good leader to periodically check-in even with a well-oiled group or person.

Leaders must find the appropriate balance between abdication and "micromanagement," just as a balance between "telling" and "delegation" must be found. The extreme ends of the leadership continuum are rarely appropriate in most organizations. The leader must go back to the situational analysis of the problem. You determine the nature of the issue and the people involved to decide which phase you will initiate to solve a problem or confront a task. If you are flexible enough to adjust your management style to whatever situation and group you encounter, you will likely lead your organization wisely and successfully. They're your cards to play, depending on the situation.

A leader has two important characteristics; first, he is going somewhere- second, he is able to persuade other people to go with him.

Maximilien Robespierre

CHAPTER THIRTEEN
Ace of Spades
Humility

All in all, I suspect this kid has a shot to make it in the poker world. Yes, he lacks experience, but his heart, courage, effort, and intellect all seemed in place. He just needs more varied poker environments and the humility to learn from his mistakes.

Roy Cooke, Telegraphing Your Thoughts, Card Player Magazine

Whether he likes it or not, a man's character is stripped bare at the poker table; if the other players read him better than he does, he has only himself to blame. Unless he is both able and prepared to see himself as others do, flaws and all, he will be a loser in cards, as in life.

Anthony Holden, Big Deal

John Baldoni (in Darwin Magazine) noted that "humility is not taught in management courses or many leadership courses, for that matter. And you can understand why. Organizations want their leaders to be visionary, authoritative, capable and motivational. Nowhere does it say anything about being humble." Humility is defined as the "state of being humble." Unfortunately, the word humble has some generally disparaging definitions such as a "low or inferior station or quality," "meekness or modesty" or, "use of unskilled work." Even worse, some who have been humbled are thought of as having been shamed. With these definitions, it is no wonder that leadership and management courses have avoided looking at humility as an integral part of leadership.

Yes, humility is integral to leadership because it is alternatively defined as "being modest in self-estimation." This definition has a leading and important part to your development as a leader. In leadership, humility is the brake on your ego. It is realizing that your position as a leader is a trust between you, the organization and the followers. It is your humility that will allow you to place follower and organizational concerns above your own needs. Your humility is the paramount connection to your followers.

Over the recent holidays, Raymond and his cousins were having dinner. One cousin, a very successful businessman involved in equity trading said, "Do you remember Christmas cotton?" Raymond and the other cousin, a successful e-entrepreneur, smiled. For us, Christmas cotton was a reminder of our connections to the past. My cousin recalled the first time he heard the phrase. Our grandmother was driving him somewhere and pointed out the last of the cotton crop. It was Christmas cotton. She explained that a small portion of the crop, the most difficult to harvest, was saved until near Christmas. It was picked to provide money for gifts – like shoes.

We talked about being only a generation away from Christmas cotton. It was clear that we had a shared sense of having been handed a gift from our parents and grandparents. It was our job to take care of the gift, to remember how difficult it was to come by and to grow it for the future. We understood that we didn't get to success alone. We found that as leaders in our own industries what we shared was a profound sense of gratitude for the trust placed in our hands. If you met the cousins individually you would see that their humility is a brake on their ego. It allows them to see different points of view, consider radical information and use feedback for improvement.

Former Secretary of State and Retired General Colin Powell has thirteen leadership rules. His third leadership rule is "Avoid having your ego so close to your position that when your position falls, your ego goes with it." A sense of humility can help leaders separate their ego from their position. It makes it easier to be wrong, to receive critical feedback and to change and learn when your ego is not involved. Indeed, a sense of humility makes being wrong easier to accept, therefore, it makes learning from your mistakes much more likely. Humility is critical to leadership success because it opens the door to feedback, learning and involvement with your followers.

Basketball coach Phil Jackson said that many have classified him as arrogant and aloof. He did not feel this way about himself. Rather, he felt he was inherently shy. He felt this characteristic, coupled with his great success as a coach, led to people putting him into a category he did not feel he belonged. Perhaps true, but people draw their perceptions from their limited perspectives, even though both perceptions and perspectives are usually wrong--and it is just a question of how wrong in matter of degree. Andrew identifies quite closely with Coach Jackson's comments. Andrew is also inherently shy, and achieved great success in his field at a very early age. This, in turn, caused people to assess him as, you guessed it, arrogant and aloof.

Andrew became aware of this perception and did not like it one bit. He worked to change the perception but found it a tough case to crack. In his path toward changing some people's perceptions of him, he found that, as a general rule, the better people knew him, the less they felt he was arrogant and aloof. This resulted in Andrew putting forth effort to get to know people better on a more personal level, rather than just in the professional sense. This had great effect and this is recommended for those of you who may find yourself in similar straits.

A caveat first though: No matter what you do, there will always be some person or group of people that will see you in this fashion no matter what you do. This is so in some cases because seeing you this way fits into their agenda. The following anecdote helps to illustrate this troubling fact.

Andrew had a regular practice of speaking with his staff members and asking their advice on how he could do a better job for them. As a command-level law enforcement officer, people were not usually very forthcoming at first. After a while though, people would usually begin to warm up and provide substantive information that could help in Andrew's quest to do the best job he could.

One particular supervisor commented on the placement of Andrew's computer, which was on a back credenza. This supervisor stated that because Andrew needed to turn his back to his office door when he worked on the computer, this was a message that he did not want to be bothered with people, and that this contributed in part to some of the "aloof" perceptions that may have been occurring.

This was valuable insight in that it was something that Andrew would not have thought of on his own. After thinking about it though, he mentioned to the supervisor that the chief of police also had his computer in the same configuration. He asked the supervisor if this was also contributing to the perception that the chief was aloof. After pondering this question for sometime, the supervisor told Andrew that it was not. Andrew then asked why it was that he could engage in the exact same behavior as the chief, and in the chief's case it was not perceived as aloof, but in Andrew's case it was. The supervisor again thought about it for some time and said, "I don't know why it's different. It just is." The moral of the story is that people are human beings and, even in a leadership position, there is only so far you can go toward displaying humility. No matter what you do, there will still be those that claim you don't possess it!

People do not lead organizations, they lead people. A sense of humility opens the door to the leader admitting they don't have all the answers and requiring follower input and help for success. If you have humility you know you can't lead on your own. You can't lead on your own because you need people to follow you. People want, need and like to be needed. Our shared need connects us. We sense and feel it. If your followers sense you need them, they will connect with you. It is the human connection that enables people to go to extraordinary lengths.

Dr. Leonard Wong, associate research professor at the U.S. Army War College's Strategic Studies Institute completed a project: "Why They Fight: Combat Motivation in Iraq." Combat studies from World War II revealed that a soldier's primary motivation to fight and overcome extraordinary circumstances was their connection to their comrades. Dr. Wong's research wanted to determine if, during our age, the connection to comrades still trumped patriotism and cause as it did during World War II. American soldiers in Iraq responded similarly to their predecessors about wanting to return home, but the most frequent response given for combat motivation was "fighting for my buddies," Wong's report said.

Making a human connection with your followers is one of the most important aspects of your leadership ability. You can only connect if you are seen as human and this is often accomplished through your sense of humility. If you display the need for human assistance, people will respond. Simply put, humility makes you human and allows your followers to see that, even though you are the leader, you are in many ways just like them.

You can help yourself to have more humility in a variety of ways. You can display and garner a sense of humility by occasionally working with your followers in their jobs. Many leaders set aside one day a month where they work directly with followers. For instance, as a watch commander in the police service, Raymond worked as a police officer's partner once a month. There is no better way to understand your follower's challenges than by experiencing them. An added benefit of spending such time with your followers is the opportunity to pick up on subtle nuances that could never be seen from "on high." If you worked your way up the ranks of any organization it is helpful to remember the days when your organization was Christmas cotton to you.

You can engender a sense of humility with followers by encouraging feedback on you and the organization. As we will discuss later in the book, one technique is to receive feedback using a 360 degree model. The idea is to open yourself up to feedback, and to demonstrate to your followers that feedback is essential to maintaining a connection and improving performance. You will demonstrate humility by recognizing that you, just as your followers, can always improve. Most importantly, if you make real efforts to use the feedback you will model humility. This emphasizes a recurring theme of this book – you cannot expect followers to behave in any way you will not or have not modeled. If you don't, they won't.

Humility breeds productive dissent, hopefully. There is dissent in every organization. In some, it is stifled and there is a false sense of harmony. The dissent hovers below the surface and rears its head at the most inopportune times. However, if you can create a workplace that engenders productive dissent and encourages followers to provide input, you can facilitate agreement. For dissent to be healthy it must be about a specific action. A follower exercising a good dissenting opinion focuses on a specific issue, has an alternative, and voices the dissent in the proper forum. It is your job to model dissenting behavior and to provide the proper forums.

When you demonstrate humility, you show your followers it is okay not to know everything and to make mistakes. In this type of environment, people readily admit their mistakes and use them as lessons for the future. The opposite environment is where everyone "covers their tracks." When mistakes are covered up and passing blame is an art form, an organization is in serious trouble. This poor environment is a leadership issue because it was caused by a leader who modeled that they were always perfect, always right and that mistakes would not be tolerated.

Perhaps humility is largely ignored in the leadership and management literature because it is so very hard to accomplish. Being visionary, authoritative, capable and motivational, yet humble, is a tall drink of water but it is a balance worth striving for.

I have never imputed to Nature a purpose or a goal, or anything that could be understood as anthropomorphic. What I see in Nature is a magnificent structure that we can comprehend only very imperfectly, and that must fill a thinking person with a feeling of humility. This is a genuinely religious feeling that has nothing to do with mysticism.

Albert Einstein

HEARTS

High-stakes poker is a game that has always attracted lawyers, perhaps because many of the skills of a good lawyer are transferable to the poker table: quick calculations, decisive decision-making, and the ability to "read" another human being.

Ken Swift

CHAPTER FOURTEEN
Two of Hearts
Action vs. Words

If you reraise a raiser, and he doesn't raise you back, you know he has kicker problems.

Crandall Addington, Texas oil millionaire (2001)

How you play your cards often gives other players information about your hand. Consider "actions" to be the cards the player holds and "bets" to be the words. If you bet inconsistently or get caught bluffing once too often, people are going to begin to draw conclusions about your play. Perhaps, more importantly, in Poker you often want people to draw incorrect conclusions about what you hold based on how you play. You may bet weak to draw them in or bet strong to scare them off. The point is that our actions send very strong messages about what we intend to do.

> **Wild Card** A "kicker" is the highest single card held by two players in Hold'em who each hold the same pair. For example, if the board in Hold'em is A-10-8-5-2, and Player One holds A-J as his hand, and Player Two holds A-Q, each player has a pair of Aces, but Player Two has a better kicker and would win the hand.

The difference between actions and words is highlighted in the role of leader. People will no doubt listen to what you have to say if you are in a position of leadership. Over time, they will compare what you say to what you do. If there is a disparity, your credibility will diminish.

Research indicates that upwards of 85% of human communication is non-verbal. Typically, we think of non-verbal communication as facial expressions, tone of voice and body language. Leader actions are also strong forms of non-verbal communication. Your followers are watching your actions and looking for consistency and modeling. The consistency aspect of leader behavior is your behavior matching your words. The model aspect is when you demonstrate your expectations. Consistency and modeling are related to two specific types of leader power: Consistency is highly correlated with referent power; and, modeling is highly correlated with expert power. As we shall see, your actions determine if you gain or lose these types of power.

Like the other players at the table, people are using your actions as a means to interpret the messages you send. Since the lion's share of communication is non-verbal, it is our mutual interpretation of each other's actions that determine which messages are received and how the messages are interpreted. Think of it as our words being interpreted in context with our actions. When your actions mirror your words, you begin to build credibility with followers and credibility is the centerpiece of referent power.

Credibility has several meanings. For a leader, it most often means the capability of being believed by followers. Credibility is to command belief or truthfulness of what one says. In other words, credibility means that whatever a leader says, he or she believes in it. However, merely being believed is not sufficient for a leader to be taken as credible, because the leader must act on what he or she says.

People must realize they can count on a leader following through. For instance, a leader who is known for following through will find that his followers take warnings much more seriously. In addition to taking your counseling more seriously, your praise will be more meaningful. Remember, if people see that your actions and words are consistent, they form the strong opinion that you believe in what you say. Therefore, if you believe an action is praiseworthy, so too will your followers. Taking the opposite tact further demonstrates the point – leaders who don't follow through are not believed when they issue warnings; leaders who are not believed are found to be gratuitous when they praise followers. By demonstrating consistency between actions and words you also demonstrate your commitment to your own words. You believe what you are saying. If you believe, your followers will believe.

LEADERSHIP IN BRIEF

The importance of leader credibility comes up over and over again in the best literature. As an example, in *The Leadership Challenge*, Kouzes and Posner state: "We know that leaders' deeds are far more important than their words. Credibility of action is the single most significant determinant of whether a leader will be followed over time."

In addition to building your referent power, consistency between your actions and words can build your expert power. Expert power is the leadership influence you build with followers through the demonstration of knowledge and experience. Often, demonstrating expert power is termed as modeling behavior or leading from the front. This type of modeling is not doing the follower's job. It is using the consistency between your words and actions to demonstrate organizational values, beliefs and goals, as well as technical knowledge.

You can only lead others where you yourself are willing to go. You must state the way and show the way. For example, in 1942, General George S. Patton took command of the Desert Training Center east of Los Angeles. Upon his arrival, all officers and enlisted men stood for inspection. Patton advised them that everyone under his command would be required to run a mile in fifteen minutes carrying their rifle and full military pack. He said, "We will start running from this point in exactly thirty minutes. I will lead."

It is an uncommon sight see a general running a mile with a rifle and full pack. That, however, is exactly what General Patton did. His actions provided a very tangible demonstration of leading by example. Patton said, "The leader must be an actor. But with him as with his bewigged counterpart, he is unconvincing unless he lives his part." What was Patton, a 57-year-old man, demonstrating when he ran with his troops? What did his 18-year-old privates think about the general running through the desert? While few enjoy running under these conditions, most will respect the leader that shows he or she can do what he or she expects the follower to do. In addition to Patton gaining respect by his words mirroring his actions, he was beginning to build his expert power by demonstrating what he valued and believed in.

Patton believed that tough, well-trained and disciplined troops would prevail in battle. His run through the desert was modeling his beliefs. His actions said that soldiers who followed their leader on an arduous run through the desert can be tough, trained and disciplined. They can prevail in battle. Patton was not showing them how to run with a rifle and pack; he was demonstrating what he believed. Leaders should always look for ways to demonstrate beliefs and values to followers. These demonstrations enhance the leader's expert power without micromanaging the jobs of followers. The essence of modeling is not showing how to do a task, it is demonstrating organizational values, beliefs, and goals.

Most of the literature on organizational studies defines a boundary spanner as an individual who links their organization with the external environment and primarily concerns the exchange of information between the organization and environment. Leaders are boundary spanners. Leaders often find themselves as the connection point between the boundaries of their organization and others outside the organization. Moreover, many researchers see these efforts at boundary spanning as not only an effort to exchange information, but as an effort to influence how information is used and perceived. This means that the same consistency between words and actions can greatly affect how those outside your organization view the organization as a whole.

> **The companion website at www.pokerleadership.com has additional information on boundary spanning and its relationship to strategic planning and decision making.**

As a law enforcement officer, Andrew felt it was important for his actions to match the expectations of the public. He believed that while driving a patrol car he was a very visible representative of the traffic laws he was charged to enforce and his organization in total. Except when driving in emergency mode, if he had been seen not signaling, or if he had been speeding, or following too closely, he would not have been an effective agent of the law nor an effective representative of his organization. Simply put, leaders live in a goldfish bowl. When people know you represent an organization they are looking for the same consistency between your words and actions. The credibility of your organization is at stake when your actions are inconsistent with your words.

Words come easier than actions, but actions ultimately tell more about you. Through consistency between your actions and words and by using your actions to demonstrate what you believe, you can build your leadership influence. It is more than doing what you say, it is also crafting what you do to represent what you believe.

What you do speaks so loudly that I cannot hear what you say.

Ralph Waldo Emerson

Example is leadership.

Dr. Albert Schweitzer

CHAPTER FIFTEEN
Three of Hearts
Communication

I've always had confidence, but I never let my ego get to the point that I think I'm the superstar, because I know that ego has destroyed many a poker career.

Jim Boyd, modern-day road gambler

The cardinal sin in poker, worse than playing dead cards, worse even than figuring your odds incorrectly, is becoming emotionally involved.

A Girlhood Among Gamblers by Katy Lederer

In several of the previous chapters and many of the chapters to come, we touch on some aspect of communication. Consistency between your actions and words, giving clear direction and having a vision are all segments of communicating. This is because effective communication may be the most challenging issue facing leaders. It is a never-ending process and one in which the effectiveness is difficult to measure. As we delve further into communication, we want to look at how both the leader and follower filter communication through a variety of lenses. As several of the great poker gurus have said, once you start to filter the action on the table through the lenses of your ego and your emotions, you're done.

But ego and emotion aren't the only filters we use to encode and decode the messages we send and receive. Consider communication filters as the internal devices we use to place communication in context. We are all using filters like our culture, previous experience, ego and emotion to make sense of the information we are sending and receiving. Often, our intended message is lost by the restrictive filters we use and the ones being used by our followers.

Active listening is one method leaders can use to improve their communication skills. Years ago, Andrew had a boss who did not give his full attention when Andrew spoke to him. Although not intentional, it was distracting when he answered the telephone, shuffled through his desk, and even clipped his nails.

The first step in active listening is giving the speaker your full attention. Imagine a "no-limit" poker game where you don't give the table your full attention. If you're ordering drinks, chatting with the gallery or even counting your money you have lost control of the table. Paying full and close attention to the speaker is just that important. If you don't, you will miss the important cues that can help you interpret the play.

Wild Card In a no limit game, there is no limit on how much a player can bet or raise. The minimum is usually determined by the current blind (the amount of the bet by the person preceding the player); however a player can bet anything up to the full amount in front of them. When a player bets all their chips, they have gone "all in."

If you cannot actively listen to an employee at a particular time, simply make arrangements to talk with that person later. Actively listening is one of the best ways to convey respect for followers and this demonstration of respect will increase your approachability.

Active listening requires a great deal of effort and patience. Often times, people make snap judgments about a person's perspective on things before they even have a conversation. This makes effective communication more difficult. To truly understand a person's view, we must actively listen to what they are trying to get across. Asking questions or paraphrasing what the person has said are good ways to make sure that you understand and did not just "hear" what was said. If you avoid interrupting and give the speaker your full attention, you will earn their respect. You will be in a better position to ask questions after the speaker is through, and you will avoid hearing an exasperated person say, "I was just getting to that."

In active listening, your questions and paraphrasing are efforts to understand what filters are in place. It is how you determine the complete context of the conversation. In order to fully understand and appreciate a message you must be able to place it in context. The only way that you can do that is to help the speaker navigate through your, and their, filters. On the other hand, we all know people who can talk on and on. As an astute leader, you should gauge the tempo of a conversation and know how to "speed it along." As an adroit leader you must master the art of moving a conversation along smoothly and ending it gracefully. Moreover, as you practice actively listening with your followers you will learn their filters and you will ultimately find that communication is not only improved, but speeded up.

Good communication is impossible when you do not care. Insincerity and the "you're wrong/I'm right" attitude eliminate rapport. Conversations are not something you can "win" and they are not always about finding a right or wrong answer. This is especially true when the conversation is about a difficult or sensitive topic. This is exactly when good communication is needed the most. If you approach others with genuine interest in what they have to say, even if it differs from what you think, effective communication is more likely to occur.

Communication is so commonplace that it is easy to become complacent and believe that everything is all right when in fact the situation may be critical, especially if there is little feedback until things go awry. Even leaders who are constantly vigilant can fail in this area. For large companies that are geographically spread out, the problem is even greater. It also can be difficult to give feedback for companies on a single site, particularly if you have employees on different shifts and different schedules. Invariably, somebody didn't "get the word."

An example of this happening is shown in the story told below:

Director Cecil B. DeMille was filming a movie and he had six cameras at various points to pick up all the overall action and five other cameras set up to film plot developments involving the major characters. At 6:00 a.m., the large cast began rehearsing. By late afternoon, they had rehearsed four times. The sun was setting and there was just enough light, DeMille looked over the panorama and gave the command for action. One hundred extras charged up the hill; another hundred came down the same hill in mock battle. In another location, 200 extras labored to move a huge stone into place. After 15 minutes of non-stop action, DeMille yelled, "Cut," and told his assistants that he was very pleased. He waved to the camera crew supervisor to ensure that all the cameras had picked up what they had been assigned to film. From the top of the hill, the camera supervisor waved back, raised his megaphone, and called out, "Ready when you are CB!"

This story is not too far off from what is happening every day in organizations. Even in companies that have good communication, problems always arise. One of the common methods leaders use to increase communication is the "open-door policy." This ordinarily means that any employee can come in and talk with a top-level boss without navigating the hierarchy. Both Andrew and Raymond have always had an open-door policy, but there are some cautions to its use.

First, you have to ensure that the employee is not "shopping" for an answer to their concern. If workers have already gotten an answer that they object to from a lower-level boss, the worker should share that with you. Sometimes employees are not forthcoming with this information and you have to be responsible for seeking that out. Secondly, the bosses under you may not be happy that their employees have direct access. You should always be wary of undermining subordinate leaders.

Warren Bennis, author of *Managing People is like Herding Cats*, has an open-door policy but his rule is that he will not give a decision without conferring with lower-level bosses to get their perspective on the situation. The authors think this is a good approach as it works to balance the needs of the employees with support for supervision and management.

Another important part of communication is an appreciation of when to keep quiet. This is particularly true for leaders because people pay close attention to what leaders say. There are going to be times when you don't know what you're talking about because you lack complete information about a subject. Those are the times to refrain from speaking until you have more information. This principle is demonstrated by the following story:

A hungry mountain lion came out of the hills, attacked a bull, and killed it. As it feasted on its kill, the lion would, from time to time, pause to roar in triumph. A hunter heard the commotion, found the lion, and shot him dead. The moral of the story is: when you're full of bull, keep your mouth shut!

There is an *I Love Lucy* episode in which Lucy ends up in France charged with counterfeiting. Ricky arrived to help, but there were major communication problems. The sergeant spoke only French, and Lucy spoke only English. However, one of the officers spoke French and German. One of the other prisoners spoke German and Spanish. Ricky, of course, spoke Spanish and English. They formed a communication line and translated French to German to Spanish to English. This very funny scene hits close to home with many organizations. Although we may all be speaking the same language, it may not always appear that way. It is the leader's duty to ensure that messages are communicated effectively.

Even when the leader communicates with great precision, things can still go wrong. In Andrew's seminars, he does an exercise in communication where he gives one of the members of the class a short paragraph to read. This person in turn is required to pass it on. After four or five people have passed the message down the line, he asks someone to repeat the message. It always comes out terribly distorted. This version of the game "telephone" succinctly demonstrates what happens when a message is passed through multiple individual filters.

The following story shows how communication easily can go astray:

Delivering a speech at a banquet on the night of his arrival into a large city, a visiting minister told several anecdotes he expected to repeat at meetings the next day. Because he wanted to use the jokes again, he requested that the reporters omit them from any accounts they might run in their newspapers. A cub reporter, in commenting on the speech, ended his piece with the following: "The minister told a number of stories that cannot be published."

JOKERS ARE WILD

Church bulletins have even been an amusing source of misleading communications, as evidenced by the following actual excerpts:

- Don't let worry kill you – let the church help.
- Remember in prayer the many who are sick of our church and community.
- For those who have children and don't know it, we have a new nursery.
- This being Easter Sunday, we ask Mrs. Lewis to come forward and lay an egg on the altar.
- Thursday, there will be a meeting of the Little Mothers Club. All wishing to become little mothers, please see the minister in his study.

Communication is invariably going to involve disagreement. There are going to be times when you must debate an issue with others and there will be times when you, as the leader, will need to mediate an argument between people. There are healthy, constructive ways to debate that promote discussion and evaluation. There are also ways of arguing that evade the issues and only end up causing frustration or insult. Think of a disagreement as a canyon with followers on opposite sides. It is the leader's responsibility to build a bridge over the canyon so that the followers can meet. The next time you are on a bridge note that they are only built across sides of the canyon that are roughly equal. It is your job as the leader to find the equal, or common ground in the dispute and build the bridge from there.

You need to be aware of where it is that a disagreement goes from normal dissent to destructive arguing. Discussion allows both sides to be heard freely and without bias. It is where people speak respectfully, rationally, stay on topic, and avoid illogical fallacies that cloud the issue. This type of debate is productive; it allows both sides of an issue to be discussed and evaluated. When you communicate in this manner, you have a better chance of getting your points across intact and faithfully representing your side. Then, the best choice can be made.

 Some fallacies to look for and avoid when disagreeing include:

- **Attacking the person (put-downs, bringing up the past, etc.) instead of the issue.**
- **Attempting to discredit the person instead of focusing on the issues.**
- **Generalizing that which may not be representative or relevant.**
- **Using fear or pity to gain support for an argument.**
- **Comparing issues or situations that are dissimilar.**
- **Excluding factors or evidence that may affect the debate.**
- **Not giving all the options or consequences of a situation.**
- **Assuming something is false because you do not know it to be true.**
- **Assuming something is true because it is generally believed to be true.**
- **Using the "slippery slope" approach where consequences**

increase from bad to worse. Example: If I let you go home early on Friday, then everyone will want to go home early on Friday. Soon everyone will want all of Friday off, and we'll get nothing done.

- Basing the argument on unrelated or improbable points.
- Attaching moral superiority or goodness to a debater and therefore to his or her argument.
- Using non-sequiturs where the conclusion does not follow from the premise. Example: Because Lily types quickly, she must be good at computer programming.
- Arguing that two contradictory points are both true.
- Concluding about the whole of something (a group, situation, etc.) when you have only discussed part(s) of it.
- Using untested or biased evidence.
- Using too broad or too narrow definitions.
- Using words or phrases that allow for varying interpretations.
- "Begging the question" when you must assume the truth of the conclusion before you can assume the truth of the premise.
- Attacking arguments that are different from what the other person is actually arguing.

In regards to communication, what's the answer for the leader? You must communicate clearly, often, and consistently. Constantly seek feedback to see if the message was sent and if it was received accurately. Practice active listening so that you truly understand the perspectives of others – never assume that you know what another person thinks before you communicate. Also, you must have a genuine interest in what other people have to say, even if it differs from your own ideas. When you face a disagreement, make sure both sides are using healthy, constructive arguments and avoiding fallacies. Good communication is not always easy, but it is an essential element for smooth operations within your organization.

When you talk, you repeat what you already know; when you listen, you often learn something.

Jared Sparks

The only bad luck for a good gambler is bad health. Any other setbacks are temporary aggravation.

Benny Binion

CHAPTER SIXTEEN
Four of Hearts
Change

Patience. And shuffle the cards.

Cervantes, Don Quioxte

Perhaps change is the only constant. It is certainly inevitable. In poker it is not just that each hand changes; nearly every factor can or does change. The players change, the deck, the order of the cards, your bank; everything is changing constantly. The winning player is able to adapt to each change, to change his or her strategies based on the environment of the table. Change is also continually occurring for organizations and is one of the most stressful events for organizations and people

There are many factors, such as fear or insecurity, which create uneasiness regarding change. Both leaders and employees are prone to resist changes. Sometimes people view it as a sign that their current work is not good enough and they become defensive about ways to improve. Good leaders recognize this and do everything they can to ease the impact surrounding organizational change.

Generally, there are two types of change for an organization, internally-imposed change and externally-imposed change. Leaders should understand that there will be situations brought about by external sources and there may be limits to how much control they have in these situations. Their only option may be a reactive posture. Internally-imposed changes offer a better opportunity to shape the organization's future in a proactive way. The one constant is that change is a guaranteed occurrence within any organization. Good leaders have the ability to adapt and also to lead others through the stressful process of adaptation. Ideally, leaders do not just react; they pro-act. It is their job to make the workplace one in which change is viewed positively.

Leaders who are new to an organization or to a particular division must remember that any changes they make may suggest an implicit criticism of the existing structure. This is going to occur despite how well the reason for change is framed. You cannot remain stagnant just to avoid offending anyone, but you must be sensitive to people's concerns. Change is difficult for most people even if the change is perceived as positive. If it is viewed negatively, there is even more potential for resistance. You can take the brute-force approach and force changes. However, good leaders understand that, in order to create a lasting effect, change must be inspired. Remember the Eisenhower string? Leaders can help their people to assimilate in several ways.

First, whether you are new to the job or implementing change in your current position, you should involve the people affected by the situation. Begin by explaining why you perceive the change to be necessary. It is always a good idea to get multiple perspectives before considering new directions. Also, this will give your employees a sense of empowerment and involvement which will ease the pressures of changing. Secondly, whenever possible, time should be allotted in the process to allow people to acclimate fully to the change. People will be less anxious if they feel that they have had enough time to prepare for a new challenge. Prior to the change, the organization's approach should be communicated in writing. Finally, if additional training is required, this training should be conducted prior to the implementation of the change. After the implementation, feedback should be solicited. It is possible that some midcourse corrections will be warranted.

Even if these steps are followed, change will still be a challenge. But, it may be accepted more easily and in a shorter amount of time. People will understand the need for the change, they will have had an opportunity for input, and they will have the confidence that they can successfully deal with the new situation. Another method for leading change can be found in Kurt Lewin's change model: Unfreeze - Change - Refreeze.

"Aboard my ship, excellent performance is standard. Standard performance is sub-standard. Sub-standard performance is not permitted to exist. Now Rome wasn't built in a day, and this ship has been sailing a hell of a long time without me, and as I say, I regard you as a splendid wardroom officers. If there's anything that I want changed in anybody's department you'll find out about it fast enough"

Captain Queeg, The Caine Mutiny

If Captain Queeg had a manual on organizational change it is likely that he would have followed it to the letter. The problem with Queeg's approach and his organizational change problem may provide insight into key leader duties during periods of change. Follower readiness for change is one of the key components of the Lewin model. Readiness can be defined as the degree to which followers' beliefs, attitudes, and intentions mirror the need for change and the organization's capacity to change. Changing follower readiness or preparing them for change is often referred to in the literature as the "unfreezing" process in organizational change. That is, a leader must unfreeze the follower's current beliefs and attitudes in order to prepare them for change.

A leader can increase follower readiness by communicating the need for change through multiple mediums such as written and verbal forms of communications as well as through the use of symbols. Communication regarding change can, for instance, help organizational members put the necessity of change in context with the environment, thereby increasing readiness. Furthermore, much of the literature about change indicates that communications decreases follower anxiety regarding change.

Explore the theories and models of change leadership on the companion website at www.pokerleadership.com

While crafting and communicating the message seems simple enough, it is fraught with difficulties. Although Queeg's message about impending change is conflicting, at best, it is unlikely that he would have been able to craft the message without a clear understanding of his subordinates, the vessel and the mission. For Queeg, all three were broad variables to which any change was dependent (his followers, his organization – the ship, and the environment or mission). Since much of the literature of change concentrates on the readiness of followers, that may have been the best place for Queeg to begin. For Queeg that would have meant considering the readiness of his top subordinates (the seaman, the writer, the socialite and the doctor). So, before a leader can begin to communicate in order to increase readiness the leader must have a deep understanding of his followers, the organization and the impending change.

Once a leader understands his or her follower's position relative to the change, a message regarding the change can be crafted. A message regarding change that is carefully crafted, demonstrated through leader actions and delivered constantly will help to unfreeze the follower and ready them for change. At the same time the leader is crafting the message, he or she should be planning out the route the followers will take in order for the change to be implemented. This plan will be the change itself.

Every turn of the cards changes the situation. A good player isn't waiting to see the next card. A good player is interpreting the environment and planning their next move to bet, call or fold before the next card is turned. The turn of the card and the reaction of the other players dictates which plan is implemented. The point is that change is planned. Once your followers are ready for change, you implement the plan.

For change to be successful it must be internalized by followers. That is, the change has to become the standard method of operation. Even if you prepare your followers by unfreezing their current beliefs and attitudes and then guide them through the planned change, there is every possibility that the change will melt away and the previous conditions, standards or methodologies will appear. The final part of Lewin's model involves "refreezing" the followers so that the change is internalized. There are numerous methods for refreezing such as rewarding the new behavior and continued communication. The key point to remember is: You must follow up and ensure that the change becomes part of your normal operating procedures.

In today's rapidly changing environment a good leader spends time preparing his or her followers for changes that have yet to happen. A constant leader activity should be the development of a nimble staff that is ready, willing and able to "march to the market." This means that you have to engender an environment of experimentation; a work location where new ideas are welcomed, tried and evaluated.

Every leader, to be effective, must simultaneously adhere to the symbols of change and revision and the symbols of tradition and stability.

Alfred Whitehead

If you want to make enemies, try to change something.

Woodrow Wilson

Change has no constituency.

Machiavelli

CHANGE ASSESSMENT

1. Employees were involved in determining the need for change and how to meet that need.
2. Employees were "in the know" in regards to the market, clients, company policy, etc., so they could recognize the need for changes.
3. Employees were involved in the planning process prior to the change.
4. Any objections employees might have had were considered during the planning stage.
5. The intended results of the change were clearly communicated.
6. The change was explained to all who would be affected by it; they knew what would be involved in the present and in the future.
7. A specific plan for implementing change was created.
8. People were allowed to voice ideas and concerns in a constructive manner.
9. All leaders demonstrated a positive attitude, which communicated that they believed in the success of the change.
10. A variety of feedback was gathered after the change.
11. Any needed adjustments were recognized and implemented following the change.

** You should have answered "yes" to at least eight of these questions. Next time you implement change, think about the areas you missed and come up with new ideas to help change occur more smoothly and easily.

CHAPTER SEVENTEEN
Five of Hearts
Dissent vs. Dissension

Once you start thinking you have nothing left to learn, you have everything to learn.

Steve Badget

Like other presidents, William Howard Taft had to endure his share of abuse. One night at the dinner table, his youngest boy made a disrespectful remark to him. There was a sudden hush. Taft looked thoughtful. "Well," said Mrs. Taft to her husband, "aren't you going to punish him?" Taft said, "If the remark was addressed to me as his father, he certainly will be punished. However, if he addressed it to the President of the United States, that is his constitutional privilege."

The current research and practitioner literature on organizations leans very heavily toward the Resourced-Based view of organizations. In this view, organizations are the sum total of their resources, most importantly their people. Competitive advantage in organizations is gained by how leaders choose to organize and use their resources thereby making them different from competitors. Think of people as a resource that is available to everyone. Essentially, all organizations hire from the same pool of human beings. Yet, some organizations use the same resources to significantly out perform competitors.

Stellar organizational performance begins with using all of the talents of your most precious resource (human beings) wisely. If you hired someone to a job, any job, you hired them to do that job intelligently and as efficiently as possible. You hired your followers for all of their abilities which includes their honest feedback on the organization, the workplace and your leadership. Moreover, people closest to the task are often in the best position to see new ways and inherent dangers. Not only do you have to be open to strong feedback, you have to teach your followers the inherent differences between dissent and dissension.

Smart leaders allow criticism under a defined set of circumstances. Healthy dissent is an important part of decision making and leading an organization. It can help to cover your blind spots as a leader. If you are not open to criticism, you will

Figure 17.1 (Safety/Expertise Axis)

Tannenbaum and Schmidt's Decision-Making Model:

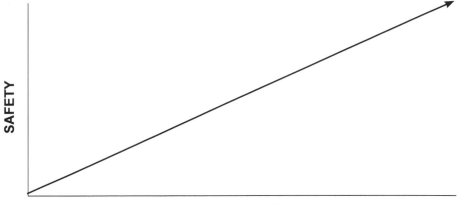

never improve as a leader or help your organization succeed. You won't be using the full talents of your human resources. You will lose competitive advantage. Your first task is to differentiate dissent and dissension for your followers and then model the circumstances under which you allow criticism or strong feedback.

We chose the words dissent and dissension in order to highlight the differences between healthy feedback and subversive activity. For our purposes, dissent means to disagree and disagreement can be thought of as multi-axis continuum. In Figure 17.1, the leader is considering two things about the follower's dissent – safety and follower expertise. Figure 17.1 gives us some clues about when to expect followers to disagree and how strongly we expect them to disagree. The vertical axis of Figure 17.1 demonstrates that the more a situation involves danger the more we expect followers to speak up immediately and forcefully. In an organizational sense, danger could be physical or some other type of danger to people or the organization. Danger could be a leader doing something that would put an organization or people at risk; it could be physical, legal or even ethical. Similarly, the horizontal axis shows that the greater a follower's expertise in a certain task, the more we expect them to speak up immediately and forcefully. After all, they are the experts.

In this instance, when something doesn't involve an element of danger and the follower has low demonstrated expertise, a good leader still expects him or her to speak up, but the manner and forum in which the follower delivers the feedback is important. On matters that are low on the continuum leaders should expect followers to deliver feedback in private, or in an open discussion forum lead by the leader.

An additional aspect of the difference between dissent and dissension is the natural interplay between rights and responsibilities. Essentially, with every right there are corresponding responsibilities. As an example, we have the right to vote; and, we have the responsibility to vote, to make a good decision, and to protect other's right to vote. If strong feedback is a follower right, the corresponding responsibility highlights the difference between dissent and dissension. Dissension occurs when the follower voices their concern and is overridden by the leader and the follower fails to fully adopt the decision. Or, perhaps more insidiously, the follower both fails to voice his or her concern and fails to fully implement the decision. Followers may not be privy to all the information available to the leader. After followers have exercised their right to dissent, they must fulfill their responsibility to implement. And, followers who fail to exercise their right to dissent still have the responsibility to implement. It is the failure to recognize the responsibility to implement that turns dissent to dissension. The key is leader modeling.

Don't kill the messenger. Whether it is bad news or a criticism of the boss's style, the messenger should not be punished, as long as the dissent does not turn into dissension. Dissent occurs when the person still supports the boss and the organization despite a difference in point of view. Dissension is when the differences erupt to the point that the person no longer supports the leader or the organization.

Some leaders work to suppress dissent, even that of the productive variety. We discourage this approach. There is a great deal leaders can learn from healthy dissent. Moreover, suppressing dissent does not eliminate it from existence; it merely forces it underground where it cannot be addressed and dealt with effectively. Dissent kept out in the open fosters trust, communication, and a respectful environment where viewpoints different from the leader's are still valued. This is healthy as long as the line between dissent and dissension is not crossed.

This can occur when the boss is not willing to hear any feedback from employees. They may become resentful that they cannot voice their opinions and have no control over their environment. It can also occur when every suggestion or opinion is ignored. If people have legitimate concerns about their jobs or how to perform them, you must be at least willing to hear them out on the matter. Obviously you will not act on every concern raised by an employee; you should at least consider them and determine when action is necessary. As a leader you also have the responsibility to occasionally tease out dissent. As we have pointed out, the lion's share of human communication is non-verbal. If you were giving direction to someone and their facial expression conveyed that they did not understand you would probably continue to explain the task. However, many leaders see body language that conveys dissent and choose to ignore it. Followers know they are sending the body language. If you ignore the signs of dissent you are not creating an environment for healthy discussion.

The truth is that as human beings we have learned that it is more difficult to hold us accountable for body language than our words. Followers who are giving off body language indicating dissent are often testing the waters. If you pick up on the dissent and lead the follower to a healthy discussion you are modeling that proper dissent is encouraged. If you don't, you are sending the follower onto the path of dissension. Another way that leaders can model the behavior of proper dissent is by setting the stage.

Many years ago, Andrew took an executive position in an organization. He still remembers his first staff meeting where he discussed his expectations. He explained his version of the "kill the messenger theory," and told his followers that he would never "kill" the messenger. What he would do, however, is deal harshly with people who neglected to deliver important messages when they should have. His followers learned to take Andrew at his word and always gave him reports, even if they were unpleasant, and he kept his word and never punished someone who conveyed the message. Even better, no one refused to bring him necessary information. Everyone learned that strong feedback was not only desired, it was required.

In Andrew's case, his followers understood the priorities. In some environments, however, the "never kill the messenger" system may not initially meet with success. The problem is that employees will resist being forthcoming out of fear or from peer pressure. Dealing with such situations can be challenging because no matter how much you try and convince them, employees generally perceive a wide divide between you and them. It may take a lot of time and patience for that divide to be bridged, particularly if you are attempting to change an established pattern of behavior.

The authors are aware of a leader who took this a step further and had a sign made up which was prominently displayed on his desk. The sign read, "Bad news welcome here." No one wants bad news, but this leader made it crystal clear that if bad news in fact existed, he wanted to know about it!

CONFLICT RESOLUTION SKILLS

1. I engage in active listening, giving the person my full attention and making eye contact.
2. I do not interrupt; I let the person finish speaking before I begin.
3. I ask questions and paraphrase to make sure I understand what was said.
4. If I disagree, I tell the person and explain why.
5. If someone disagrees with my idea, I listen. I do not become defensive or punish the person.
6. I recognize that the person has the right to his or her opinion, even if I disagree with it.
7. I focus attention on solving the problem, not arguing or bringing up the past.
8. I maintain my calm and discuss the situation rationally; no name-calling or put-downs.
9. I distinguish between condemning the idea and attacking the person.
10. If I find that I cannot control my anger, I step back and take a break. I wait until I have calmed down to discuss the problem again.
11. When I am wrong, I admit it and take responsibility. I do not try to cover my error or blame others.

** You should have answered "yes" to at least eight of these questions. If you did not, you need to think about ways you can improve your conflict-resolution skills.

Leaders often inherit an established culture wherein strong feedback was previously discouraged. If you are a leader in this type of environment you probably have deeper problems with follower norms and values. You may find that your efforts at creating an environment wherein followers have feedback Rights and Responsibilities is part of a larger effort on your part to change the current culture. The key consideration is using your human resources to their fullest potential in order to create competitive advantage. Remember, everyone draws from the same pool of human beings and it is your leadership that will draw out stellar performance.

When two men in business always agree, one of them is unnecessary.
William Wrigley, Jr.

CHAPTER EIGHTEEN
Six of Hearts
Integrity

The key is transparency, full disclosure. If everybody knows who has an interest in the outcome of a player's results, the likelihood of impropriety is significantly lessened. It also creates opportunities for examination of the play of hands, a higher standard of scrutiny for those who have an interest in each other. Such transparency, of course, is not an easy thing to enforce.

Roy Cooke, Card Player Magazine

Kouzes and Posner have done extensive survey work in attempting to determine what people want most in their leaders. They found that, among other things, people wanted their leader to be intelligent, fair, competent, and inspiring. The integrity and ethics of leaders have become increasingly important issues. To get workers to be productive and loyal, they must have faith in their leaders as ethical persons.

Integrity is one of those concepts that is voiced but often ill-defined. By looking at how the term is used in other venues and seeing it as a metaphor for some kind of human conduct we may be able to understand it more fully. Generally, integrity as a concept outside of human relationships means to establish an impenetrable barrier. A ship with hull integrity is water tight. Water doesn't pass through the hull and sink the ship. Think of a destroyer on the high seas. A destroyer with the most advanced weapons technology, fastest engines and best trained crew is going to sink if the hull is breached. Integrity of the ship's hull is the barrier or bond that keeps it all together.

Integrity at the poker table is always playing well. It is using all of your strengths and talents all of the time. It is also using your strengths to bolster your weaknesses. Few are good at everything. Suppose you are a player that is good at reading other players, but not so good at calculating your odds. You play to your strength. A player's integrity is consistently recognizing your own limitations and strengths and playing within those boundaries. For destroyers, poker players and leaders, integrity is a measure of the strength of the barrier or bond of other concepts. For instance, integrity is a measurement of your honesty. If you are always honest, you have a high degree of integrity in your honesty. It is impenetrable. If you have low integrity in honesty you are perceived as sometimes honest – and, of course, your honesty is always in question.

Honesty is part and parcel with integrity. Leaders should be honest for a variety of reasons. First, it is the right thing to do. Morally and ethically speaking, one should be honest in dealings with other people. Second, presumably, one wants employees to be honest. How can you expect this behavior if you do not model it yourself? Also, your level of honesty has direct impact on how people perceive you in other important areas, such as trust, credibility, and dependability.

Even people who are naturally honest sometimes have difficulty with this issue in the workplace. It is not easy to confront someone in a brutally honest fashion; it is not easy to criticize people in a straightforward manner; it is not easy to deal with sensitive matters in direct terms. However, good leaders make every effort to be honest with people at all times. Although difficult, this is what people really want from a leader; they want honesty with empathy. The combination of empathy with honesty demonstrates how integrity is a measure of the strength of the bond between the two.

Children often give us some of best examples of honesty not tempered by empathy. Think of a time when your children uttered something in the grocery store that was true, but perhaps best left unsaid. Absolute truthfulness is not a demonstration of integrity. Balancing truthfulness with tact, diplomacy and empathy demonstrates integrity. How you deliver the truth is as important as the truth itself, a lesson it took both of the authors a long time to learn. You should be as kind and respectful as you can when delivering bad news because it will help others accept the information more easily. It will demonstrate the strength, or integrity of the incorporation of all your skills or traits as a leader.

Like the child in the grocery store, in the workplace there are times the truth will not enhance a situation and may be better left unsaid. For example, if a secretary is a marginal but satisfactory performer and has no chance for promotion, is it necessary to disclose that fact when it is obvious that this person is performing at his or her highest skill level and is happy in the position? It makes no sense to use the truth when nothing is to be gained.

People today are looking for more than just money out of their jobs. They are seeking out a higher meaning in their lives, both professionally and personally. They want inspiration and fulfillment from their work. In evaluating their lives, they look to their own and their companies' morals and ethics. This includes company policies regarding themselves, other workers, and society at large. They are also looking closely at the character of their leader. Integrity, as an organizational and leader characteristic, is the strength of the incorporation of norms and values into actions. When an organization or a leader has situational or "sometimes" ethics, honesty or other traits, it is viewed by followers as low integrity. It is the consistency or strength of the barriers and bonds that make something water tight.

One reason this is so important is that it is directly tied to employee retention. The bottom line is that people want a leader with integrity. To get loyalty from employees, employees must see concern for themselves and others, fairness, honesty, and good moral values from their organizations and leaders. For workers, the leaders are the personification of the company. If they see you consistently emulating these virtues, they will have better feelings for the company and will tend to be more loyal. When employees realize that these essentials are missing from their workplace, turnover will increase. Most people do not want to compromise their own integrity by working for a company that does not maintain high values.

Therefore, leaders should create a workplace that employees feel good about from a moral point of view. Think about the impact that any action will have on your staff, your company, and society. First, you must define what integrity means to you and your company. As an organization, create an outline of your most important values. Look to your vision statement and create a code of ethics that will help guide you. Discuss how these values apply to day-to-day operations, how they could be compromised, and how to deal with such situations. By discussing and demonstrating the vision statement or the organization's code of conduct, you are taking steps toward increasing the strength (or integrity) between actions and words. Employees should feel comfortable enough to raise concerns they have about ethical problems in their jobs or in the company as a whole.

Once you have defined your values, make sure that you apply them consistently in every aspect of your organization. Again, you must lead by example. No one is going to believe you are ethical simply by what you say on the subject. Your actions must parallel your words or you will be perceived as having low integrity. Remember that it is in the little things that a moral code is demonstrated. If you ignore small ethical transgressions, you are sending a message that, despite your announcements, ethics are situational at best.

There are signs to look for that suggest your employees are dissatisfied with the integrity of their workplace. These signs point to the fact that a leader is adversely affecting company morale. First, as we said before, loyalty is tied to integrity. If you have a high turnover rate, chances are that something is wrong. Although it is easy to make excuses, it may be that you are to blame. There may be a number of reasons why people are unhappy at their jobs. However, if you are seeing higher numbers of workers leaving, it is definitely time to take a look at the organization's overall integrity, including your own.

Low productivity or morale and increased absenteeism are also signs that something is amiss. It is likely that your organization's commitment to certain norms and values were weak and became replaced by sub-group or individual norms and values. Consider that, at an organizational level, the strength of individual or sub-group commitment to organizational norms and values is a measurement of integrity. When people are unhappy, they do not work as productively. You should investigate the causes of such behavior even if it is not related to integrity concerns. Finally, look for signs that employees are not comfortable approaching you. If they do not seek you out for answers or to talk, something is wrong. Check to make sure that employees are sharing information with you. If you are not receiving any feedback and employees are avoiding you, you have a bad situation brewing.

For leaders and poker players, strength in one skill is not enough. It is strength in all skills and alignment of those strengths with weaknesses that demonstrate integrity. Moreover, an inability to temper or bolster one skill with another demonstrates a lack of integrity. The ability to anticipate the leader makes a good follower. Without integrity in action and word, followers will never develop the ability to determine how you want them to act. If the follower can't anticipate the leader or the organization, they cannot follow effectively.

The person who is slowest in making a promise is most faithful in its performance.
Jean-Jacques Rousseau

The straight and narrow path would be wider if more people used it.
Kay Ingram

CHAPTER NINETEEN
Seven of Hearts
Attitude

The strong point in poker is never to lose your temper, either with those you are playing with or, more particularly, with the cards. There is no sympathy in poker. Always keep cool. If you lose your head you will lose all your chips.
From The Gentleman's Handbook on *Poker* by William J. Florence

There are days when we go to work and we are not feeling our best. Our goal on those days is to act in such a way that no one is able to identify that we are not in top form. Leaders do this because they take their position very seriously. It is your responsibility to be upbeat, even when you're not. Most leaders do not appreciate how much they impact people. If the boss is clearly having a bad day, it can become a bad day for the entire organization. As a leader, you are part cheerleader, and you never see an "on-duty" cheerleader in a bad mood!

This is not an easy burden to bear. Kouzes and Posner have researched this issue and in *The Leadership Challenge*, they state that many leaders describe "putting on a happy face each morning" as one of the most difficult, exhausting, and crucial performance requirements of the job. Despite the burden, good leaders do this every day. There is a payoff; fewer bad moods within management mean fewer throughout the organization.

Maintaining a good mood, even when you do not feel it, does not have to mean lying to employees or being deceitful. You can be honest and forthright when there are factors that may impair your ability to be a good leader. However, staying upbeat means that you do not complain about the little things and you certainly do not complain to your team members. There are lots of reasons to be in a bad mood; however, in the workplace and at the poker table, expressing your mood is telegraphing way too much information. People will act on that information. At the table, if you telegraph that you have been dealt the fourth straight loser hand, or a weak hand, the other players are going to take advantage of you. Perhaps more importantly, when your attitude suddenly changes, everyone around you begins to fold.

There are several ways to fight the bad attitude. First and foremost, learn to know yourself. When you have a poor attitude you should acknowledge it to yourself. Once you've acknowledged your own feelings you may be able to isolate what is irritating you. If you can determine the source of your poor attitude you must next decide what to do about it. Most of the time, the things that drive us into the dark zone of our personalities are things we can't act on. However, if it is something you can act on you should first initiate your own personal "tactical pause."

Remember when your mother told you that if you were angry you should count to ten before you act? That is a tactical pause. Give yourself some space and time before you do something that you will spend an inordinate amount of time trying to undo. Moreover, a tactical pause isn't just counting to ten – it is more than taking a little extra time to speak. It is often putting some distance between yourself and the problem. A tactical pause can be either spatial or temporal. Space and time can help to change and manage your attitude.

Raymond uses the technique of personal debriefing to help manage his attitude. The commute to and from the workplace are devoted to decompressing and preparation. During your commute, think about what has happened to change your attitude and begin to plan what positive actions you are going to take. Raymond uses the space and time provided by his commute to work out what has happened and to prepare for what will happen. It is critical that you begin to plan in terms of positive steps. As an example, you leave work after a very rough day. You can avoid taking it home by going over the difficult parts of the day, then deciding what positive things you are going to do at home. If you continue to think about the workplace, even if you begin to positively plan for the next day, you will take work home with you. However, if you acknowledge that your day was a "crap storm" and move to plan for home, you will begin to decompress. Your commute becomes one of your tactical pauses.

The ability to disengage from work on your way home is crucial, just as is your ability to disconnect from trouble at home while enroute to the job. To the extent possible, we recommend compartmentalizing work and home. The ability to do so creates a better chance for success in both locations. Those who work primarily from home may need to do a couple of laps around the block!

Another approach is to take a brief journey in your mind. Think of some of your favorite "spots" in the world. For Andrew, there is a place on the Island of Catalina, a bed and breakfast in Santa Barbara, and even a quiet spot in his backyard. Quietly picturing himself in one of these locations helps to ward off the troubles of the day, even though he might not be able to be physically present at the location. Visualization is a powerful tool. Don't be afraid to use it!

A 15-minute tactical pause in the middle of your day can also be useful. Often, if you will just take a few minutes, walk around the building and begin to positively plan what the rest of your day will be like, you will change your attitude. If you plan positive actions, you attitude will change and become more positive. The purpose of the mid-day tactical pause is not to ruminate on what is bothering you. That will make it worse. The purpose is to plan out positive steps you are going to take.

Positive planning can be very simple. Recently, Raymond was preparing to leave for a Rotary service club meeting when he received disappointing news. As he drove to the meeting he realized that he was "down in the dumps." But, as president of the local Rotary Club he really could not lead a meeting if he had a bad attitude. Raymond stopped his car, pulled out the meeting agenda and began to go over it. He then wrote down the names of five people in the club that he was going to compliment on something they had done. When he walked in the door of the meeting place he immediately put his plan into motion and sought out the first member on his list.

Walking up to the member, Raymond shook Dale's hand, smiled and said, "Dale. I really like your idea about handling the menu. I think that is going to work out well. Thank you." Dale and he chatted for a few minutes and Raymond moved onto the next person on the list. Soon, the early disappointment had faded into the background. The positive interaction with people, the working of a positive plan, the warmth of human contact and reciprocal smiles had done the trick. During your tactical pause recall five people in your workplace you need to compliment or recognize, shake their hand, smile, look them in the eyes and tell them about the good thing they have done.

The United States military relies heavily on the "buddy system." In 2004, Professor Gregory J. W. Urwin, of Temple University wrote an article on Discipline, Camaraderie, and Luck: A Tale of POW Survival. He noted that " The Wake Island Marines also acted on their own to institute "buddy systems"

–interlocking networks of mutual support – to improve their prospects for survival. "In order to survive, you couldn't be an island," stated Pfc. Borne. "You had to help other people." These buddy systems became the basis for the many types of group assistance available in the Shanghai War Prisoners Camp. They formed the glue that held the community together. If a man stumbled, he knew somebody would help him get back up. If a POW saw someone going down, he felt honor bound to aid a comrade in need.

Andrew attended a management class many years ago in which one of the main presenters was a Vietnam veteran and former prisoner of war. He spoke of creating a positive attitude under truly the most adverse of conditions. He even talked of learning to play the piano while he was a prisoner! Every man had a variety of skills and each chose to teach those skills to everyone else as a method to pass the time and a way to stay positive. Surely if this man could learn to play the piano in such a situation and without the benefit of the piano, we can all do our best to stay positively focused in our daily struggles.

The buddy system has become part of the U.S. military doctrine. The point is that you, the leader, must also have a buddy you can turn to for mutual support. Selecting a buddy is about finding a peer outside your chain of command that you can confidentially turn to and express yourself. Your buddy must be a leader of similar responsibility in a similar organization. Someone who will understand the pressures of your position and you can trust to "blow off a little steam." This is not about finding a best friend, a drinking pal, or even someone you occasionally play racquetball with. It is about finding a peer who you can trust to add perspective to your view.

Civic groups can be a good place to start your search for a buddy. You are likely to find a peer and be able to develop a long-term, trusting relationship. Moreover, as a member of a volunteer or civic non-profit group you can extend your network outside of your own organization and add perspective to just why you are a leader. It will probably take you awhile to find the perfect buddy, but along the way, your work outside of your organization can serve as a reminder of why you chose to become a leader. Volunteer work helps to give you perspective and perspective is one of the best defenses against a bad attitude.

If you watch one of the televised poker tournaments you will ultimately see some player wearing sunglasses. They are wearing the glasses to hide their eyes; really to mask their attitude. When you walk around, keep a smile on your face.

Don't let body language give away how you feel inside. Masking, in the short-term, can help you maintain a positive, up-beat, team-oriented image in the eyes of your followers. Surprisingly, research shows that if you act upbeat, chances are that you will begin feeling that way. So, unlike the poker table where the player tries to hide his attitude, a little bit of masking can help to turn the leader's attitude around.

Your buddy can help you with perspective, but if you need to voice concerns over policies, decisions, etc., do so to your supervisor or someone who holds the same or higher level of authority as you do. Complaints of this nature should run up the chain of command, not down. Hopefully, your boss is modeling the same open door policy that you are and is open to listening to your complaints about the workplace. However, going to the boss just to complain is usually not a good idea. Going to the boss to express concerns, offer options and alternatives is a good idea. Anytime you are going to express something negative, take a tactical pause. Figure out how and what you really want to express.

If you are feeling stressed, find some ways to relax and rejuvenate. All work and no play will ruin your perspective. Perhaps the perfect play activity is something that combines physical activity with mind activity. Find something that you enjoy, gets you up and moving about, and engages your mind. Play will help you keep work in perspective.

There is little difference in people, but that little difference makes a big difference. The little difference is attitude. The big difference is whether it is positive or negative.
Clement Stone

I have never seen a monument erected to a pessimist.
Paul Harvey

CHAPTER TWENTY
Eight of Hearts
Fairness

In order to say anything meaningful about whether there has been poker justice requires, like in basketball, that we ask process questions like: did the players play voluntarily, did everyone obey Hoyle's rules of poker (poker law), were the cards unmarked, was there honest dealing? If affirmative answers can be given to each of those questions, then any game outcome was fair or just.

Walter E. Williams

Poker is fair because fairness is not about outcome, it is about process. Sometimes in poker you get a poor hand, but the process is fair; the cards are shuffled and dealt. Everyone understands the rules and has an equal chance of receiving cards that make a good hand. Poker is fair because everyone understands the rules, they have similar expectations and the rules are applied to all. If you think of fairness as an outcome, then something could only be fair from a particular point of view. In other words, what is fair to you would not necessarily be fair to others. However, if you look at fairness as a process, it becomes clear when something is fair or unfair. Fairness for the leader is about conformity with rules and standards, making impartial judgments based on objective information and treating people equally.

In a future chapter, Treating People Differently, we will explain how people should be treated differently. "Ah," you say. We have given you conflicting information. Well, in that chapter we are talking about treating people unequally in an outcome sense. As an example, a high performer should be rewarded more than a marginal performer; that is about performance. In a fairness sense, treating people equally means applying the same rules and standards to all; high performers and marginal performers. Moreover, fairness can also be viewed through two different mechanisms – rewards and consequences.

Fair treatment through the consequences mechanism begins by the leader having a complete understanding of the workplace rules, norms and goals. First, in order to make sound judgments about the actions of your followers as they relate to the rules, you must have an understanding of the expectations. Secondly, a good leader models the workplace expectations. Followers will immediately perceive that it is unfair if you enforce workplace arrival times while being late yourself. Understanding expectations and modeling them creates a positive environment for your followers. It demonstrates that you are fair.

Just as you must understand the rules, so must your followers. There are a number of ways to ensure that followers have a complete understanding of what is expected of them. You could post important rules in a conspicuous place. Indeed, there are many local, state and federal regulations that require certain workplace rules be posted. Occasionally, you should hold meetings wherein you not only discuss expectations but the logic behind them. If your followers understand the necessity of a certain rule or regulation, they will be more likely to perceive the enforcement of the rule or regulation as fair.

A major problem with the enforcement of rules is their "situational interpretation." Situational interpretation can either be an action or inaction by the leader. An example of a leader action would be deciding that a certain rule doesn't apply to a certain employee. Favoritism is one of the most frequent complaints workers have about management. All leaders are human beings. It is natural to have likes and dislikes and this extends to people as well. As a leader, you must distance yourself as much as possible from becoming too intimate with employees or letting your feelings dictate how you behave. Decisions should not be based on how you feel about a person. You are paid to be objective and take into account all sides of an issue.

> **Research at Western Electric's Hawthorne plant, near Chicago, from 1924 to 1932, has become commonly known as the Hawthorne Experiments. The experiments centered on worker productivity and became the foundation for much of the research on motivation during the 20th Century. You can explore the results of the Hawthorne Experiments and the continuing research on motivation at the companion website at www.pokerleadership.com**

Situational interpretation also results from leader inaction. Work groups are going to form informal norms in the workplace. The Hawthorne Experiments of the last century clearly demonstrated that employees are going to form norms and values that control the behavior of the workplace. When a leader is inactive in reinforcing organizational expectations, informal norms will grow and take the place of organizational norms. The informal norms of the work group become the lens through which employees judge the fairness of actions.

Typically, leader inaction allows the growth of informal norms and then something happens and the leader must take action. A sudden intervention – the enforcement of the organizational norm that is out of alignment with the informal norm – will be seen as unfair. Followers will view this as selective enforcement of expectations by the leader. If you have let the workplace develop norms that are out of alignment with organizational norms, you are doing a disservice to your followers and your organization.

One technique for double checking your workplace is the "fresh eyes" approach. This approach assumes that it is always best to intervene and correct norm alignment during non-crisis times rather than a sudden intervention. There are two ways to conduct a "fresh eyes" assessment of your workplace. First, you decide to walk around and say to yourself "What if I had just walked in here? What would a visitor or new leader find disturbing?" Observe your workplace through fresh eyes. Are there informal expectations? A second technique is to ask a peer to observe your workplace. A very good technique is to trade places with someone for a day. You observe their workplace and they observe yours. Honestly appraise each other and develop co-action plans to increase alignment between your followers expectations and organizational expectations. It is much easier and ultimately fairer to conduct a planned intervention to bring your workplace into alignment than suddenly imposing a work standard that has been ignored.

You should encourage subordinate leaders to use the fresh eye approach. You could have a meeting of all your subordinate leaders and explain how the workplace often drifts toward the growth of informal norms and ask each of them to partner up. After they trade work groups for a day, they can then develop action plans to improve their group. This is also a very good team building exercise for your organizational leaders. Have a second meeting wherein each team discusses their findings and action plans. If you do this, follow up and ensure that your subordinate leaders are working their plan. Sometimes, despite making employees aware of expectations, leaders find themselves having to enforce workplace rules through negative consequences.

Andrew had to handle numerous disciplinary cases in his career. Normally, it was his responsibility to review the misconduct in question and recommend a consequence to the chief executive. There have been several instances when he supported employees on one issue when, on the whole, he felt they were undeserving based upon past conduct. However, he was able to separate his personal feelings about the person from the individual facts of the current case. Raymond refers to this as "stringing beads." It is very difficult to decide the consequences for the act based solely on the act. We really see this concept clearly in personal relationships. Many times, people will have disagreements about an issue and then begin to bring up everything else that has happened in the relationship. It is as if they were stringing the beads of the negative stuff together and then presenting it to you at once. Andrew has had other managers question his decision because they knew the employee had behaved inappropriately in the past. Both Andrew and Raymond feel strongly, however, that this is the way to be consistently fair.

In their book, *Putting Total Quality Management to Work*, Marshall Sashkin and Kenneth Kiser list ten specific areas of action that help to create an organizational climate of fairness:
1. Actions that develop trust, such as sharing useful information and making good on commitments;
2. Acting consistently, so that employees are not surprised or taken aback by unexpected management actions or decisions;
3. Being scrupulously truthful and avoiding "white lies;"
4. Demonstrating integrity by keeping confidences and observing ethical; guidelines to show concern for others;
5. Meeting with employees and defining what is expected of them;
6. Treating employees equitably and not playing favorites;
7. Giving people meaningful influence over decisions about their own work, especially how to accomplish their work;

> 8. **Adhering to clear standards that are just and reasonable;**
> 9. **Demonstrating respect toward employees; and,**
> 10. **Following due process, or procedures that are open to public scrutiny and that permit everyone to participate actively in their application.**

While you judge the act based on the act, you will face a situation wherein two different employees have violated a work standard and yet common sense says their consequences should be different. As an example, consider the scenario wherein a follower with 15-years in your organization is late to work. On the same day, a second employee, with three months experience is late to work, for the fourth consecutive day. Today, they were both late to work. Fairness does not mean that since you have decided to dismiss the second employee you should dismiss the first. Fairness means that both employees face consequences. However, fairness also means that the penalty for the transgression fits the act. If you separate out your judgment of the act from the judgment of the consequences you will see the fair path.

Fairness also involves how behavior is rewarded. This issue is most clearly demonstrated when there is an internal promotion. If you start with the premise that not everyone is going to agree with your decision, but they can agree that the process for the selection was fair, you will be on firm ground. Your followers must know what types of behaviors and qualifications are necessary for promotion. They should be told how behaviors and qualifications will be assessed. Also, they should see that the process for promotion (the assessment and then ranking of behaviors and qualifications) is consistently applied to all candidates. The inherent problem with a promotional process is confidentiality. While you want the process to be transparent, you must keep confidential the reasons one employee was assessed as more qualified than another. This is one of those times that perception is much more powerful than reality.

Your followers do not have access to the reality of the process. They aren't privy to all of the facts that went into making your decision. Followers only know what they know, and if they had more information they would probably reach a similar conclusion. Your most powerful tool for bridging the gap between what followers can possibly know and what they believe is by consistently demonstrating fairness. If you are fair with your followers, they will learn to trust you. They will learn to trust your judgment and, if you make a decision they can't quite understand, they are more likely to give you the benefit of the doubt if you have been fair in the past.

A great deal may be done by severity, more by love, but most by clear discernment and impartial justice.

Goethe

Men are by nature unequal. It is vain, therefore, to treat them as if they were equal.

J.A. Froude

CHAPTER TWENTY-ONE
Nine of Hearts
Praise and Criticism

Is that the game where one receives five cards? And if there's two alike that's pretty good, but if there's three alike, that's much better?

W.C. Fields

In order to use both praise and criticism effectively the leader must first understand that both concepts have a single purpose: to reinforce workplace expectations. In the last chapter we looked at fairness as a process. The discussion of workplace rules and standards concerned official actions. We were interested in those times that the leader must take official action and saw that it was critical to be fair in our application of the rules. Praise and criticism involve modifying behavior before it becomes something requiring an official action.

Praise tells employees when they have met or exceeded workplace standards. Criticism, on the other hand, tells employees when they have failed to meet expectations. The critical component of both is that they involve some aspect of the workplace standards, norms and goals. As an example, complimenting someone because they are wearing a great outfit doesn't necessarily meet the standard of workplace praise. Indeed, there are instance where comments about appearance might be taken wrong or even be inappropriate. However, if appearance is critical to your organization and an employee has previously been told they need to improve their appearance, the praise might be appropriate. Also, you might praise someone on their appearance for the purpose of sending a message to employees on the workplace standards. As an example, if your employees wear a uniform, meeting or exceeded minimum uniform appearance might make for an appropriate moment to praise.

Ken Blanchard and Spencer Johnson make some interesting observations about criticism and praise in their book, *The One Minute Manager*. They recommend that praise be given when someone does something approximately right. Their contention is that if we wait for perfection in order to praise, we will never praise. Indeed, praise is something a good leader uses when an employee is moving toward the attainment of minimum expectations. In this instance, if you think of praise as sign posts for the employee, you are telling them they are on the right path and how far they have to go.

A good leader gets into the habit of praising and learns the simple actions they can take that are praise. For instance, interest is the simplest and perhaps most overlooked form of praise. If a follower tells you or shows you something, your level of interest can be praise. Raymond related that one way to show interest was by finding out what employees were doing. When Raymond worked in a large organization, he would walk around on every Friday afternoon with the candy jar he kept on his desk. He would visit each employee, offer them a piece of candy and sit a chat with them for a few minutes. The candy was a device. A way to walk around innocuously and ask, "So, what are you working on?" This invariably opened the door to some aspect of the followers work performance that could be praised – both by interest and through verbal affirmation.

A second method of seeking opportunities to praise is by recognizing employees during meetings. Recognition can be as simple as asking the employee to relate some aspect of their current work project to the group. This sends the message that their work is important and meaningful and opens the door to the leader praising some aspect of the work. Praise can also be a more formal recognition such as the delivery of a certificate of achievement or completion. Formal or informal, praising before the group reinforces individual and group behavior.

There are some key factors to remember that will make criticism easier to give and easier to take. When you criticize, start with the positive, such as examples of what has been done well and then pinpoint what needs to be done differently. Try to end on a positive note. Ending on a positive note is most easily accomplished if you tell the person how the task should be done differently. Focus on the behavior, give specific examples of what was done incorrectly and provide specific examples on how to do the task correctly.

Reprimands should be brief and timely. Negative behavior needs to be corrected as quickly as possible. The closer the criticism follows the behavior the more likely it will be taken as positive, corrective action. A good leader should not "string beads" or gather negative information over time and then bring it to someone's attention all at once. There is less chance that the behavior will actually be corrected if a person cannot remember it. Reprimanding a whole list of wrong doings at once will send the message to that person that nothing they do is right. Try to stick to one point at a time. If you string beads, you will be perceived as criticizing the person and not the behavior.

As Blanchard and Johnson remind us, leaders are reprimanding behavior and not the person. We should be as gentle with the person as possible. Criticism and reprimands don't have to be harsh; they must be timely and specific. People should walk away from the conversation thinking about their own behavior, not the behavior of the boss. By reprimanding the behavior and not the person, you create a better chance that the person will actually consider what was done incorrectly and how to improve. When you are aggressive or offensive while correcting behavior, you put people on the defensive. Although timeliness is critical in criticism, if you need a tactical pause before you deliver the criticism, you should take it. You must have your own emotions under control so that the follower doesn't focus on their feelings instead of what needs to be done.

Although you should not be hesitant to criticize someone, you should make sure you have the facts before you move forward. If you are always willing to praise, your followers will be more open to criticism. People who have been praised in the past will be more open to criticism because they trust that your intentions are good. When you do have to criticize them, there will be an overall balance of praise and criticism. They will be more open to the suggestion because you have dealt out both praise and reprimand equally and honestly.

Remember the old rule about criticizing someone's performance: praise in public and reprimand in private. The object of criticism is not to embarrass but to improve performance. There have been occasions, though, where both Andrew and Raymond have reprimanded someone in front of others. This is only for extreme cases where someone is just refusing to follow directions properly. Neither of the authors particularly like to use this method, but when all else fails, it can be effective. Under normal circumstances, this is unnecessary and unprofessional. Corrections should be between you and the other person involved; the entire staff does not need to be included. Use this technique only as a last resort.

When you criticize, you should be constructive and precise. To tell people that they have bad attitudes may be a true statement, but you must elaborate. Explain to them exactly which of their behaviors leads you to the belief that they have attitude problems. This is not always easy because sometimes the problem, like a bad attitude, is easy to recognize, but hard to describe. Specific criticism helps employees to understand precisely what you expect and what they need to do to meet your expectations. It is also helpful to explain why the correction is needed. If people do not understand why something needs to be done differently, they are less likely to change. Also, let employees participate in discussions on how to make corrections. Get people to think of their own ways to improve so they are more personally involved in the matter.

Finally, be as gentle as possible with your criticism. Consider how you would want to be treated. Words can injure deeply, and although you may not see the damage visibly, it can be quite devastating. Leaders often have more impact with their words than they realize. Many people are able to recount in great detail criticism they received from their bosses a decade ago. Do not be afraid to criticize but think about it beforehand and choose your words very carefully.

You want to create a workplace where criticism is given constructively. You should never allow mean-spirited or vindictive motives to pervade criticism. This is true when you or your employees critique others. When everyone in the workplace feels that criticism is being given honestly and by people who care for one another, the potential for improvement is unlimited. Share these steps on how to criticize constructively with your employees. If everyone understands how to criticize in a productive manner, your workplace will be a healthy environment where improvements can take place.

A final word on criticism comes from this story about Jay Leno's effort to keep criticism in the proper perspective:

When Jay Leno replaced Johnny Carson on The Tonight Show, he started to take some heat. Critics unfavorably compared him to Johnny, and from all that criticism, most people thought his stay as the host would be short-lived. However, Jay never really worried. In fact, he kept a stack of unpleasant reviews on his desk for inspiration. One critic said, "Too many soft questions." Another said, "He's being too nice." These unkind words did not bother Leno though because they were written in 1962 and were directed at Jack Paar's replacement – "an awkward nobody named Johnny Carson."

Remember that being the boss is not just about reprimanding mistakes. Too often, we focus solely on the negative. Most people do not mind working hard.

However, they become frustrated when no one seems to appreciate their efforts. Lack of appreciation is a dangerous thing that can quickly destroy employee morale. All people hope for certain rewards in return for their work. If they don't receive them, they become discouraged.

Some managers operate with the attitude that people are getting paid and that is all the reward they need. The effect of this is potentially demoralizing. People that feel their efforts are not being recognized may begin to develop resentment toward their job, which in turn can impact the quantity and quality of their work. Unhappy and neglected workers tend to be unproductive.

When a man points a finger at someone else, he should remember that three of his fingers are pointing at himself.

Anonymous

Sandwich every bit of criticism between two layers of praise.

Mary Kay Ash

I have yet to find a man, whatever his situation in life, who did not do better work and put forth greater effort under a spirit of approval than he ever would do under a spirit of criticism.

Charles Schwab

CHAPTER TWENTY-TWO
Ten of Hearts
Empathy

Before you criticize someone, walk a mile in his shoes. That way, when you criticize him, you will be a mile away, and you will have his shoes.

Chuck Humphrey

Typically, people think of empathy as simply being able to identify with the emotions of another, but it is more than that. In leadership, being empathic includes understanding the emotional state, cultural beliefs and norms of another. For the leader, empathy encompasses the full range of background noise with which people interpret their surroundings. Empathy and sympathy are two very distinct concepts. Sympathy comes from the Latin "sympatha," or to be affected by like feelings. You are sympathetic when you share someone's feelings. That is, when their feelings are similar to yours. On the other hand, empathy is the ability to imagine oneself in another's place. Perhaps, sympathy is "I feel your pain," while empathy is "I understand your pain." Not everyone has a good capacity for empathy, as shown in this story:

Many years ago, a preacher from Kansas was returning home after a visit to New England, and one of his parishioners met him at the train station. "Well," asked the preacher, "how are things at home?" "Sad, real sad Pastor," answered the man. "A tornado came and wiped out my house." "Well, I'm not surprised," said the unsympathetic preacher. "You remember I've been warning you about the way you've been living. Punishment for sin is inevitable." The layman responded, "It also destroyed your house, Pastor." "It did?" the pastor asked, momentarily surprised. "Oh my, the ways of the Lord are past human understanding."

The degree of empathy a leader has tells you quite a bit about the leader. For instance, to be empathic you must be able to interpret what your followers are saying. It is much more than just detecting sadness or regret; it is the ability to understand a full range of human emotions and guide your followers based on their current situation and their long-term personal beliefs. Empathy is not something you pull out when needed. It is something that pervades everything you do as a leader. It impacts how you treat people, how you talk to people, and the level of care you have for people. In short, it impacts every human interaction you have and any managerial action you must take.

It is fairly clear for most people that empathy is called for when someone faces a tragedy not of their own making. If a follower receives news that a loved one has died, it is fairly easy to imagine yourself in that position. In this instance, your sympathy rapidly becomes empathy because you not only share the feelings but are able to imagine yourself in that position. The lion's share of our ability to empathize comes from having similar occurrences in our lives. For instance, as a leader you were once a follower so you should be able to understand the follower's point of view when you are giving them direction. Indeed, the best leaders are the ones who have not lost their ability to be empathetic

Certain people seem to lose their ability to empathize when they become leaders. While some may have never had the capacity for it in the first place, other leaders suffer memory loss. They seemingly cannot recall how it felt to be in certain situations. It is difficult to relate to your employees if you do not remember being one. As we rise through organizations, the nature of the task often changes. If you were in a line position more than a decade ago, it is very likely that the task has become more complex. Technological and sociological changes often have increased the complexity of line tasks. It is difficult for the leader to be empathic if the task has changed so much that they really don't know what their employees are experiencing.

Mark Twain's *The Prince and the Pauper* had some very poignant lessons on empathy for the leader. Recall the Prince becomes a commoner and experiences a life he never knew existed. A theme from Twain's work is that leaders should make an effort to discover how their followers are experiencing the world. In Raymond's last assignment before retirement from the police department he was in charge of seventy-five detectives. Their primary mission was to seek out and capture fugitives. Every month, Raymond took a case and worked it with a different partner. Usually, the case would take a full eight hours away from his leadership duties, but it helped to keep Raymond's basic officer-survival skills and investigative skills intact, and it helped him understand the problems his followers were experiencing. For instance, when the jail introduced new screening and paperwork requirements the process for booking a suspect became much more time consuming. You simply could not fully understand how these changes affected your employees unless you experienced them yourself. Sometimes, it is good for the leader to get back into the trenches; see the view, the problems and the challenges. It may help temper your next decision.

Having empathy for workers does not preclude you from making hard decisions or taking tough action. It is merely one component of an overall approach. In some cases, you may take the exact same measures, regardless of whether or not you are concerned for the individuals involved. However, if you have strong empathy for people, you will find that it will occasionally sway your decisions. Being empathetic will also change the way that you implement decisions. That may be just as important as the decision itself.

How does a leader develop empathy? The easiest way is to analyze consciously how a particular decision would make you feel if you were in the same situation. That's the classical Golden Rule approach and, while somewhat useful, it has many drawbacks. To be truly empathetic, you must be aware of a person's complete background, history, education, culture, morals, social position, financial status, interests, thinking patterns, and social status. It is virtually impossible to really do that; we can only hope to approximate it.

Being aware of the culturally diverse nature of the workplace is a first step. Becoming informed of the differences and nuances of different cultures is another step. Finally, being sensitive to the position and social dynamics at play makes a leader more effective at employing empathy as a powerful ingredient in decisions. In fact, it is the predictive power of empathy that leaders often overlook. Consider how the poker player watches the other players. He or she is using his or her observations of the other's play and their reactions to the play in order to predict how they might handle succeeding hands. As a leader, if you understand the context with which followers place communications and tasks, you are better able to predict how they might react.

As an example, consider that you have two followers. Both are inexperienced at a certain task. One enjoys new challenges while the other tends to be apprehensive about new situations. Being empathetic to their skills and their personal make-up you might give them different direction. If someone is inexperienced yet eager, you could probably just tell them what you want done, tell them where resources can be found and let them experiment with the task. On the other hand, with the less emotionally able follower you might provide more support. Perhaps, more specific direction and clarification are in order for the less emotionally able.

Another example might be an employee who has recently been turned down for a promotion. Your job as a leader is to guide the person through what they are feeling. Now, we are not recommending that to be a good leader you must provide your employees with therapy. But, what we are strongly suggesting is people are going to react differently based on their emotional and cultural state. You have to work with all of them and for you to be your most effective you should consider how they feel about what is happening.

Sometimes leaders are called on to deliver very bad news. Most typically, this involves terminating someone's employment. Some leaders believe that once it has been decided that an employee should be terminated there is no other organizational responsibility. If you have that opinion, you would just call them into your office, terminate their employment and take their keys. Raymond knew a leader who faced a very difficult termination. This captain of police had an employee who was facing felony charges. The captain could have simply had the person arrested, but, he didn't. He went to the employee's home, picked him up and personally drove the employee to the police station. He explained that the person worked for him and it was his responsibility to care for the person up to the exact moment of termination. He knew this person was going to be devastated by the consequence of his own actions. The captain also explained that the person would ultimately recover and likely go on to lead a productive life in some other venue.

The captain felt that his kindness and caring even during this difficult time would help the person to heal and recover from their own mistakes. Perhaps, more importantly, the captain demonstrated to his subordinate leaders that people were the most important part of the organization and as long as they were members of the organization they should be cared for. It was a powerful example and message.

One of the most poignant of all human experiences is empathy – the ability to feel what others feel when suffering from pain or loss.

Louis West

CHAPTER TWENTY-THREE
Jack of Hearts
Fun on the Job

Last year people won more than one billion dollars playing poker. And casinos made twenty-seven billion just by being around those people.

Samantha Bee

Andrew had the great pleasure of meeting and talking with four of the twelve men who have walked on the moon. As a space enthusiast, he had many questions for each of them. He was struck by a common thread that ran throughout their answers. The thread was best summed up by what the late Pete Conrad told Andrew as he spoke of their "heroics." Conrad said, "We weren't so great; we just did what we had fun doing." The space program and the moon landings were perhaps the greatest and most audacious human efforts ever. The training requirements and pressures put on these men were enormous. They were literally putting their lives at risk, but they viewed it as merely having fun. If under such serious conditions these men can perceive their work as fun, it is okay for the rest of us to do so also.

Why do you think people spent twenty-seven billion dollars playing poker in 2004? Sure, some of them are probably addicted to gambling, but for most the cost is worth the enjoyment. People enjoy challenge, risk and potential reward. As human beings we like to be challenged. Abraham Maslow's hierarchy of needs tells us that once people get past being worried about their shelter and security they are looking for a challenge. That is when life and work becomes fun; when it is challenging.

We have all experienced bosses who thought that it was their job to ensure that people were not having fun. They perceived that more fun would equal less work. Conversely, there are also bosses who practically demanded that we enjoyed ourselves. This type of leader believed that work should be pleasurable.

The leader thinks that if you are having fun at what you do, you will be happier and work more productively.

Both Andrew and Raymond agree that work can and should be fun. Granted, there are some jobs that lend themselves to this more than others. However, every boss would do well to make the work environment fun and exciting. While this means that amusement and laughter should not be foreign to the workplace, it also means that work should be challenging and the environment of the challenge should be positive. Happy people truly are more vital, creative, and productive. They have more personal concern for the organization and therefore, work harder to accomplish its goals.

The more people enjoy their work and environment, the more likely it is that they will stay with the organization. Happy and fulfilled employees tend to be more loyal and dedicated. Absenteeism and employee turnover are also reduced. So, all you leaders, keep repeating after us, "It's okay to have fun at work. It's okay to have fun at work..." To illustrate in better detail, let's separate out fun as in amusement and fun as in challenge.

The perceptive leader can distinguish between a healthy amount of fun and the point at which it begins to disrupt production. The line is almost imperceptible, but once crossed, it can negatively influence morale. That probably accounts for some leaders' fear of allowing any joviality; they don't know where the line is and are fearful of finding out that they have crossed it inadvertently. The art of leadership involves feeling confident enough in your judgment to know the limit and having enough faith in your employees to know they won't abuse it.

A survey of over 700 CEOs found that 98 percent favored job candidates with a sense of humor over those without. A second survey also found that 84 percent of the executives thought that employees with a sense of humor did a better job. So, what is a sense of humor? Humor is the trait of appreciating (and being able to express) the humorous; and, the ability or quality of people, objects or situations to invoke feelings of amusement in other people. Humor can be any form of human communication (verbal or non-verbal) that invokes feelings of laughter or happiness. The key points of this definition are that humor is both verbal and non-verbal, and that humor encompasses activities that make people laugh or feel happy. For the leader, fun on the job or a sense of humor involves both laughter and making people feel happy about what they do; happy they work in your shop.

There are a few rules about fun on the job:
1. Don't over do it.
2. Don't violate workplace rules and regulations.
3. Laugh with people, not at them.
4. Laugh loudest at yourself.

There are many ways that leaders move fun into the workplace. Sam Walton, the founder of Walmart is famous for losing a bet with his employees and walking down Wall Street in a hula skirt. Another CEO took a chocolate pie in the face. You really have to be a special type of individual to pull off these types of physical humor. Quite frankly, they aren't recommended for most leaders. Indeed, being too quick witted can be a detriment to your leadership ability. But, there are some things you can do.

Learn to celebrate. From birthdays to anniversaries, to any major internal accomplishment - celebrate with your followers. Raymond inherited a large work-group that held monthly all-staff meetings. They were two hour sessions, dreaded by all. After the first one, Raymond made some changes. One change was to recognize all of the people who had a birthday in that month. Along with the recognition, he brought a cake to the meeting and had the birthday people cut and serve the cake to their peers. Birthdays are highly recommended as times to celebrate. They are the only holiday that is just about the one person. They should be seen as that person's special holiday.

Find a great big smile and wear it most of the time. There are times smiling and laughter isn't appropriate, but most of the time, smiling will lead to other people smiling. Smiles are like yawns; they are somehow infectious and lead to a positive attitude. Smile and emphasize the positive. There is usually a bright side to everything. Now, we are not suggesting that you become some kind of "Polly Anna." Clearly, not everything has a bright side, or perhaps the bright side is inappropriate to mention at the time. Nevertheless, look for the positive in situations and emphasize them with your followers.

The very successful Trader Joe's specialty grocery store takes their fun very seriously. CEO Dan Bane meets with all employees whenever they open up a new store. The last thing he tells them is to have fun. More specifically, he tells them that at the end of 30 days if you're not having fun, please quit. He gets some startled reactions, but he simply believes that people are spending too much of their life at work to not be having fun.

Part of making the workplace fun is energizing your followers. You can energize the workplace by using games to build teams and teamwork. There are a large variety of teamwork, discovery and ice breaking exercises. At first blush, some leaders are reticent about using games as a means to teach concepts and strengthen workgroups. Okay, so don't think of them as games, think of them as exercises. Raymond has used gaming exercises as a means to build his subordinate leaders skills and strengthen their ability to work as a team. Workplace team building games (or exercises) are a very purposeful and powerful tool for the leader. And, they can be fun.

SKILLS OR ATTITUDE?

People believe skills are the most important attributes for a worker and should be the organization's training and educational priority. Many organizations spend time and money on skills when, in fact, establishing norms and changing attitudes will probably have the largest impact. You can use a game to demonstrate to your workgroup why this is so. This game is good for large groups, but works best with groups of seven to ten. If you have a large group you can split them up and appoint several facilitators. Use a flip chart, or white board and brainstorm with the group. Ask them to name great leaders and managers. These can be business people, leaders in your field, military leaders, political leaders, even fictional leaders. After you have a collection of names, put those names aside (where they are still visible). Ask the group members to name the attributes most associated with the various names of the board. List them. It really doesn't matter what order. Now, choose one of the most dominant members of the workgroup (we are certain you can identify these persons). Ask them to come forward and circle the skills associated with the leaders. There won't be many. Then, ask one of the quieter group members to come forward and circle the attitudes. You guessed it. It's mostly about attitude.

Facilitate a discussion with your group. While you need a minimal skill level for any job, what separates stellar performers from mediocre performers is attitude. Gaming is fun, engaging and educational. You will find a list and directions to a number of team building games at the companion website for this book at www.pokerleadership.com.

The supreme accomplishment is to blur the line between work and play.
Arnold Toynbee

The human race has only one really effective weapon, and that is laughter. The moment it arises, all our hardnesses yield, all our irritations and resentments slip away and a sunny spirit takes their place.
Mark Twain

Work like you don't need the money, love like you've never been hurt, and dance like you do when nobody's watching.
Anonymous

CHAPTER TWENTY-FOUR

Queen of Hearts
Moral Courage

It's hard work. Gambling. Playing poker. Don't let anyone tell you different. Think about what it's like sitting at a poker table with people whose only goal is to cut your throat, take your money, and leave you out back talking to yourself about what went wrong inside. That probably sounds harsh. But that's the way it is at the poker table. If you don't believe me, then you're the lamb that's going off to the slaughter.

Stu Unger, three-time WSOP Champion

Both Andrew and Raymond worked in an industry where physical courage is literally part of the job description. Both authors have seen many acts of physical courage over the years. However, Mark Twain probably summed it up best, "It is curious, curious that physical courage should be so common in the world, and moral courage so rare."

To be a good leader, you need to have moral courage. What does this mean? Many of the chapters in this book speak of areas in which moral courage must be present in order to be effective. Leaders who are good at making tough decisions and who are honest and fair possess an internal component of moral courage. Moral courage is generally not about the physical world. It is not about putting your physical person at risk. Rather, it is about facing mental and emotional risk. It is about facing down the challenges to your reputation, the challenges to your beliefs and the challenges to your sense of well-being. Indeed, physical courage may be more prevalent because moral courage is so much more dangerous, albeit in a different fashion.

Moral courage is recognizing your values and beliefs and not letting them be compromised regardless of the circumstances. When temptation cannot lead you to abandon your principles, you display such courage. Good leaders do not practice situational ethics but are resolute in their beliefs. You must face the consequences whenever your morals are challenged; either you will protect your values or you will desert them and lose your integrity. There are times when our sense of right and wrong, our sense of justice, lead us to physical acts of bravery. This too is moral courage. The key point is that moral courage involves risking danger because of something we value or believe in.

A reading from the core values of the British Army may help to further identify the concept of moral courage: "All soldiers must be prepared for tasks that involve the use of controlled lethal force: to fight. They may be required to take the lives of others, and knowingly to risk their own; to show restraint, even when doing so involves personal danger; and to witness injury or death to their comrades but still continue with the task in hand. This requires physical courage, and soldiers will depend on each other for it. Moral courage is equally important. That is the courage to do what is right even when it may be unpopular, or involve the risk of ridicule or danger; and to insist on maintaining the highest standards of decency and behavior at all times and under all circumstances. In the end this will earn respect and foster trust."

Ethical conduct can be a manifestation of moral courage. Because of the competitive nature of business, it is easy for some people to lose sight of ethical conduct. Focused intently on the bottom-line, profits, or expansion, they lose perspective of what is acceptable behavior. Essentially, they begin to value the material over the ethical. As an example, is it acceptable to use sweatshop labor to increase your profit margins; or, is it okay to pollute the environment in order to reduce costs?

These are large, complex issues that leaders face, but you must also remember to recognize the smaller, daily questions of moral behavior. Will you speak up when someone is being treated unfairly? Will you look the other way when others use expense accounts for their own personal use? Moral courage involves not only knowing what you stand for but also actually standing up for it.

Andrew observed a particularly troublesome lack of moral courage once in an organization he worked for. A loyal, long-time employee was to be fired. Although there were some performance problems involved, politics involving the leader's personal favorites were really the driving force behind the termination. It was the responsibility of the leader to notify the employee. This particular manager's level of moral courage was not his strongest point. Instead of facing the employee, the manager called in an outside organizational consultant to do it! He couldn't stand up and do the job because of his own lack of moral integrity.

If you are in a leadership position, understand that having the moral courage to take the right action is a job requirement. To be a good leader you must take actions now to ensure you will have a solid footing when your moral courage is needed. The first step is to clearly define your personal beliefs and values. What are your deeply held beliefs? What do you value? Are the things that you value ranked? Could you choose between them, or are they all equal? Next, you must clearly define your organization's beliefs and values. Look past your mission statement or written documents that talk about your organization's values. Look to what is really going on around you. What does your organization value?

Once you have clearly defined your beliefs and your organization's beliefs, you must search out any discrepancies between them. Explore the discrepancies. Can they be resolved? Can you change? Can the organization be changed? If there is major discrepancy between what you value and believe, and your organization's values and beliefs, you have a major problem. You will always be faced with making difficult choices, never really being true to either. But, if you can resolve the differences, or if there is a high degree of congruence between the two, you have a solid foundation for moral courage.

Once you are on a firm footing, look around your workplace and identify followers and co-workers who have a high-degree of moral courage. These are the people with whom you should associate. As you lead, recognize, celebrate and reward followers who demonstrate a commitment to your organization's beliefs and values. We are not talking about people who demonstrate some overt moral courage, although they are important and should be recognized. You build an ethical workplace by rewarding those who demonstrate they have incorporated the beliefs and values into their everyday patterns. Through these public acknowledgements you send the message that the beliefs and values of your organization are the foundation of everything you do. You are building an atmosphere where your followers and you can, if the need arises, demonstrate moral courage.

On those occasions when someone decides to stand up, even if they stand alone, you must stand with them. Retired Navy Master Chief Carl Brashear is a man who has demonstrated both physical and moral courage. Brashear was born on a rural Kentucky farm to poor sharecroppers and ultimately became the subject of a major motion picture entitled "Men of Honor."

Brashear says seven acts of courage marked his way:
- Leaving the farm to join the Navy;
- Persevering against all obstacles in pursuing his dream to become the Navy's first African American deep sea diver;
- Taking on the challenging curriculum of the deep sea diving school with only a seventh grade education;
- Completing the first class divers school;
- Rushing in to rescue his divers from an accident -- an act that severely damaged his left leg;
- His decision to have his badly-infected leg amputated; and,
- His battle to be restored to active duty in the Navy as an amputee.

In January of 2000 he was a guest aboard the aircraft carrier Nimitz. He told the crew, "I don't claim to be a hero but I do have bragging rights. I have bragging rights that you can do whatever you put your mind to. No one can stop you. And as long as you have a can-do spirit and a positive attitude you can make things happen." He went on to say, "I hope after sharing some of my acts of courage and triumphs this morning you will also feel inspired to meet your goals, follow your dreams and overcome your adversities through commitment, action and perseverance."

A great example of courage was demonstrated by the passengers aboard United Airlines Flight 93 on September 11, 2001. These heroes showed bravery above and beyond what any of us will likely ever have to face. When they discovered their plane had been hijacked with the possible intention of crashing it into a populated area, a small group banded together to try to save thousands of lives. Knowing that it might be their last act, they attempted to overtake the plane before it could be used to cause the death of even more people.

These heroes displayed the highest form of heroism – to die for the noblest of causes. The number of lives they saved that day cannot be measured and neither can the amount of bravery that they demonstrated. They will forever be remembered as examples of true heroes who faced adversity, fear, and death with dignity and courage.

Moral courage is the most valuable and usually the most absent characteristic in men.

General George Patton

CHAPTER TWENTY-FIVE
King of Hearts
Morale

You cannot survive without that intangible quality we call heart. The mark of a top player is not how much he wins when he is winning but how he handles his losses. If you win for thirty days in a row, that makes no difference if on the thirty-first you have a bad night, go crazy, and throw it all away.

Bobby Baldwin on Poker

Morale is incredibly important in any organization; it affects everything. It affects how people treat one another, their work quality and even the way in which they answer the phone. It is elusive in nature but palpable in its impact. If morale is low, it is a problem even if everything else in an organization is strong. Karl Von Clausewitz, a Prussian military general and military theorist, identified morale as a fundamental military principle. Since Clausewitz published *On War*, morale has developed into a concept seen as critical to organizations. Unfortunately, morale is difficult to define and in many circles has become somewhat synonymous with motivation. But, morale is not about motivation.

Research indicates that high morale creates a more productive and safe workplace. When morale is high employees are enthusiastic, dedicated, and creative. They have a personal investment in their work and gain a sense of fulfillment from it. The quality of work and the quality of the workplace are both increased when morale is high. Traditional definitions of morale include: the mood of individuals in the workplace; attitude or spirit; how a unit feels about itself and its abilities; and, even a state of individual psychological well-being. As you can see, these definitions go back and forth between the individual and groups. We all have good and bad days. Yet, as individuals who occasionally wake up on the wrong side of the bed, we generally don't affect the mood of the entire unit. As our personal attitude ebbs and flows, the morale of our unit is marching to a different drummer. In a previous chapter we talked about your individual attitude as a leader. Here, we are looking at the overall attitude of your work unit.

Morale is about groups and it might be defined as how a group feels about what it does. For instance, this group feeling can be an expression of how high or low the group values an activity. If a group of detectives have their job suddenly changed and they find themselves working in uniform and issuing traffic citations, they may have lowered morale because they place a low value on working in uniform and issuing citations.

For the detectives, their normal working conditions do not involve uniformed activities nor issuing citations. The activity is outside their group norm and not highly valued. Morale is about sub-group norms and values and their alignment with larger organizational norms and values. For our hapless detectives, working in uniform and issuing citations is not the norm nor highly valued by the group. Therefore, when the larger organization imposes new norms and values, if the group maintains its previous norms and values there is a misalignment which manifests itself as low morale. The detectives will show-up in uniform and issue citations but because of the misalignment between group and organizational values we can expect them to have lowered morale and probably not issue many citations.

A norm is the behavior expected within a group of individuals. It is a belief shared by the group about what is normal and acceptable. In groups we establish norms so that we can anticipate and judge the actions of other group members. In law enforcement, we have a strong safety norm. We expect our peers to be tactically sound and safe. We place a high value on this norm. Value is an expression of worth we place on an activity. In other words, groups can have many norms (safety and productivity) and they can place differing values on those norms. For instance, we generally value safety over productivity.

If your organization developed a new rule, policy or procedure that seemed to value productivity over safety, morale would most likely be lower. Employees would have the previous value scheme wherein safety was more important than productivity. They would not feel good about the change. Also, like the detectives who were asked to issue citations, if the organization rapidly changes the norm, employee morale falls. It is the imposed change in the value or norm that lowered morale.

Changes and challenges to sub-group norms come from both inside and outside the organization. If a police officer is killed, especially in the line-of-duty, many group norms and values are challenged. Police officers face dangerous situations daily. The norm is that police officers, as individuals or members of a team, overcome those dangers. The death can represent an inability to overcome danger thereby challenging the norm. Moreover, we value human life as well as, the individual person who died, and safety. An on-duty death can shake all three values. This outside challenge to the norm can lead to a lowering of morale.

Sub-group changes from within are somewhat more subtle. A sub-group with high congruence to organizational values can find itself drifting towards new sub-group norms and values and experience lowered morale. As an example, weak small-unit leadership can lead to deviant peer group behavior becoming the norm. Perhaps the leader allows a clique to grow within the workplace. A clique will develop its own norms and values. Typically, it will value clique membership more than wider workgroup membership. This change in values leads to a change in normal behavior which manifests itself as a reduction in workgroup morale.

When groups feel good about what they do, they experience high morale. Certainly, high morale can lead to improved productivity and quality. If we accept the proposition that morale is an expression of sub-group alignment with larger organizational norms and values, an increase in productivity and quality makes sense. As an example, if the sub-group and the larger organization both value traffic citations, traffic citations will be issued.

For law enforcement, sub-group alignment with larger organizational norms and values is even more critical. Police officers work in a high-discretionary environment. Basically, we choose when to intervene and what to do. The use of discretion is driven by our norms and values. In other words, our decisions will reflect our alignment with organizational norms and values. Consider the impact of norms and values alignment on high-discretionary activities like the application of reasonable suspicion, probable cause, use of force, and vehicle pursuits. Simply put, high morale leads to greater group and individual integrity. As you can see, morale is critical to your organization.

In most organizations, management as a whole is collectively responsible for morale. This is fine in theory, but generally does not have a practical application because morale is such an inclusive and intangible attribute most closely associated with sub-groups within an organization. Through experience, Andrew has developed a technique that can improve morale as a whole by breaking it down into more manageable pieces.

The leader's first step is to seek absolute clarity in understanding your organization's norms and values. You should understand how your organization's mission, goals or objectives support the norms and values. After it is clear to you, it is time to express it to your unit subordinates. For the leader, increasing morale means drawing a direct connection between workplace activity and the group norms and values. Moreover, it means assuring that your workgroup has high congruence with organizational norms and values. You simply can't feel good about doing something you don't value.

Andrew had three top-level managers reporting directly to him. Andrew considered himself responsible for their morale, although he knew that he did not have absolute control over it. In his conversations with his three direct reports, Andrew regularly asked them about their own morale, and routinely observed whether they appeared to have good morale. Andrew discussed morale, or how they felt about what they were doing, with his direct reports. Raymond adds, "The next time you offer praise, instead of praising the action, praise how much the action reflects the norms and values." The idea is to get your followers to feel good about what they are doing by having them value the activity.

Andrew continued morale building by requiring his direct reports to be responsible for the morale of the people directly below them, the line supervisors. Andrew expected that his managers do just as he did. Just as Andrew sought clarity with organizational norms and values, he now expected his direct reports to seek clarity and then to make the connection between workplace activity and values with their direct reports. Andrew specifically made his direct reports responsible for the morale of their units. Most importantly, he gave them the tools to improve morale. This concept of improving your direct reports morale through making a connection between workplace activity and norms and values continues down the chain of command. Everyone is responsible for morale.

Andrew's technique for morale improvement involved bringing it full circle. He would regularly check throughout the entire organization to ensure that his directions had been followed and to make sure that the process was operating as it should. There are some people whose morale you just can't seem to improve.

Some people are not happy with their lives in general. How could we possibly expect them to be happy at work? There are probably 10% of the people who are going to be unhappy no matter what. Likewise, there are 10% who are going to be happy no matter what because it is just in their nature. The remaining 80% could go either way depending on the circumstances. Leaders must focus on this group when trying to impact morale.

Although Andrew's technique is not the ultimate answer to improving morale, it does lay a good foundation. It requires certain people to be specifically responsible for certain individuals' morale. It also creates regular opportunities for the subject of morale to be discussed. It transforms morale from an intangible, lofty idea to something that can be worked with and examined. Finally, it encourages people to speak out when their morale begins to slip. Sometimes, when you can catch morale problems early, small problems can be prevented from becoming larger ones.

There are some signs to look for that may suggest there are potentially serious, underlying problems with employees and their morale. Employees with low morale levels tend to be late or absent from work more often and may want to leave early. They may display poor attitudes, act or speak in insubordinate ways, and become argumentative. They may complain more often, make more careless mistakes, and have below-average performance. You should also pay attention to any increase in violations of policy, loss of inventory, missing documents, and cash shortages. There may be abnormal amounts of customer complaints, personal calls and e-mail, and missed deadlines. What you are looking for are those times when employee actions are out of alignment with overall organizational norms and values. It is not normal to be late, rude or to steal. Many times, negative behaviors are the first sign morale is weakening, which means that employees are beginning to value something other than what the organization does.

What you should watch for is a marked increase in these events and a widespread occurrence of them. One or two people behaving this way may not mean that there are general problems with the organization's overall morale. It may just mean that there is a problem with a limited number of individuals. However, if you notice problems occurring with a large group of people, it is vital to take a closer look. Employee morale is a key component to an organization's productivity; so don't ignore any signs of trouble.

My theory is that an army commander does what is necessary to accomplish his mission and that 80% of his mission is to arouse morale in his men.

George Patton

Morale is faith in the man at the top.

Albert Johnstone

CHAPTER TWENTY-SIX
Ace of Hearts
The Little Things

If scientific reasoning were limited to the logical processes of arithmetic, we should not get very far in our understanding of the physical world. One might as well attempt to grasp the game of poker entirely by the use of the mathematics of probability.

Vannevar Bush

Leaders often overlook the fact that little things mean a great deal to people. We see leaders continually underestimate their impact on people in their organizations. You do not have to slay giant dragons daily as a leader. Sometimes, you just keep paying attention to small matters and the big things seem to take care of themselves. Poker demonstrates the value of how the little things add up. Everyone has an equal chance of getting the same cards, yet some are consistent winners and others losers. One of the things that separate winners from losers is attention to the little things. It is the little things, the nuances in how your opponent plays, that gives you insight and advantage. As human beings, we pick up on the little things. We use them to make judgments when we lack perfect information. You may not know the cards a person has, but if you watch them long enough you may be able to make an educated guess on the strength or weakness of your hand as it relates to their hand.

Employees need to know that you care. For the leader, demonstrating that you care is in the mind of the follower. How often in life has something unimportant to you turned out to be very important to someone else? Certainly you can show them this care by doing the big things, but the major issues do not come along very often. Small things come along all day, every single day, and provide leaders with great opportunities if they are only perceptive enough to recognize them.

All leaders are constantly developing. Recall in the chapter on Life-long Learning, we demonstrated the need to continually refresh yourself in your art. However, as valuable as learning is, practice is even more valuable. The little things give you the opportunity to practice your art, to stay in-tune with your followers and to begin to recognize big problems while they are minor matters. While you are learning and practicing your art, through the little things you will discover how big the little things seem to your followers.

As you begin to notice and act on the little things you will find out that many of them are the surface ripples of a huge under-current. Leaders have called sick employees to check on their welfare and discovered that the follower wasn't merely out with the flu, but was undergoing chemo-therapy. Leaders have noticed a small change in a follower's attitude and discovered they were dealing with a run-away teen at home. Often, upon reflection, we say that we noticed something was happening, but at the time the signs were small. They often go ignored and grow past the point of an easy correction. Perhaps just as important, if you had an employee who was calling in sick or had a change in their attitude, your judgment and actions would probably be different if you knew more about what was going on.

Leadership, like life and poker, is about consistency. As a leader you simply do not have the opportunities to regularly demonstrate your leadership ability in a big way. The opportunities to lead your people throught difficult, complex or even dangerous situations simply do not come along often enough, but your followers need consistency in leadership. They need to know consistently that you are there, you are engaged and you are capable. The little things give the opportunity to demonstrate your leadership consistently.

It is the consistency in leadership that engenders follower loyalty. Consistency makes people feel comfortable. If they have seen you act in many small ways they are able to predict how you will likely act with large issues. It is the consistency in small actions over the long-run that help you build follower trust and loyalty. When people trust you and are loyal, they are much more likely to interpret your actions positively. For the leader, the small things are like deposits into an employee "trust" fund. The more you put in, the more your organization will receive.

We know that these are not seemingly significant issues, but we can assure you that people remember when you do such things. They really are important to people and, if you are on the lookout for such opportunities, you will find that there will be plenty of them to act on. This is the part of leadership that requires extreme sensitivity to the needs and mood of your workplace. It is an area in which demonstrated loyalty to employees on your part can reap tremendous personal and organizational rewards.

TEN SMALL THINGS FOR LEADERS

1. If the member of a follower's family is hospitalized, call the employee, send a card, send flowers or even go to the hospital. Their family is your extended family.
2. If a follower is involved in an accident, even a minor traffic accident, again, follow-up with a visit, a call or a card.
3. If your workplace provides coffee or some type of refreshment, try to include various types, like decaffeinated, teas, or hot chocolate. Make sure there is something for everyone.
4. Celebrate your follower's victories. If they have a birthday, anniversary, promotion or even if a family member does something noteworthy, celebrate it publicly.
5. Help your followers through defeat and disappointment. If an employee fails at promotion, speak with them, offer encouragement and offer to help the next time around. Make every defeat a learning experience.
6. When someone comes to you, give them your full attention. Stop what you are doing and focus.
7. Recognize cultural and religious differences. Send cards on the appropriate holidays. Find out the proper greeting for the follower's holiday and recognize them with their traditional greeting.
8. Follow-up on all changes in routine or appearance.
9. Each of your followers has hobbies and interests. Seek this information out. When you are walking around and talking to your people ask them about how their hobby or interest is going.
10. Ask questions. Your followers know you don't know everything. Indeed, they may even share this knowledge behind your back! Ask them about their area of expertise. Seek their input.

We suspect that many leaders don't follow-up on the small things in a personal way because they do not know how to do so. This kind of consistent caring leadership was not demonstrated and taught to them. Consequently, the first time you do it you may feel wooden or awkward. Welcome to the learning curve. Being able to engage people consistently on a personal level is a learned skill. You will probably sound wooden to yourself and surprise the heck out of your followers the first time you call and ask how their spouse is. However, if you are reading this book, you care enough about your people to want to provide them with better leadership. Your care and concern will come through. Besides, you will become more comfortable and better at engaging your followers on the small things.

People are not concerned about big, faceless corporations. They are not loyal to companies that show no concern for them. As the leader, you are the representative of your company. You have the ability to shape how employees view their own organization by how you treat them. You have the opportunity and, indeed, the responsibility to create a positive, loyal workforce by using your observation, sensitivity, and empathy to provide employees with a positive work environment. This is a critical point of leadership. People do not have relationships with organizations. They have relationships with people. People do not trust, care for or even blame organizations. People trust, care and blame people. As the leader you are the manifestation of the organization. Bad leaders severely impact organizations not only by major bad decisions, but by everyday actions that turn employees away from the organization.

Leadership is about building relationships. The cornerstone of any relationship is trust, and this takes time and effort to build. The authors view their efforts more as an investment than a time expenditure. Andrew shared that he had a long learning curve as a leader in this regard. Although he "got it" instinctively that it was important to connect with people, he thought that it needed to be over significant issues.

Through trial and error though, he learned it was not that important what you connected with people about, merely that you did. Common interests in cars, music or even a television show can bring this about. Although leaders and followers may have different positions in the organization, followers want to look at their leaders and see a bit of themselves. These kinds of "small connections" can help to build and achieve meaningful follower – leader relationships.

One of retired General and Secretary of State Colin Powell's leadership rules is to "Check Small Things." Any organization, task or project is the sum total of its parts. As each of the parts is put together or acting in concert with each other, the weakest of the parts makes the whole weaker. Who hasn't heard the adage that a chain is only as strong as its weakest link? Part of leadership is intuition. Leadership intuition is the type of intuition that can view the small parts of the organization and make a good, generalized conclusion about the organization, a task or a project. But what small things do you check?

Checking the small things is not about looking over everyone's shoulder and beginning to micromanage your organization. Truthfully, if you have to watch followers so closely that you might as well be doing their job, you have a real leadership and/or organizational problem. Checking small things, paying attention to the little details is not about micromanaging as much as it is about knowing where to look for danger signs. Checking the small things involves knowing where and when in your organization a small problem may indicate that a larger problem is looming over the horizon.

You've probably met someone like this. The leader who can walk out into the workplace and spot a problem, or pick up on some small cue that things are beginning to go sideways. Like the sorcerer's apprentice, these leaders make magic. They seem to be able to predict where and when a crisis is brewing. They can step in, take some small corrective action and accomplish two things. First, they take action without micromanaging because they are spotting a distinct, yet small deviation. Second, they are taking action early, when it is easy. A huge leadership maxim is that taking action usually doesn't get easier; on the contrary it often gets messier and more complex. The leaders who can spot problems early by checking small things are not magicians. They have learned, in a very specific way, from their past experiences.

As a leader you have to learn this skill. While we all have previous experiences and most of us have learned from them, in order to be attuned to the small changes in the environment you have to learn a specific talent. That talent is learned by working backwards from your problems. The next time a follower brings you a problem, no matter how small or large, look backwards in time and dissect the problem. Where were the critical points in the brewing problem that you were temporally and/or spatially involved? Spatial involvement is being nearby when the problem was brewing. You can only check small things if you were close enough to spot them. Temporal involvement is similar to spatial in that you must be in the right places at the right times. Moreover, temporal involvement often means scheduling yourself during critical moments of production.

You first assignment in this debriefing/learning experience is to determine if you are "nearby" enough of the time. You can't spot the small problems if you are barricaded in your office behind your in-box. If there weren't enough times for you to have been nearby, you should think about the amount of time you spend involved with your staff. If you determine that you were nearby, the next question for yourself is what were the danger signs? Thinking back on it, what did you miss? Using your 20/20 hindsight, what was readily apparent? What would you have done differently? Where were the points you could have easily intervened and put the ship back on course?

You may find only a few, but if you do this exercise enough times you will begin to see patterns in your workplace. There are natural choke, connecting and transferring points in every workplace. Once you spot these areas you can focus your efforts to be "nearby." Secondly, you will see patterns of conduct. It is very likely that as you go through this debriefing exercise with yourself you will begin to recognize that there are behaviors, albeit small ones, that indicate all is not well. It could be minor tardiness, an increase in overtime, an increase in wastage, or some other relatively minor cue. The magic in checking the small things is building your intuition to be in the right place and look for the "wrong" behaviors, consistently. You can be the sorcerer's apprentice of taking small corrective action – but it takes effort.

To make sacrifices in big things is easy, but to make sacrifices in little things is what we are seldom capable of.

Goethe

Kindness can become its own motive. We are made kind by being kind.

Eric Hoffer

DIAMONDS

Poker players look for their opponents' "tells"—unintended signals that people send when they have drawn aces or are just bluffing. If a good player watches an opponent long enough, she can begin to detect a pattern. Serious poker players strive to disguise their tells with sunglasses or use eye drops so that their pupils don't dilate as they take in a spectacular hand, but it's not easy to control the emotions that bubble up to the surface. Negotiators have their habits, too, though it takes time and patience to discern their meaning.

Michael Wheeler

CHAPTER TWENTY-SEVEN
Two of Diamonds
Teamwork

Is it a reasonable thing, I ask you, for a grown man to run about and hit a ball? Poker's the only game fit for a grown man. Then, your hand is against every man's, and every man's is against yours. Teamwork? Who ever made a fortune by teamwork? There's only one way to make a fortune, and that's to down the fellow who's up against you.

Somerset Maugham from Cosmopolitans

Everyone probably knows at least one "individualist" who is a nonconformist and cannot fit into a group or function as part of a team. Successful entrepreneurs are often portrayed as members of this class of rebels, along with writers and artists, who shun traditional organizational structures to "do their own thing." Of course, at first blush, poker doesn't seem like much of a team sport. Or, is it? The facts are quite different from the perceptions. While you could find poor team players in any field or in any organization, entrepreneurs or small business owners must have exceptional team skills to recruit and retain the right people. There are actually quite a few similarities between poker games and organizational teams.

Teams are created for a purpose. In sports, the purpose is to play a game, with all members of one team working to out perform, or out score, the members of the other team. In poker, while the players are playing against each other as individuals, they have come together as a team with a purpose – to play the game. The first concept about forming a team is that it has to have some purpose, some ultimate goal. If your organization has formed teams to just form teams it will be an unsuccessful venture. There is a distinct difference between work groups and workplace teams. First and foremost, workplace teams must have a team purpose. Moreover, because there is a difference between a team and a group, they are treated and led differently.

The second characteristic of a team is that the goal cannot be achieved by the individual. While we have video games that replicate play, you cannot, in reality, play poker, football or baseball by yourself. The only reason to form a team in the workplace is because the ultimate goal can best be achieved through teamwork. The key concept is in team formation is "best be achieved." Certainly, many workplace functions can be accomplished by individuals or groups of individuals, but if by some unit of real measurement, you can better achieve the goal with a team, form a team!

Next, there is something about teams that you can measure. Perhaps, it is a measurement of the different skills or how the combined effort eases production, increases motivation, creativity or even integrity. The importance of measuring teamwork is illustrated in the following anecdote:

At a county fair, the townspeople held a horse-pulling contest. The first-place horse ended up moving a sled weighing 4,500 pounds. The second-place finisher pulled 4,000 pounds. The owners of the two horses decided to see what these horses could pull together. They hitched them up and found that the team could move 12,000 pounds. By working separately, the two horses were good for only 8,500 pounds. When coupled together, their joint effort produced an added 3,500 pounds.

Teams also have the distinct characteristic of defined rules for the attainment of the goal. Consider the poker game; the rules define how the goal of playing the game will be achieved. Although playing against each other, the players are bound by the same rules. These rules are designed to facilitate the play, or the attainment of the group goal – playing poker. Workgroups are very similar. Rules are a primary difference between groups and teams. Teams may have rules that require closer cooperation and reporting than groups. For instance, teams are often required to meet to discuss the progress of the task whereas groups tend to meet and discuss items general to the workplace. Teams may have specific rules such as timelines for task completion, or perhaps order of task completion. Simply put, teams are more structured by rules than groups.

Teams have a greater ability to learn from their prior experiences than groups. Again, let's return to the poker table. One of the most interesting phenomenon of the poker table is the rapid development of a "table personality." Games differ not because the rules have changed but because the players are intent on discovering each other's "tells." The individuals playing poker exhibit a key aspect of teams in that they are learning from their experiences. Teams differ greatly from groups because teams learn by the behaviors and use that information to guide their future actions.

As teams learn, they develop their own languages, norms and values. If you have a workplace with several teams you will note that even though they might all perform well, they will develop significantly different ways of completing tasks, mediating team disputes and rewarding team member behavior. Teams are much more complex than groups and along with the benefits of teams comes the need for special leadership talents in guiding them.

 TEST YOUR TEAM –
HOW WELL DOES IT FUNCTION?

1. We get along well. We are respectful and courteous to one another;
2. We support each other. We share ideas and opinions openly;
3. We respect differences in opinion and give constructive criticism;
4. We listen actively to one another and we communicate effectively;
5. We have a common goal. We understand the team's vision and strive to accomplish it collectively;
6. We agree on the basic values of the team;
7. We give praise to each other and feel free to challenge ideas constructively;
8. The team has clear goals and expectations;
9. Each member has the necessary equipment, skills, and resources to accomplish a task;
10. Each member is accountable and responsible for individual actions;
11. Each person follows through on commitments;
12. We each support team decisions, even if we voiced concern over them; and,
13. We trust each other. We are concerned with the team's success and not just individual success.

**You should have answered yes to at least nine of the questions. If not, you need to look over the questions and determine in which areas your team could improve.

The concept of "team player" is often used without an adequate definition. What is the basic tenant of "team" action in business? Some purists would say that in a team, the individual's self-interest is subjugated to the team's objectives. Others would argue that "being a team player" merely implies a loyalty to the company and dedication to the job. In much of American business, work has been broken into projects, which are then assigned to corporate teams. This "project-oriented" workflow has become increasingly popular. Then, there are those who would argue that "team" concepts have been too enthusiastically applied in business. Indeed, it is very likely that the word "team" and "group" have been inappropriately used as interchangeable. When Japanese teamwork constructs were introduced in U.S. businesses, some American workers chafed under the burden of the teamwork environment. They were not always so willing to put the interests of a team above that of their own careers. One cannot dismiss the individualist as a heretic just because they do not work well in a "cooperative team" of four or five people. "Team players" may not be the perfect employees, especially in a small business. In situations requiring unique solutions or intense creative work, other workplace personalities may be more effective.

If you are going to have work teams because the task is better achieved through teamwork, then you must use different leadership strategies in order to help the team become effective. Small businesses often function as one team. There is little distinction between members of the executive group and workers. This works well in many situations because the small group exhibits all the tenets of a team, not a group. On the other hand, the older chain-of-command approach may be more appropriate in a larger business.

Whether your organization is a full team-oriented organization, a traditional chain of command, or a hybrid, the full commitment to the organization by each participant is critical. If a leader is to expect high-quality production, this must be communicated and modeled by the leader's own behavior. There are several leader behaviors that can foster teamwork.

Let's decide whether you have a group or a team. First, go back over the beginning of this chapter – how many of the characteristics does your team/group exhibit? If you're still undecided, there is a sure fire way of finding out. Go to our website at www.pokerleadership.com and pick any of the short team building exercises. Try it on your team/group. You will find that the reason so many leaders are disappointed with team building exercises is that they have tried them on groups and not teams. A team will take to the exercises like fish to water. When you debrief the exercise the team will have learned something about the team and the team members. Groups will look at you like you are from Mars. Team building exercises don't work well with groups because they are not teams. Remember, teams:

- Have a specific goal;
- The goal is best achieved through team effort;
- The effort is measured;
- There are team rules for achievement;
- Teams learn; and,
- Teams develop their own languages, values and norms.

Begin to develop your team by clearly stating the goal. When leaders do this, people notice. Good teamwork creates a synergistic effect where combined efforts are much greater than the sum of the individual parts. One of a leader's most important duties is to create an environment where teamwork can thrive. Teamwork often produces greater results than individual efforts. In essence, teamwork divides the effort and multiplies the effect. Explain to your team how you envision their team efforts being superior to individual efforts. Concentrate on their talents, experience, etc. Moreover, tell them how these efforts are measured. What is the yardstick you will use for success?

In the beginning, the leader will have to formulate team rules, such as: when they meet; how the work will be assigned; and, when tasks are due for completion. Because teams learn, the leader should be able to gradually back away from intensely directing the team to the position of coaching them. Because your team will develop a sub-organizational culture, you must be attuned to any norms or values that begin to walk away from the organization. This can be a danger point for the leader. Sometimes, teams will begin to take short-cuts that the organization would disprove of, in order to achieve goals. You want your highly functioning team to have its own personality, but it must be consistent with your organization.

Wild Card The Senn-Delaney Leadership Consulting Group has created a list of nine guiding behaviors that help to forge good teams. An analysis of these behaviors can serve leaders when working toward building a better team. These behaviors are:

- Acts for the long-term benefit of the company even when it may detract from short-term personal benefits;
- Develops positive working relationships with peers;
- Supports fellow teammates to succeed;
- Involves others in discussing issues and resolving conflicts;
- Acknowledges others who demonstrate teamwork;
- Informs and involves teammates whenever possible;
- Seeks win/win solutions;
- Shares information and resources with others; and,
- Credits others for their contributions.

No matter how much work a man can do, no matter how engaging his personality may be, he will not advance far in business if he cannot work with others.

John Craig

CHAPTER TWENTY-EIGHT
Three of Diamonds
People Are Watching

You have to learn what kind of hand this guy shows down, watch that one's moves, watch the veins in his neck, watch his eyes, the way he sweats.

Johnny Moss (1975)

As a leader, people are always watching you, even though in many cases you may be unaware of it. People watch how you dress, how you decorate your office, how you conduct yourself, even where you park your car. While you cannot completely control what others will think of you, you do have the ability to shape their perceptions by how you conduct yourself.

By nature, Andrew is a very logical person. While employed by a municipal police department, he had several options for entering the building. He used the seemingly most logical entrance, the door closest to his office. By using this door, he only had to go through one door, instead of two. The other entrances required entering multiple doors and generally a longer trek to his office. He thought nothing about his choice of entry, although he did note that others did not normally use this door.

In the meantime, people were taking note of the door he entered and making assumptions about what his choice meant. One of the assumptions was that he was being aloof because he did not choose one of the more commonly used entries to the building. As ridiculous as this may sound, it presents a good example of the fact that, as a leader, people are watching everything you do! They are also making judgments, some warranted and some unwarranted. There are a few reasons people may take notice and draw conclusions on our simple and often unconscious actions. Recall that we have noted several times that most of human communication is non-verbal. We simply have more practice as human beings interpreting what we see instead of what we hear. Indeed, Raymond's grandfather often said, "Don't believe anything you hear and only half of what you see!" As human beings, we naturally attach some communication meaning to what we see others do. Unfortunately, the interpretation of our action is left to the follower unless we, as leaders remain vigilant and use our actions directly. Secondly, people's perceptions may have to do with consistency and regularity.

Consistency and regularity are two distinct concepts that impact followers' perceptions. Consistency means doing something the same way, so that your followers can understand you and be able to reasonably predict your behavior. The ability to predict how someone will react makes us more comfortable with them. Regularity has to do with the frequency of your actions. Often, especially with new leaders or new followers, leader actions must be both consistent and regular. So, your consistent and regular small actions are used by followers to predict your behavior.

Andrew's followers' assumption about the meaning behind his choice of doors was without merit. But, for some people the perception, despite the fact that it was a "misperception," became reality. People don't always behave based upon truth and reality. Their behavior is based upon perception and interpretation. Leaders must realize that almost every action they take may be scrutinized, and they should behave accordingly. There is an old joke that goes: a man jumps off a ten-story building. Do you know what he said for nine floors? He said, "So far, so good." The man's perception was to that point, everything was fine. For most people who work in organizations, perception is reality. As a leader you cannot change this. What you can do is recognize it, and when you have a chance, correct misperceptions and realize the power of your actions as a leadership tool.

After a great deal of reflection and after overcoming some personal stubbornness, Andrew ultimately changed the door he used. Although he knew he had no aloof feelings in his heart, the adverse perceptions became too much of a distraction and he chose to eliminate it. Regardless of what decision you may make when faced with such a decision, the important concept to understand is that no matter what you do, people will be watching and drawing conclusions. This does not mean you have to alter your every move, it just means you need to be aware of every move.

If you don't believe that minor actions cause your followers to make large assumptions about your behavior, try an experiment. Alter some minor aspect of your day. Watch the reactions. As an example, Raymond recently conducted Andrew's "door experiment." Andrew and Raymond are faculty advisors at the same university. As with Andrew's police department, there are several doors to enter the building. Raymond always uses the front door even though it means passing one side entrance that is much closer to his office. Now, Raymond doesn't really do this for any other reason than it gives him the opportunity to pick up his mail before going to his office. So, even though the side door is closer, it is a shorter trip and saves time if you pick up your mail first! Using the front door also gives Raymond the opportunity to "chat" with the receptionist and then pass most of the offices and "chat" with his colleagues.

As an experiment Raymond began to use the side door. After using the side door, Raymond went to his office and then took essentially the reverse path to his mail box, still "chatting up" everyone. It took two days for the receptionist, the financial aide director and the assistant dean to ask him if something was wrong! The dean and the receptionist had drawn the inference that Raymond was going directly to his office and "hiding out" because of some problem. In reality, Raymond went to his office, put his briefcase down and then walked the reverse course, with essentially the same behaviors. While not a very scientific experiment it is very suggestive that small actions make a big difference. If you don't believe it conduct your own small experiment. Andrew comments that it has been his experience that when people don't have accurate information, they tend to fill in the blanks on their own, more often than not with negative perceptions. Through constantly being aware, you can work to combat this destructive force.

You should also be aware of the fact that you, as a leader, represent your company or organization to the outside world. The image that you portray to customers, other companies, and the general public will affect how these people view your organization. Your overall image includes your personality and lifestyle and also how you conduct business. If you are fair, moral, and conscientious, this will reflect back on the organization's reputation. Leaders must be aware of how their actions and words can either jeopardize or benefit their companies.

If you present the qualities of a good leader (professionalism, understanding, dependability, and strength through your actions and speech) you will be perceived that way. You do not have to compromise your basic personality to please everyone, but it is important that you present a persona people can respect. People are more apt to follow willingly and support the visions of a respectable leader. Being aware of all your actions, however minor they seem, helps you to present yourself as the type of high-quality leader you aspire to be. Once you realize how important your unconscious actions are you can begin to explore how powerful your conscious actions can be.

In his article for the United States Command Studies Institute, *Invoking Force of Will to Move the Force*, Dr. Jack J. Gifford recounted how General Matthew Ridgeway understood that people were constantly watching the leader. According to Gifford, "When General Walton Walker died in a traffic accident on 23 December 1950, General Matthew Ridgeway replaced him as commander of the U.S. Eighth Army in Korea. At the time Ridgeway took command, the Eighth Army was in a defensive position and posture near the 38th parallel after completing a 300-mile retreat following Chinese intervention in the Korean War and the Eighth Army's stunning defeat on the Chongchin River in November."

Gifford tells us that "Part of Ridgeway's answer to raising morale and fighting spirit was to use showmanship. Patton, with his pearl-handled revolvers, had employed this method with the Third Army in World War II. Ridgeway hoped to do something similar in the Eighth Army--but different enough that no one would compare him to Patton. Earlier, General Walker had tried to show a Patton-like facade but failed. Ridgeway, on his part, displayed his own distinctive persona, by wearing a hand grenade and a first aid pouch strapped to his battle harness. Next, he visited the front lines, believing that a commander has to see the action and be seen at the front if he is to have credibility with his troops. He must give the impression that he is sharing, to some degree, the same hardships and hazards as his men. Ridgeway believed and voiced the notion that a commander should never ask his troops to do what he himself would not do and his troops knew he would not do."

Gifford continued, "Ridgeway believed a commander should publicly show a personal interest in the well-being of his soldiers. He should do something that attracts notice and displays his concern for the front-line fighters. Finding that one of his units was still short of some winter equipment, Ridgeway dramatically ordered that the equipment be delivered within twenty-four hours. In response, the Logistical Command made a massive effort to comply, flying equipment from Pusan to the front lines. Everyone noticed. Ridgeway also ordered-and made sure the order was known-that the troops be served hot meals, with any failures to comply to be reported directly to the commanding general."

You can choose the message your actions communicate. Good leaders look for symbols they can use to help followers understand the leader's message. Symbols and symbolic actions are the meat of non-verbal communication. Often, people think of a good leader as part actor. This is only part of the story. Acting is difficult; it really means being something you aren't. Using symbols and symbolic actions to communicate your message is not acting. It is using complex, rich and multiple mediums to communicate with your followers. You are not acting some leadership part; you are using non-verbal communications tools as part of your leadership methodology.

A leader is also an actor and must consciously act the part of the leader.
Alan Axelrod in *Patton on Leadership*

CHAPTER TWENTY-NINE
Four of Diamonds
When the Cat is Away...

There are few things that are so unpardonably neglected in our country as poker. The upper class knows very little about it. Now and then you find ambassadors who have sort of a general knowledge of the game, but the ignorance of the people is fearful. Why, I have known clergymen, good men, kind-hearted, liberal, sincere, and all that, who did not know the meaning of a "flush". It is enough to make one ashamed of the species.

Mark Twain

Mark Twain's comments on people who don't know poker remind us of leaders who haven't prepared their followers. If you were playing a high-stakes poker game would you turn your hand over to someone who didn't know how to play? Or, would you be comfortable turning your hand over to someone who knew how to play, but did not have your experience at the table? They don't know the people or your strategy. Well, every time you turn the workplace over to followers that you have not prepared, you are turning your hand over to someone who doesn't know the game. Of course, the follower is going to lose your money!

Our proudest moments as leaders have been when we have returned from an extended absence. Some people think this is odd, but we do not. To the authors, the most important duty we have as a leader is to mentor and develop people to accomplish organizational goals even when we are not around. When you return from an absence and everything is running smoothly, you should be proud. For us, this means that we have properly prepared people to succeed in our absence. Raymond received his first glimpse of the importance of developing people to act independent of the leader during basic training.

As a seventeen-year-old, Raymond received basic training in basic ship-board damage control and firefighting. Although nearly thirty years ago, he clearly recalls the primary message – if there was a fire aboard ship you needed to be able to perform the necessary actions where you were, with what you had and without somebody telling you. If there is a fire aboard a ship, there is nowhere to go. There is no 9-1-1. The ship sails or sinks based on the ability of every member of the crew. Since a fire can occur at any time, and you could be in a part of the ship with which you weren't familiar, you still needed to know the basic equipment and duties. If you waited for someone who knew it better, or waited for someone to tell you what to do, you would soon be wading in the water. Good shipboard leaders made sure their people knew the basics on hatches, fire equipment and shipboard communications. The phrase, "it's not my job" did not apply.

The United States Army also uses a very similar concept on preparing subordinate leaders. It is a primary duty in the Army to prepare your subordinates for your job. This is a simple, yet powerful, tool. On the battlefield, if the leader has prepared the subordinates and the leader becomes a casualty, the mission doesn't fall apart because the subordinates are prepared and expected to step up and carry out the mission.

The paradigm is clear and obviously applicable in the military or in emergency services. It is also applicable in the private or non-emergency services public sector. Developing your followers to replace you is the surest way of ensuring your longevity as a leader. Your followers are going to act in your absence the way you have developed them to act. By absence we are referring to both planned long-term (such as vacation and travel) and short term (such as the daily decisions your followers make without you). Followers can only act as if you were present if you prepare them to act that way.

Throughout the book we have talked many times about the necessity of being clear with organizational goals, norms and values. Instilling them in your followers is the first step in preparing them to act without you. This should be your foundation for action, therefore, you should make sure your followers have the same foundation. Think of it this way – goals, norms and values are the rules of the game. They tell you the basics of play, but they don't tell you how you should play every hand. Each hand depends on the cards, the table and you. You can know the basics and still lose, but if you don't know the basics you will lose – that is if they even let you play.

Once your followers have the basics, they know how to play, but they don't yet have enough information to play well. You must teach them to play well. One of the most interesting leadership tools is the relationship between teaching and leadership. Consider that from Kindergarten through your senior year in high school you were programmed by the state to respect the teacher as the leader. A teacher combines all of the power bases that were discussed in Chapter Four to influence your behavior. Indeed, next time you attend a training seminar watch how people react to the teacher. Even the "hardcore" eventually sit down and display respect. They listen and often learn. Teaching is perhaps the simplest way to combine multiple powerbases and increase your leadership and the knowledge of your followers.

Begin by observing your followers as they work through real-life problems. You often don't need to be present because you can get an idea of what is going on through written and verbal reports. Look for their good work. Find the things they are doing well and identify people in your shop that have significant institutional knowledge. Find out who knows how to do what. At your next staff meeting, ask one of these people to talk about how they worked through the problem. Encourage them to share their knowledge and expertise with your workgroup. Two things are going on: you are beginning to develop subordinate leaders by recognizing workplace expertise (a power source); and, you are setting the stage for future conversations about things that didn't go so well.

After someone relates how they correctly worked through the problem, simply ask them if there is anything they would have done differently. This can open the door to frank discussions on training and educational needs in your workplace. Listen carefully to what they would have done differently. It will provide you with clues as to what type of training and education your followers already recognize that they need. Based on their identified needs, provide them with the training.

Things can almost always be done differently. There are often no right or wrong solutions to problems. Moreover, people can become defensive if you tell them they were wrong, but most people can tolerate thoughts on how to do something differently. The critical point is to keep the discussions appropriately structured by using positive words and phrases. Help your followers explore alternatives. This experimentation with "near-histories" is a good way to increase follower ability.

Some of your people may never learn anything new if you don't give them something new to learn. Delegating your tasks is a controlled way of modeling your expectations for when you will absent. Give your followers an experience base. When you turn your hand over to them, make sure they not only know the rules, but that they actually have had some experience playing the game. In Chapter Thirty-five we will spend more time looking at delegation as a leadership tool.

Your followers must know mission specifics. There are times that you can't divulge information to followers but there are probably fewer such times than you would think. Both Andrew and Raymond have worked for leaders who withheld knowledge and information. People who do this without purpose are mistaking power with leadership. Certainly, if I know something you don't, I may have power over you. But it is only power and most importantly, it is only power that can be exercised when I show you what I know and you don't. This is just a foolish power game. Your followers should know as much as it is possible to tell them.

"There is more than one way to skin a cat." While we are certain that this is true, we are uncertain why you would want to skin a cat. But, that aside, the sentiment is clear. The authors have worked for leaders who weren't happy unless something was done exactly as they would have done it. This type of leadership creates a no-win environment for the follower, and the follower can always default to doing nothing. If leadership in business is "like herding cats," then leadership in volunteer organizations is like herding fish. At least in business you are paying someone to do a task and there is an expectation that they will do it the company way. However, with volunteer organizations, it takes all of your leadership and motivational skills to get things done.

Raymond recounts a recent event as a volunteer leader that highlights the concept of allowing followers the ability to do it their way. As the board of Raymond's organization prepared for the upcoming year, a relatively new member agreed to chair a fundraising activity. As the group moved closer to the event, a long-time member began to complain to other members that the newer member, "Mike", was not organizing the event as he, "Stan", had organized it for the last several years. Raymond met with Stan. None of Stan's concerns were substantive; they were matters of style.

Raymond explained to Stan that Mike, a prosperous business owner and volunteer, was doing the job. Probably not the way Stan would, and perhaps not even the way Raymond would, but Mike was doing it. It was Mike's event and it was everyone's responsibility to support him. The truth was, Stan and Mike just couldn't stand each other. For Stan, Mike couldn't do anything right and for Mike, Stan was a micromanaging idiot. Unfortunately, Stan had some very valuable insights, but because he continually interfered with every decision Mike made, Mike stopped listening. Both men were prosperous, effective business owners, and good-hearted volunteers.

Raymond bridged the gap by constantly praising Mike in person and in front of the group. Raymond also made sure that he communicated each of Stan's substantive ideas to the fundraising committee. But, Raymond always made sure that the ideas were communicated positively and made sure Stan knew his ideas were being respected. If Raymond had not intervened between the two, Mike would have quit! The point is that if you don't allow followers the freedom to complete a task, even if it is not exactly how you would do it, they will be very much less likely to do anything without your specific instructions.

Part of developing your followers to continue in your absence is exposing them to your boss. It takes practice to effectively communicate with your boss. While you don't want people "jumping the chain of command" you do want to encourage an environment wherein your followers feel comfortable dealing with your boss, in your absence. Take your followers along to staff meetings. Allow them to interact with your boss. Have your followers prepare and deliver briefings. If you take the time to develop your followers, "When the cat's away," nobody will even notice. Although it may at first be difficult to accept that you are "replaceable," at least temporarily, the reality is that such a scenario is the best evidence of your ability and success as a leader.

The final test of a leader is that he leaves behind him in other men the conviction and the will to carry on.

Walter Lippmann

CHAPTER THIRTY
Five of Diamonds
Surround Yourself with Excellence

The guy who invented poker was bright, but the guy who invented the chip was a genius.

Big Julie

One of the emerging themes in the academic literature on organizations is the "Resource-Based-View." In a nutshell, this view says that organizations are more or less competitive based on how they use their resources. Time and again, a dominant theme rises when organizations are studied and that theme is people. Technology and structure as organizational components pale in comparison to the power of finding and leading the best possible people. In the author's view, the only way to create an excellent organization is to hire the best people available. There are many companies with great equipment, good training, competent management, and clearly defined goals; these are relatively meaningless if you don't have top-notch people.

Hiring the best employees starts long before you have the need to hire. Your recruiting efforts begin by creating the best possible workplace. As a leader, if you create a place where people want to be, you will attract the best. This is most clearly demonstrated in large organizations wherein employees have the ability to transfer to different workgroups. As the reputation of the workplace grows within the organization, people take notice and begin to consider a transfer to your unit. Even if you hire from outside your organization, the reputation of your workplace can either attract or dissuade people from applying.

The phrase "first class people hire first class people" is often taken to mean you should hire the smartest, or the best. What do "smartest" and "best" mean? First, the terms are relative not only to the job, but the workgroup in general. Self-evaluation and evaluation of the current employees and organization is needed in order to hire wisely. The boss must know where the strengths and weaknesses of the organization are and the dynamics that will help it reach its highest potential. You should hire people who fit the workplace's style and who can complement the skills of the rest of the organization. They should be the smartest and the best in the skills you need to round out your group.

Think of your hiring efforts as a poker hand. You don't just want the highest cards. You want the best cards. If you go for the highest cards and end up with Ace, Queen, Jack, Ten and Nine you have five really high cards, but not a Straight. The person with a pair of twos is going to take your money. The person with the pair of twos has the cards that fit best in the hand. A win during the hiring process is finding a person with the right skills for your group.

Near where Raymond lives there is fast-food restaurant that generates one of the highest sales and profits in a national chain. It also has one of the highest turnover rates for employees. The franchise owner has a dirty little secret. If you go into the store you will find it is clean, efficient and friendly. Yet, you will see new employees all the time. The owner admits to running an employee development program more than a restaurant. Her idea was to establish a reputation among the area's young people as a place where the best and brightest go to get their first job. She takes them in at $6 an hour, but many of them leave within six months for an $18 an hour job. By word of mouth, the young people in the community know this is the place that you go to learn to get that really good job. If you talk to the owner, she will tell you that she can teach the cash register but she can't teach drive and dedication. She knows what she is looking for when she is hiring. If you have a great workplace and know what skills will round out your team you're half way home to surrounding yourself with excellence.

 Here are some questions to ask yourself when considering new candidates for employment:

1. Do they have strengths and skills that your organization lacks?
2. What are their areas of weakness and how will these affect their job performances?
3. Do they fit with the group's work style?
4. How do their work histories demonstrate their abilities?
5. How much training do they need and is it available?
6. Do they have good attitudes and interpersonal skills?
7. What are their ambitions within the organization?

Wild Card Dewey Decimal Classification or Dewey Decimal System is used by libraries to classify non-fiction publications into subject categories. The subject is indicated by a three-digit number followed by decimal points that indicate the order and location of books on a library shelf.

You should not be hasty when it comes to selecting your employees. In the long run, it will save you time and resources to carefully select the best people, even though it may seem a difficult and arduous process. Most leaders are not in a position to hire a new team every six months. Most of us are hiring someone for the long-run. To assist you in finding the right person you should spend time exploring what types of skills are necessary to complete the tasks of the job in question. The longer you are looking for someone to be employed, the more complex and important the task of hiring and selection. Indeed, many large firms have Human Resource Departments that develop skills and competency lists which should mirror task requirements.

It is important to note that task and competency lists are minimal requirements. In reality, minimal requirements should simply help you screen out non-qualified candidates for your interviews. There are many ways of conducting and scoring interviews. The best advice is to remember your goal is to surround yourself with excellence. When you enter the interview room, you should know what "excellence" in your workplace means and how someone would demonstrate it.

Even if you know what excellence in your workplace would look like, how do you tell if the prospective employee has those qualities? You can't judge a book by its cover, but the Dewey Decimal System can give you an idea about the book. In other words, one way to delve into the character and qualities of a potential employee is by looking at with whom they associate or would choose to associate. Questions like "Who is your hero?" and "Whom do you admire?" when followed up by "Why?" give you insight about a person. The critical part is why. Why a potential employee wants to be like someone (as in a hero) or would associate with someone (as in admire) can tell you a lot about their core values and beliefs. How closely do the potential employees core values and beliefs align with your organization's?

Once employees are hired, it is important to focus on training and evaluating them extensively during their first year or whatever normal probationary period your organization has. This period is actually the last and most important part of the selection process. You should make it clear to potential employees that the probationary period is an extension of the selection process. People need to know that they are still under examination for a fit to your workgroup.

You have to be almost ruthless in your approach to probationary employees. People are expected to excel during this period. This is especially true if you have made it plain that the probationary period is an extension of the selection process. This is probably when you will get the best effort and attitude from them. If they are marginal at this point, the chances of them improving after they pass the probationary period are slim. Although it is conceptually possible, never, during either of the author's careers, have they seen someone who was below average during a probation period go on to become an outstanding performer.

Once you are satisfied with the people you have hired and trained, it is important that you let them know that they are valued. Great employees are priceless additions to your organization. No matter how outstanding the leader is, an organization will never thrive without the work and dedication of an excellent staff.

The best executive is one who has sense enough to pick good men to do what he wants done and self-restraint enough to keep from meddling with them while they do it.

Theodore Roosevelt

Wild Card Here are some questions to ask yourself when an employee is nearing the end of their probationary period – the final part of selection:

1. Works well with coworkers. Shares ideas and assists others;
2. Understands organization's or group's vision and objectives and strives to accomplish them;
3. Listens to others and communicates effectively;
4. Contributes positive, useful ideas to the group;
5. Meets deadlines;
6. Has a good attendance record;
7. Quality of work is high; errors are kept to a minimum;
8. Continues to develop and learn new skills;
9. Has initiative and is able to work with minimal supervision;
10. Recognizes problems, both actual and potential, and solves them proactively;
11. Recognizes errors or weaknesses and strives to correct them. Can take constructive criticism;
12. Follows guidelines but is also imaginative and innovative;
13. Has a positive, cooperative attitude; and,
14. Is self-motivated.

**You should have answered yes to at least ten of these questions regarding your employee. For a more in-depth exploration of hiring and selection visit the companion website at www.pokerleadership.com

CHAPTER THIRTY-ONE
Six of Diamonds
Consensus

Hold em is to stud what chess is to checkers.

Johnny Moss

Leaders have the right to do what they feel is best for the organization. The smart leader, however, involves people in decisions and attempts to gain consensus whenever possible. Communicating your visions and goals and clearly outlining directions are keys to successful leadership, but listening to your employees is also very important. Paying attention to the feedback and ideas your staff provides works to your advantage. There are two main reasons for this.

First, employees working at the scene of the action are generally going to know more about what is currently happening than their organizational superiors. Not many bosses like to admit it, but the smart ones know this to be true. Good leaders rely upon their trusted workers to give them up-to-the-minute information and feedback. They use this information when forming decisions on how to proceed. Also, this communicates trust and respect for employees; one of the most important messages any leader can send to workers. It lets them know that you value and respect their work.

Secondly, when you gain consensus, people are personally invested in the initiative. A leader can tell people what to do without asking them, and they will most likely make an effort toward compliance. However, when people are actively involved in creating the direction, their commitment to it increases enormously. When possible, collaboration with your employees creates numerous benefits. It makes the project more personal for them, and it may bring new perspectives or ideas to a situation. This is the type of involvement and consensus that helps to create success in an organization.

The authors went through long periods of their careers believing that being "right" was the one and only acid test for how to proceed on something. Only after traveling the long and winding road did Raymond and Andrew recognize that, many times, gaining consensus was ultimately more important and productive than being "right."

Andrew applies this type of concept to his family relationships as well. For a long time in his life he felt that as long as he was "right," he had "carte blanche" to move forward. He ultimately learned that except for the most cornerstone of ethical matters and beliefs of the heart, placing both consensus and peace above being right pays long-term dividends. This is not to say there aren't times to "dig in" and forcefully put forward your beliefs, whether in a personal or professional arena. It is simply to say that there is more to life, work, and relationships than being right. It's okay to believe you're right, but if you can put that belief into broader context, you might be better served in the long run.

Consensus building has application inside and outside your organization. Indeed, the higher you climb your organization's leadership ladder, the more likely you are to find yourself building consensus with other stakeholders. For instance, in large organizations it is not unusual for multiple workgroups to participate in a project. As the leader of your group, you might be called upon to build consensus on how the problem will be tackled by the involved groups. Or, if you are manager in the public service you might be working with another agency or even involved in consensus building with stakeholders outside your organization, like the community.

 For further information on identifying stakeholders you can access a short article on our website at www.pokerleadership.com.

People often find consensus building difficult because they confuse the process with trying to seek unanimity. Consensus means that group members overwhelming agree on the decision. It means that a large percentage of the group agrees on the course of action. While it would be great to have everyone agree, the more diverse your group is the more likely there are to be people who find their interests outside the group agreement. If your consensus building efforts are internal, involving just your workgroup, holdouts are probably going to be less of a problem. This, of course, is a two-edged sword. Stable groups (like a workgroup) can bring a lot of pressure on individuals to conform. This can be good in that it can help manage holdouts. It is bad if group pressure deteriorates to "groupthink."

When you are working to build consensus external to your workplace, holdouts are much more of a problem. When working with external stakeholders, it is important to determine their interest. An interest is the reason someone takes a position. This is an important concept because while it is difficult to meet all positions, if you get to the underlying interests – the need the group or individual must satisfy – you will find that it is easy to satisfy interests rather than demands. This is because people often mis-frame their positions when trying to satisfy their needs. Moreover, think of the position as the hard shell of an egg protecting an interest, or the yoke. The shell is brittle and you can't mold it. But the yoke is much more fluid; more easily mixed. You will know you have reached consensus

Wild Card Groupthink is a term coined by psychologist Irving Janis in 1972, to describe a process by which a group can make bad or irrational decisions. In a groupthink situation, each member of the group attempts to conform his or her opinions to what they believe to be the consensus of the group.

with either an internal or external group when the group agrees that they can live with the final proposal. Consensus is working to satisfy most of the interests or needs of the individuals who make up the group; it is not unanimity.

The first step in seeking consensus is the identification and recruitment of group members. As the leader, you must determine who has a stake in the problem and the solution. Getting the right people to the meeting is critical. If you are working external to your workgroup, getting the right people means getting the people who have the expert knowledge of the interests they represent and who can commit their group or organization to the consensus. It is very frustrating to reach consensus with an external group only to find out that the person who helped you reach consensus cannot commit their organization. If you don't properly identify and recruit, you cannot possibly reach consensus.

> ## JOKERS – WHEN IT AIN'T CONSENSUS BUILDING.
>
> **Tyrants are poor consensus builders. One of Andrew's bosses would hold staff meetings and discuss specifically how he wanted to handle each issue. Only after going on record with his position would he ask for group input. Obviously, this inhibited feedback as he had already made it clear what he thought was the best approach to each issue. In one case, he went so far as to say he would be damned if we were going to do things any way other than the way he had described. Then, as usual, he asked for input on how we should handle this issue!**

Then there is the phony consensus builder for a boss. Here is an example of his approach: there was an important community member who had a pet project that involved the use of police resources. The leader made a commitment to the person that they would have the department's support. After doing this, it would have been career suicide for the leader to back out. Rather than informing the department of the project they would be involved in, he created a committee. He went before the committee and explained what the project entailed. He said the department would not be involved in the project unless there was consensus in the group. He ended by asking what we thought and whether or not the group wanted to do the project. Based upon his position in the organization, no one felt comfortable turning him down, but many people in the room felt that the process was a charade. In many people's view, his integrity was compromised.

After your group is recruited, the first task for the group is to design the process by which the problem with be resolved. As an example, if the group is the board of a non-profit agency the path to consensus is the organizational by-laws often implemented through Robert's Rules of Order.

> **Robert's Rules of Order is a handbook written in 1874 by General Henry A. Robert. It is a set of parliamentary procedures that are often used as an operational authority for decision making in groups. The rules were designed more for use by citizen groups, like corporations and volunteer organizations rather than for use by government bodies, such as legislatures. For a copy of Robert's Rules of Order, visit the book's companion website at www.pokerleadership.com.**

Conversely, if the group is new you may want to use one of the techniques like "forming, storming, norming and performing." The choice of model depends on the group. However, this is just as critical as finding people who have intimate knowledge of the various interests.. Defining the problem is the next phase. Once you have recruited the group and decided how to go about solving the problem, the group must succinctly define the problem. How the problem is framed is going to heavily influence how the problem is solved. A key point for the leader to remember is that the group may define the problem differently than you initially envisioned. As the leader, remind yourself that you decided on a group decision making process because you didn't know everything about the problem and you did not represent all of the interests. The more diverse the group, the more likely the problem is to diverge from your first blush.

 "FORMING – STORMING – NORMING – PERFORMING"
is a model of team development proposed by Bruce Tuckman in 1965. Tuckman maintained that all phases were necessary and inevitable for team or group development. The model has become a fairly frequently used model for team or group development.

After the problem has been defined, your group should begin the search for alternatives. By looking for alternative solutions rather than the ultimate solution, you engender a fuller discussion. It is during this phase that stakeholder interests can be identified. As you listen to the various solutions put forth by the members, look for clues on how they see the problem. People tend to define and offer solutions to problems based on their point of view and their point of view is heavily influenced by their interest.

Once alternatives have been identified you must lead the group toward a solution. Each alternative should be fully discussed. One technique is to list the alternatives on a white board and, under each list the benefits and drawbacks to the solution. Then, look for places where the benefits and drawbacks from the different alternatives are similar. Ultimately, as you move toward consensus, group members can see how you may not use their exact solution, but the solution you use contains benefits similar to their recommendation. It is very important during the decision phase that all group members understand and agree upon the benefits and weaknesses in the various alternatives. Once you have made this agreement, at least on the available alternatives, you are a long way toward consensus.

The next to the last step is to finalize the decision. Note that we have separated the decision making process from the decision. They are, often, two different phases. How you reach the decision is dependent on the earlier work you did on defining the group process. If you decided that the decision would be by vote, as in the case of a non-profit board, the final decision making process is the vote. As you can see, the early phases of the process become critical as you work toward consensus.

The last part of the consensus building process is the implementation stage. This is much more than simply putting the decision to work. It involves supporting all parties as they implement their portions of the decision. In many decisions we make we are affected by a "cooling off" period. Think of the last time you made a purchase. Have you ever experienced buyer's remorse? Sometimes, group members experience a form of "buyer's remorse," and like you and I after that new car purchase, it occurs within 48 to 72 hours. So, as the leader, follow-up with your group members. You are not re-opening the consensus building process. You are providing emotional support and keeping your group on track.

Decisions reached by consensus are like many other decisions that leaders implement in that they need definable check points. A major portion of the implementation process are the decisions that are made about who is going to do what, when. This is the time to reinforce commitments to the consensus and define check points. As the leader, the implementation process lasts as long as the decision is being implemented. You must continually follow-up and hold group members accountable for their participation.

Reaching consensus is a long and often difficult process, but the benefits can be huge. A leader who can bring different interests together and encourage them to work toward a common goal has a definitive set of skills. Because consensus building requires a special set of skills, you may want to consider bringing in outside talent. Often, the use of a professional facilitator is valuable when seeking consensus among those with diverse interests. That being said, as a leader, you should still strive to hone the skills necessary to work with your group and use the consensus building process to play all of your follower's skills.

You can employ men and hire hands to work for you, but you must win their hearts to have them work with you.

William Boetcker

CHAPTER THIRTY-TWO
Seven of Diamonds
Recognizing Weakness

If, after the first twenty minutes, you don't know who the sucker at the table is, it's you.

Unknown

We have all probably come in contact with people who think they have all the answers. What passes for complete arrogance is often an attempt to hide immense insecurity and self-doubt. When leaders act as if they have all the answers and are free from any weaknesses, those around them can suffer from the charade. One of the interesting side effects of success seems to be failure. You really see this in poker. Players with an early series of successful hands begin to believe they know more than they do. It generally goes like this. During the first part of the game the player is careful. They realize that they have certain weaknesses as a player. Perhaps they don't calculate odds well or they have difficulty reading people. Because they recognize those weaknesses they compensate through careful analysis of each hand. Because they know they have a weakness, they compensate with a strength. This is hard work. As they build up a string of successful wins, they begin to minimize their weaknesses. The next thing you know they lose some monster pot of chips, and in retrospect, they knew better.

Leaders do this. When you start out you know your weaknesses. As time passes and you are successful, you minimize your weaknesses. You forget about them. The result is that you think you are playing a strength, when you are falling down on a weakness. Just when you think you know everything, someone is going to demonstrate how little you actually know.

No one should expect perfection from themselves or others. What is important though, is that you recognize your weaknesses and not try to cover them up. Instead, seek self-knowledge and then compensate or correct the weaknesses. Some people are good at identifying their weaknesses while most of us are not.

How do you identify your weaknesses? If you evaluate your own performance, you can become aware of some points; they are the easy ones. What is difficult is identifying weaknesses you can't see. We are all blind to certain aspects of ourselves. The first step in compensating for any weakness is knowing that it exists. Ask yourself - How can you know what you don't know? This is a critical point. You must find a way as a leader to remove your own blinders and open yourself to knowing your weaknesses. One way is to ask your superior, a peer, or your own workers for an assessment. This can be a delicate situation. Some people will be forthcoming when you ask, but many will not. Some of what they say may be valuable and some may be a pure putdown or be spurious. Regardless, you may still gain valuable insight that will help you evaluate yourself.

Some organizations are now using formal "360-degree" assessments on their leaders. Such an assessment requires that superiors, peers, and subordinates all evaluate management personnel. This concept takes feedback beyond the standard evaluation you may receive from your boss. Peers and subordinates will have their own perspective regarding a leader's performance. Compiling information in this "360-degree" fashion creates a much more diverse and comprehensive evaluation of one's performance. A formal "360 degree" assessment can minimize negative commentary based on observer bias because it is a compilation of many views. In other words, the feedback of the individual who would use the process as a "put down" is minimized by the incorporation of other views.

Part of the process is also a self-evaluation. This will show how you are doing versus how you think you are doing. All this information is compiled and shared with the leader in an effort to improve performance. Designing and implementing a "360 degree" or full circle review is actually less than half the solution. As a leader, you must be ready, willing and able to take honest feedback and use it for improvement. Identifying weaknesses requires honest self-assessment. People who have gotten to a leadership position are usually strong, confident individuals, so it may be hard for them to admit that they cannot do something well or that they need help in a certain area. You must keep in mind that being the best leader you can be is going to require continual work. As in many areas of life, natural talent will only take you so far; you must learn and practice to rise to the top.

Assessment also requires that you have the ability to listen critically to others when they give you input. It is difficult to hear criticism without getting angry or becoming defensive. Here again, the natural confidence that got you the leadership position in the first place may cause trouble. Never let yourself fall into the trap of believing that no one has anything to teach you or that you alone come up with the best ways to do things. Be open to the suggestions of others, even when these suggestions deal with your own performance. Show your employees that it is beneficial to take healthy criticism by being the one to model this behavior.

On the other hand, be careful in how you interpret such criticism. If you appear too eager for feedback, peers, bosses, and subordinates alike may perceive you to be weak, indecisive, and lacking in self-confidence. Getting feedback about your performance when you are the leader is a delicate operation. It is also a learned skill. You must learn to seek, evaluate and act on feedback about your performance. Because it is a learned skill, it is also a skill with a "shelf life." That is, if you don't use the skill, it will atrophy. It will become weak and useless. Conversely, the more you use the skill of seeking, evaluating and acting on feedback the more comfortable and adept you will become.

As you identify weaknesses, you have to assess whether it makes sense to devote effort to rectifying them or whether you can just as well compensate for them. For example, a leader who has no knowledge of financial analysis may find it better to have a good analyst on staff rather than go through the struggle of attempting to become a financial expert. If you have a gap in your knowledge, skills or abilities, you must decide if you must fill that gap or if someone else is better suited to fill the gap. You may staff some expertise or you may hire it on a short term basis. If you are a really fine leader you have developed a network of experts you can call and ask. Better to get the right information at the beginning. Sometimes, improvement may be a joint effort: compensating in part while you get up to speed on the basics.

Once you have identified the weak points that you are going to remedy, do not put off implementing a plan for improving them. For example, many years ago, Andrew realized that he had poor computer skills and he knew he should strengthen his knowledge in this area. He bought a laptop computer, attended instructional courses, and read all of the *Computers for Dummies* books he could find. He made a lot of progress, but there were a couple of times when, in his frustration, he almost ended up tossing the computer out the window. Ultimately, he became proficient. Now he presents leadership and career-development seminars using a fancy PowerPoint presentation, something he would not have thought possible many years ago.

As Andrew and Raymond began this project they discussed many leadership topics, their own successes and failures, lessons and skills. Computer skills have been a somewhat regular topic of discussion. Raymond has the "computer gene" and Andrew does not. Raymond's expertise has even reached the point where he is the author of a nationally-recognized book on the use of technology within the criminal justice system. Raymond has learned the hard way (which is typical for him) that even though he can work through a problem with his computer network, sometimes it is a sink hole. Raymond has the rudimentary skills to work through most problems. But, it can take a long time. Rather than spend three hours figuring it out, Raymond makes a ten minute telephone call and pays for the real expertise. Knowledge isn't the same thing as a strength. A strength is something you know how to do well.

As you identify and come to know your weak areas, you need to surround yourself with people who help balance them. It is human nature to select those who are just like you, but smart leaders intentionally pick a variety of people to get an overall balance of strengths and weaknesses. Surrounding yourself with exceptional people reduces the likelihood that a weakness will cause a problem. No single person is going to be able to give the organization everything it needs. When you have others around who excel where you are weak, you can focus on what you really do best. Organizations with diversified staffs succeed because they have the ability to meet any challenge.

Experience is very valuable. It keeps a man who makes the same mistake twice from admitting it the third time.

Brook Benton

CHAPTER THIRTY-THREE
Eight of Diamonds
Promotions

Being able to pit your wits against literally hundreds of other people is really exciting and ultimately the biggest single challenge for a poker player.

Tim Page

When you're playing you either win or lose. What softens the loss at the table is the knowledge that you know the rules of the game ahead of time. You know that everyone has an equal chance at the cards and that it is the skill of the players which primarily determines the outcome. Of course, it's gambling and therefore sometimes what seemed to be a winner turns out to be a loser. Poker and promotions are a lot alike. If your followers know the rules of promotion and they see that the process is fairly applied across the board they will understand loss and victory. Sometimes, it is when the rules are not clear up front, or they seem to have been unfairly applied that followers have difficulty with the leader's choice.

Promotions within your organization make statements so loudly that almost every other action you take as a leader can be drowned out. People see who gets promoted and who does not, and they make a variety of judgments accordingly. This process is called observational learning and it is the "hidden" process that always impacts leadership decisions. Your followers are learning what is rewarded and punished based on promotions. They can learn to emphasize behaviors that they determine resulted in promotion and they can minimize behaviors that they believed did not lead to promotion. When followers learn what behaviors are valued they then make judgments about organizational values. Promotions can be seen by followers as the lens through which to interpret the difference between was is said or written in your organization and what actually goes on.

If the person promoted is intelligent, hardworking, capable, and honest, then workers will believe that these are the traits that the organization values. Those who also wish to be promoted will tend to emulate these traits. Moreover, even those without a desire for promotion will make a determination on what is valued, what is rewarded, and what they should be doing. Your promotional selections are doing much more than filling a position. You are defining your organization for your followers.

On the other hand, if the person promoted is perceived to be deceitful, lazy, or incompetent, other employees may not be motivated to be any other way themselves. Although their internal self-regulation may keep them from sinking to this level, they may not be enthused about the organization in which they work. High turnover and low morale invariably occurs when employees do not believe in the integrity of their organization or leaders. The integrity the followers are judging is the alignment between what you said and what you did with the promotion. If your organization tells members that customers should be treated fairly and your promotional process is not followed and therefore patently unfair, followers will also begin to pay lip service to the concept of fairness.

 Here is a list of characteristics you should look for in an employee before promoting:
- **Attitude of enthusiasm and "can-do" mentality;**
- **Builds esprit de corps;**
- **Team player who contributes and compromises;**
- **Dependable, reliable, works to potential;**
- **Innovative, recognizes opportunity, thinks imaginatively;**
- **Has the training, experience, and aptitude to be successful at the next level; and,**
- **Has the desire to be promoted.**

Promotions should be undertaken with great seriousness. Although you may have a mission and value statement posted on the wall, it means nothing if your promotions are in contradiction to the mission and values. As was mentioned earlier, people will sometimes believe what you say, but they will almost always believe what you do. Defining the process of promotion for your organization and the followers is the critical first step. What attributes, skills and behaviors should be promoted? Not, "who" should be promoted? A leader's primary task is defining what you value and how the ultimate promotion will demonstrate those values.

Like many other leadership processes, the promotional process begins long before you have an opening. It is quite likely that, if you listed the minimum qualifications for promotion the vast majority of your followers would qualify. As you begin to sort through your followers you could probably begin to rank them according to their ability to be effective at the next level. In addition to seeking a qualified candidate, your organization wants to promote those with ability who exemplify the organizational values through their work. Therefore, in addition to determining the "task" qualifications, you want to develop the "values" qualifications.

Once you know both the task and value qualifications, a method to measure them must be developed. The promotional process in the public sector, particularly law enforcement, is very competitive but also very systemized and regimented. There is usually at least a written test and an oral examination. Ultimately, a promotional list is developed. Most agencies have a "rule of three" which allows the chief executive to choose any candidate among those who scored in the top three. This allows some flexibility. There are times when certain people who are good test takers come out high on the list; however, this does not automatically mean that these are the best people for the promotion.

The problem in the private sector is that promotions may or may not be subject to any system. In some industries, the "time-and-grade" system still exists (where promotions are based almost exclusively on seniority). In other companies, the process seems to depend on the whims of management. Both of these approaches can lead to apathy, since promotions may have little correlation to performance. In the most enlightened organizations, promotions are based upon a competitive system with clearly defined job requirements. In these companies, candidates for open positions are sought from within the company before positions are advertised outside. Whatever scheme is chosen by an organization should be followed so that it is interpreted as being a fair system. This means that followers should know beforehand the qualities for promotion and the scheme for measurement.

Ultimately, leaders must ensure that the person promoted is the person who is modeling the core values of the organization. Otherwise, there would be a contradiction between the organization's words and its actions. Other employees will certainly recognize this and react accordingly, either with anger or lack of motivation. Don't think that only employees who wanted a promotion are affected by the promotional process. Even those who have no desire to promote are taking very strong cues about your organization from your choices. Promotions are simply one of the largest rewards for behavior. Who is or who is not rewarded sends a strong message to all followers.

At several points in this book we talked about developing your followers. Part of your development program should be identifying and readying followers for promotion. Sometimes leaders prepare followers for promotion by expanding their duties or allowing them to work temporarily at the next level of the organization. These types of development steps are also rewards and send messages to your followers. People can tell when someone is being groomed for the next level. As we have said, they are watching you.

There are several post-promotion considerations. Some leaders promote and forget. The promote and forget crowd is assuming that the follower will magically translate their previous skill set into the new job. After all, it was the follower's use of their skills in their previous position that was used to judge them as the best candidate. Those skills don't necessarily translate into being effective at the next level. People who are newly promoted need just as much support and guidance as a new employee. You may have to be much more diplomatic and tactful on how you provide the support. You may want to avoid direct intervention which might undermine the person in their new position, but you still must provide support.

A good line-employee is not automatically a good supervisor. A good manager in one firm is not necessarily going to be a good manager in your firm. This is especially true if you promote and forget. It is likely that newly promoted people have a general idea on what they want to accomplish within the organization. This is good, but it is your job, as the leader, to provide them with the support which allows them to develop new tools.

It is a fine thing to have ability, but the ability to discover ability in others is the true test.

Elbert Hubbard

CHAPTER THIRTY-FOUR
Nine of Diamonds
Motivating Others

I've often thought, if I got really hungry for a good milk shake, how much would I pay for one? People will pay a hundred dollars for a bottle of wine; to me that's not worth it. But I'm not going to say it is foolish or wrong to spend that kind of money, if that's what you want. So if a guy wants to bet twenty or thirty thousand dollars in a poker game, that is his privilege.

Jack Binion

Knowing the difference between individual and group motivation is your first step in learning the leadership skill of motivation. In Chapter Twenty-Five, we looked at morale. Recall that morale is how the group feels about what it is doing. In contrast, motivation is about the individual. One of the greatest failures of leaders is attempting to use the same motivators for all employees. The fact is, all people do not want or need the same things, therefore, they are not all motivated by the same incentives. Leaders often erroneously assume that what personally motivates them now or what has motivated them in the past will be effective motivating factors for everyone.

There are a large number of theories on motivation. The theories that assume a leader can make a difference in employee motivation begin with the premise that follower behavior results from conscious choices among alternatives in order to minimize pain (like workplace sanctions) and maximize pleasure (whatever motivates the person). One theory that can help understand some employee behavior is Victor Vroom's Expectancy Theory.

Vroom's Expectancy Theory is based on three core concepts - Valence, Expectancy and Instrumentality. Valence, or value, refers to the emotional orientation a follower has with respect to a reward. It is a measurement of the depth of the desire by the follower for the reward. Furthermore, rewards can be viewed as either extrinsic, like money or a promotion, or intrinsic, like satisfaction.

Finding out what will motivate employees is not a simple task, but the first step is simple – you ask them. You may find that even a casual conversation reveals a lot about how employees view various motivational factors. Also, pay attention to how they work and what they like to do. If there is a particular job that someone likes, you can use this as a reward. It can also work in the opposite direction. If there is a task that someone really dislikes, assigning it to someone else can be a positive reinforcement. Once you have given a reward, watch to see how it influences performance. If quality and amount of production increase, it was a good motivator. In this experimental manner, you can judge what motivates followers and what does not. You can then adjust your rewards accordingly.

 The expectancy theory says that individuals have different sets of goals and can be motivated if they believe that:

- **There is a positive correlation between efforts and performance;**
- **Favorable performance will result in a desirable reward;**
- **The reward will satisfy an important need; and,**
- **The desire to satisfy the need is strong enough to make the effort worthwhile.**

The Expectancy portion of the Vroom theory may be the most obvious yet least explored portion for leaders. Expectancy has to do with a follower's perception of the task. Can they do it? If people want something, yet they know they lack the skill or the confidence in their skill to complete a task in order to get a reward, they will be de-motivated. This is fairly clear when you introduce a new task. If you install a new software system in your organization you will undoubtedly hear groans. Your followers know they have something new to learn and this unfamiliarity may cause their motivation to drop. This concept is less obvious with long-term employees. If you are looking to motivate someone, your first stop should be with their skill set. Do they have the skills to complete the job? Do they have the tools and resources to complete the job? Many times motivation can be improved by providing followers with the skills and tools necessary to complete the task.

As a leader, you should be concerned with eliminating factors that can negatively impact motivation. These factors could include things such as poor working conditions, inadequate equipment, or lack of knowledge. Workers will not be motivated to perform well when the essentials that their jobs require are absent. Only when the basics are in place can a leader attempt to make a positive impact on motivation.

The final portion of Vroom's theory involves the leader's ability to actually produce the reward or instrumentality. Leaders who promise what they can't or won't deliver ruin motivation. Indeed, it may be that instrumentality is the most restrictive part of the theory for the leader. You may be unable to actually deliver what the followers want. If you don't control pay, you can't use pay as a motivator. For an employee to be motivated they must: want it; be able to do it; and, know if they do it well, they will get it. Whatever it is.

So, what is it that people value? Why do some people want milk shakes, some wine and others want to play poker? Real motivation comes from within. Everyone has a certain natural capacity for motivation. This ebbs and flows over the years, depending on a variety of different factors. For each person, at a different time in life, there will be certain factors that are more dominant and factors that have no effect. Abraham Maslow, a leader of the humanistic school of psychology, devised a "hierarchy of needs." It puts the basic needs, such as housing and food, at the bottom of the pyramid and self-actualization at the highest level. In between there are a myriad of factors. Consider just a few: position; title; pay; incentive; compensation; working hours; benefits; office; responsibilities; recognition; coworkers; and, "perks."

Maslow's "hierarchy of needs" provides some interesting discussion points. It seems clear that someone who is hungry is motivated by food, whereas once you are full, food is not as strong a motivator. Many of our employees are beyond the need to make income to support the needs at the bottom of the pyramid. This is because they have the skills to go to outside your organization. They can make enough money to provide the basics so anything you offer them as a reward that they can get elsewhere will not be a strong motivational incentive. Also, because followers are generally realistic about their skills and ability, they know that there is only so much money they can make.

Compensation as a motivational tool is somewhat limited. Yes, in sales there are "bumps" and rewards for making a certain level of profit, but they are fairly common. Monetary compensation schemes are not motivators because the follower can find similar schemes outside your organization. If you're good you can get promoted anywhere. If you're good you can make a certain level of income anywhere. So, why stay? Why perform well? Motivation for long-term commitment to an organization may be more about recognition and meaning than pay or perks. Many years ago Raymond had a conversation with his grandmother that helps to illustrate recognition and meaning. She worked in a factory for over 35 years. Raymond's grandmother made thermostats for the largest producer of them. Every month, for over three decades, she was the top producer. She had hundreds of certificates. One day, as she was putting yet another certificate in a folder, Raymond said to her, "They must pay you a lot of money for making more than anyone else." She smiled and replied, "Well, they pay me a little more, but I really don't do it for the pay. I guess I like two things. I like being number one. I like them telling the factory that I am the best. But, I also know I make so many, when I go into someone's house I see a thermostat from my company and I know that because I have made so many they are probably using one I made. I keep people warm."

Many of these factors are things over which you do have some control as a leader. You can have an impact on employees' levels of motivation. At a minimum, you can recognize their performance and help to translate their efforts into something meaningful. But in order to be successful, you must analyze your employees and know what each person wants and values. It makes no sense to use a motivator that has no material impact. Once you know what will motivate employees best, you can begin to use positive reinforcement to encourage them. Remember that everyone is motivated by different concerns. They may value money, security, or respect. Others may value flexibility, recognition, or self-expression. Leaders often fail to motivate others because they assume that what works for the leader is what will motivate their employees. You must identify what factors reinforce your employees to work to their highest potential.

There are a few more points to discuss regarding motivation. First, hire people that have demonstrated a high level of motivation in their life and in their work history. If their backgrounds suggest a great deal of achievement these people are probably driven by nature. Secondly, do everything within your power to create a work environment that will allow people to motivate themselves. Let them know that there will be rewards for optimal performance. Promotions, recognition, or raises are all long-term goals that keep most people focused on working hard.

Finally, if you have done all of these things and certain individuals still cannot be motivated it may be time to have a sincere talk with these employees about their ability to continue in the organization.

Wild Card　**EMPLOYEE MOTIVATORS**

There are many factors that can motivate employees. Everyone is different in regards to what motivates them and why. As a leader, you can have an impact on your employees' attitudes. Begin by evaluating your organization. Look to see if key motivators are present. Here are some of the most important things people want out of their jobs:

- Possibility for growth and development;
- Potential for advancement;
- Responsibilities;
- Recognition and respect;
- Meaningful work that allows for self-expression;
- Demonstrated concern from their leaders and organization;
- Positive work environment; and,
- An organization that conducts itself morally and with integrity.

People are born equal but they are also born different.

Erich Fromm

CHAPTER THIRTY-FIVE
Ten of Diamonds
Empowerment and Delegation

The reality of delegating is, almost anyone of reasonable experience can do the work. The bigger question is how much time and effort will be necessary on your part to make sure the delegated task is handled properly. One way to think about delegation is a poker game. Almost any hand you are dealt can win the pot, but some hands require more strategy and effort to be victorious than others. The pool of employees you draw from for delegating is much the same way. The relative strengths of the individuals on your team will vary, and you are pretty much left to choose the best "hand" you can for the project.

Henry Wolford, Delegation Strategies: Playing the Hand You're Dealt

You are definitely empowered in a poker game. All of the responsibility and authority is delegated to you. You, the empowered one, live and die by your own hand. Empowerment in organizations can be just as risky. The rewards for both the poker player and the organization are huge.

Empowerment is one of the big buzzwords used in management circles. It is also one of the most subverted and abused words currently in use. Are there any managers currently working who will say that they do not empower their employees? If there are, we haven't met them. True employee empowerment comes when you delegate responsibilities so that employees can grow in their skills and knowledge. Empowerment is the process of allowing and facilitating followers to take control of their job. True empowerment encompasses the freedom to think, behave and work according to one's own beliefs, values and norms. Most leaders fail at empowerment because it is not something you can give to followers. You really can't empower them. How could you? Empowerment comes from within the follower. What a leader can do is create an environment where a sense of empowerment can grow.

The logic of empowerment is that it creates ownership. It creates a sense of personal responsibility in people. When people feel responsible for a task they are much more likely to complete the task well. Moreover, when they feel personal responsibility and empowered they are much more likely to look for alternatives, innovations and excellence. Leaders who say they empower their employees need to understand the entire concept. It involves giving employees high levels of trust, understanding the attendant risks, and accepting failure in stride. If a leader is unwilling or unable to fully accept this notion, their "empowerment" is just a facade with no real substance.

In Chapter Three, Clear Direction, we wrote quite a bit about delegation. Hopefully, you reached the conclusion that delegation is the best way to efficiently manage an organization. Leaders must realize that there is only so much time and they cannot possibly do everything themselves. Delegation requires balance. You must take into consideration the situation at hand and the abilities and the skill levels of your employees.

When you delegate too much responsibility, employees may feel overloaded and incapable of handling the task. This sets them up for failure. If you do not delegate enough, employees do not have a sense of personal involvement in their jobs. When employees have a sense of control over their responsibilities and organizational decisions, they begin to feel empowered.

The problem with empowerment is not the concept. The problems start during the application stage. In several of the preceding chapters we put forth the notion that your followers are your most valuable asset and that it is how you use that asset that determines your level of competitiveness in the market place. If your followers are your most valuable asset and the only way to compete, decision making must be decentralized and pushed down to the lowest appropriate level. It involves risk on the part of the organization and requires management to be supportive during both successes and failures. It gives more power to people in the lower levels of the organization than they ordinarily have in a traditional management hierarchy. The decentralization of decision making is a step toward creating an environment where a sense of empowerment can grow from within your followers.

It sounds good, doesn't it? It does to us. Unfortunately, managers have a tendency to butcher this concept into an unrecognizable state. The first problem is a lack of trust regarding employees. Most managers will not admit it, but many do not really trust their employees. Some managers see it as their job to catch people doing something wrong. Most leaders mistake leadership for management or worse, supervision. A supervisor without leadership skills often feels that, unless employees are being watched, they will not work properly. Although this may be true from time to time, many managers feel it is true in all cases. They do not think that employees would make good decisions if left on their own. If you hire wisely and think through the delegation process before you begin it, this mistrust will abate. Employees need to have the confidence that their leader believes in their skills and judgment. It is the demonstration of your trust in your followers that grows their sense of empowerment and ultimately the follower themselves.

The second problem involves risk taking. Giving more power to lower-level employees is potentially risky. If they do not use the power properly and wisely, many things can go wrong. Some managers do not want to be involved in such risky situations and are not about to give up control over the outcome of a situation. This is only further exacerbated by the fact that you only delegate authority, not responsibility. Even if you empower your employees to act, you are still responsible for their failures. Engendering a true sense of empowerment means that you delegate the credit for success and absorb the responsibility for failure. Stellar leadership involves risk taking. But, if your leadership is strong in all of the areas we have addressed you are unlikely to experience catastrophic failure.

The third problem directly involves failure. When employees are empowered there will be an immense amount of progress, but there are going to be the inevitable cases of failure. Many managers like to assess blame when something goes wrong, fearing that errors will reflect on their own performance. They do not view failure as a potential steppingstone to success. They may also see failing to maintain control over the organization as their own failure. They see relying on others as a weakness.

In *The Secret of a Winning Culture*, Senn and Childress state, "The kind of empowerment that creates exceptional results is made up of two major elements: the letting go of tight controls by leadership; and, the acceptance of personal accountability by all employees." These two elements work together to form the essence of successful empowerment.

Leaders must first decide when they are going to involve workers through delegation and to what extent they will do so. To begin, you must decide which employees are capable of taking on the added responsibilities. Delegation works best when you pick the right employee. Not all employees are interested in or have the ability to be involved in the process. Most workers enjoy responsibility and the chance to build their skills, but others simply want to be told what to do and then do it.

The employees you select should understand and agree with the major goals of the organization. It is critical for empowered employees to have very close alignment with organizational norms, values and goals. If they do, when they act from their own value base, their actions will be aligned with organizational expectations. They should have experience relating to the situation and, if possible, previous involvement making decisions. They must have an understanding of the situation and an interest in it and its resolution. You should select people who are autonomous and seek out responsibility. People who need firm directions may not thrive under these conditions because these situations inherently involve a level of uncertainty. If you choose the right person, delegation has a high probability of succeeding. In the end, you will have more experienced employees who will be able to handle even more responsibility.

The leader's own style also plays a part in how delegation occurs. Some leaders believe that workers should have a large amount of participation in the workplace, while others see this as shirking responsibility on their parts. Leaders with a high tolerance for uncertainty have an easier time delegating assignments. They must be able to release some control over the outcome of the situation when they delegate it to someone else. Also, some leaders are naturally more comfortable sharing decisions and working with employees. Others are more inclined to solve problems on their own and order others in a more structured way.

The task must also be contemplated when deciding to assign it to a worker. Some jobs are more easily delegated than others. If the problem is commonly known throughout the organization and its outcome will directly affect the work of employees, their input can be valuable and necessary.

You must also understand that shared decision-making takes more time than does authoritative leadership. In the long-term view, delegating work will save you time because you will not have to do all the work by yourself. However, if it is a crisis situation where decisions must be made quickly, it may be best to keep the task for yourself.

Empowering workers through delegation is best done a little at a time. Incremental changes in the work environment are easiest for everyone to adapt to. As the employee's skills and knowledge increase, you can feel more comfortable giving them more responsibilities. When delegating a task, give clear, precise directions on what is to be accomplished. Also, let employees know when you need a task completed and any applicable restrictions. Check to make sure the employees understand the task at hand.

The first time an employee performs a new responsibility, you can walk through it with the person, seeking his or her ideas on what to do before sharing your own. It is okay to let the person know what you would do but be sure to communicate the fact that you respect other views. Afterwards, follow through with the assignment and the employee to make certain that everything ran smoothly and was accomplished.

Empowerment of employees has many far-reaching benefits for the organization. When there is a strong delineation between management and employee responsibilities, it stifles the creativity and motivation of workers. They feel that they should only do what they are told to do and nothing more. They do not think outside of their own job description. Empowerment motivates workers and gives them a sense of accomplishment.

When you do not delegate any authority to act, you can frustrate and anger employees. This may lead to negative attitudes, apathy, and high turnover rates. It creates an oppressive workplace where creativity, imagination, and innovation are stifled. In such an environment, the most talented people will leave for better opportunities. Trying to do everything, the leader can become stressed and lose sight of the organization's direction. Major initiatives may be put aside because the leader is focused on all the minute details. This myopia can lead the organization to failure.

Empowerment and delegation can improve the quality of work and decisions simply because there is more than one perspective involved and empowered followers have a sense of personal responsibility about the task. Office relations may be improved because a sense of cooperation is incorporated into the group dynamic. Individuals develop because they are allowed the chance to grow and learn. All of these results will have a long-term positive impact on your organization.

In an empowered organization there are bound to be a lot more disagreements because we value open and direct communication; we give people permission to disagree.

Robert Hass, CEO Levi Strauss

CHAPTER THIRTY-SIX
Jack of Diamonds
Developing People

I must complain the cards are ill shuffled till I have a good hand.
Jonathan Swift, "Thoughts on Various Subjects" (1728)

In *Managing People is like Herding Cats*, Warren Bennis stated that the organizations that would succeed were those who believed that their competitive advantage depended on their people. These organizations would constantly develop their employees and take actions designed to improve the quality and morale of the employees. Clearly, Bennis held the resource-based view that we have told you about.

The authors developed the idea of this book during a conversation on leadership. Raymond told Andrew that he thought of leadership like five card stud poker. You were dealt five cards and those were the five you had to play for that hand. You didn't get to draw anymore cards. Leadership is like that. In many instance you are dealt your followers. Like the poker table, different leaders can be dealt the same five followers. Some leaders turn their followers into a stellar, competitive and well-run team. Other leaders complain until they are dealt better followers.

People are the most important resource in any organization. From a purely financial standpoint, employee salaries are a huge part of any company's budget. This valuable resource must be managed wisely and effectively. We believe in constantly teaching, training, and mentoring workers. It is the key to enhancing productivity and increasing morale. The difference between the leader who works the hand he or she is dealt and the one who complains is simple. Good leaders know that for the most part we are playing with the same cards and we have the same followers. Most of the time, it is how the leader works with the followers that makes the difference.

Developing your followers is the key to the big pay-off. Employee development usually moves along two fronts. The first part of career development is the mastery of job skills. That is, your followers learning to do their job well. Good leaders do not take a "train and assume" posture. If you provide employees with training and assume they either understood it, or will remember it, you could be headed for trouble. Recall from the previous chapter we talked about the correlation between the ability to do the job and motivation. After a follower has been trained, consider follow-up training or some kind of check to make sure they understood and can apply what they learned.

The more complex your follower's assignment, the more likely they will need continuous refreshing and updating on their skills. Many organizations face a problem of critical skills that are rarely used. In other words, your follower rarely uses a skill but when they do, the follower and/or the organization are at risk. These are the types of skills that should be regularly refreshed, whether or not the follower has used them. Continuous updating of skills may be necessary because your workplace is changing. Technology, legal matters and some social aspects of the workplace can evolve rapidly. Anytime a change takes place, followers should receive training.

In addition to job mastery, professional development is a component of overall employee development. Whereas job mastery is working on today's skills in today's job, professional development is preparing followers for tomorrow's skills in tomorrow's job. Typically, organizations use cross-training of followers for other jobs as the centerpiece of professional development. This can increase follower value and versatility. It may also help followers grow into other roles in the organization, including promotional opportunities. Moreover, cross-training can give employees a sense of what is going on elsewhere in your organization. Cross-training may be particularly useful for workgroups who service internal customers. If your follower's product or service is primarily used by your organization, cross-training them in what their customers need can be very valuable and lead to innovation.

While cross-training may be the centerpiece of most organizational effort, the hallmark of professional development is working on skills and knowledge that go beyond the scope of today's job. Real professional development is investing in a follower's future. This type of professional development requires high participation by the follower and leader. The follower is career planning and the leader is facilitating the process.

It is very likely that your followers have not really thought through their career plans. They may not have asked themselves where they want to be in two, five or ten years, but this is the beginning of professional development and it is your job as the leader to begin the process by introducing the question. Often, you must be tactful and diplomatic. You don't want to leave a follower with the impression that today's job is not valued by the organization and, by extension, the follower is not valued. A good opening is a one-on-one conversation wherein you ask the follower how they see their job changing in the next several years. How will technology change it? Will the market influence the job? Will new skills be necessary?

Once you open the door to the possibility of developing new skills, you can start by looking at the current job. How can the follower's job be expanded vertically or horizontally? Typically, this is termed job enrichment and job enlargement, respectively. Horizontal expansion is the addition of new tasks but not more control whereas vertical, or enrichment, is the addition of new tasks and more control. You can probably see the mistake many leaders make – they call enlargement (giving the follower more to do, but less control) enrichment (which is actually more work, more control).

Ralph Brown, in *Design Jobs that Motivate and Develop People*, said it well:

"Job enrichment doesn't work for everyone. Some people are very resistant to more responsibility or to opportunities for personal growth, but...researchers report that some people they expected to resist, seized the opportunity. Enriching jobs is a particularly effective way to develop employees provided the jobs are truly enriched, not just more work for them to do."

So, ask the follower. What parts of your job could be expanded to give you more control over what you do? As the leader, you should be exploring your own workplace. Is there a way to redesign the jobs or your group so that people are enriched by learning new skills, increasing their responsibility and increasing their control over the task? In addition to asking and helping your followers explore, you must create an environment where your followers don't feel they should "check their brain at the door."

Innovation, creativity and just plain "thinking it through" are behaviors you must model. Raymond recalled working as a manager in a large organization. There was a notification that an event had occurred that required action by his workgroup. This notification took a circuitous route through the organization causing up to a week's delay. After Raymond had been there only a few days one of the followers complained about the delayed notification and the problems it caused the workgroup. Raymond asked the follower to fully explain the implications of the delay for the group. The implications were very serious, but this apparently had been a continuous problem for many years. It was one of those things the group complained about but learned to live with. Every time a delayed notification of this kind arrived, the group stopped what it was doing so that the notification could be acted upon.

Raymond told the follower, "There may be a good reason this happens. Let's find out." He and the follower spent three days tracking down the reasons and history for the delay. It turns out that the system for notification was based on how the pneumatic tubes in the old building had been laid out. Over forty years prior, the pneumatic tubes were laid out according to the planned physical location of the building and paperwork was shuffled accordingly. Unfortunately, our workgroup didn't work in that building any longer – it had moved 15 years before. Needless to say, we were able to convince the organization that the notification had to be routed differently. More importantly, Raymond was able to launch a "why do we do it this way" campaign.

Truthfully, the more followers become involved in being innovative and creative about their work, the more work there is for the leader. As followers think of new ways and question the old, there is going to be a lot of refereeing to do. That being said, the payoff is huge. Creative and innovative followers naturally enrich their own jobs. And, their search for creativity forces them to explore new tasks and skills. As they experiment and explore you will find many opportunities to informally direct and teach them.

Indeed, teaching and training are not just limited to formal courses or seminars. In fact, most of the time, the training and teaching are informal, on the job, and done on a day-by-day basis. If a leader makes training and teaching a priority, this filters down through the organization. Managers and supervisors become mentors and teachers to their employees, and the whole company becomes a "learning organization."

In his book, *Principle-Centered Leadership*, Stephen Covey makes some excellent observations in regard to teaching and training employees:

Recognize and take time to teach. With differences come supreme teaching moments. But there's a time to teach and a time not to teach. It's time to teach when

1) people are not threatened (efforts to teach when people feel threatened will only increase resentment, so wait for or create a new situation in which the person feels more secure and receptive);

2) you're not angry or frustrated, when you have feelings of affection, respect, and inward security; and

3) when the other person needs help and support (to rush in with success formulas when someone is emotionally low or fatigued or under a lot of pressure is comparable to trying to teach a drowning man to swim).

Remember: we are teaching one thing or another all of the time because we are constantly radiating what we are. Make a commitment to develop your followers. A good leader can enrich their lives and performance by teaching and training. It is the best investment any company can make.

Tell me, I'll forget. Show me, I may remember. But involve me, and I'll understand.

Chinese Proverb

Treat people as if they were what they ought to be and you help them become what they are capable of becoming.

Goethe

To teach is to learn twice.

Joseph Joubert

CHAPTER THIRTY-SEVEN
Queen of Diamonds
Supporting People

Jack Canfield, the editor of the Chicken Soup for the Soul books, describes what he calls the "Poker Chip Theory of Self-Esteem." Imagine a game of poker where one person has twenty-five chips, one person has ten chips, and another person has one chip. In this game, which person is more likely to risk more, bet more freely, and enjoy himself? Obviously, it is the person with the twenty-five chips. Why? It is because he can afford to take more risks and lose more chips while still remaining in the game.

Making a Difference: The Art of Community Connecting

A long time ago, when Andrew was relatively new to the workplace, a supervisor told him that as long as he was right, he would support him. Even as a newcomer, Andrew recognized that if he was right about something, he would not necessarily need his support. The times that Andrew would need his support would be the times when Andrew was wrong. This meant that the only time Andrew would receive the support of this supervisor was when Andrew did not really need that support. Perhaps not so coincidentally, Raymond heard very similar remarks from a supervisor. Do followers need support when they're right? When they're wrong? How about constantly?

It is likely that not much has changed in the way some leaders choose to give or withhold their support. It is important to support your employees at all times, especially when they are wrong. That does not mean you must always support the behavior. Remember that when workers make mistakes, you can disapprove of the behavior but still support the people. Let them know that what they did was incorrect but that you still believe in their ability to do a good job.

Likewise, if you cannot support a person, let your reasons be known so that the person can avoid the same mistakes in the future. You should, however, support the worker if that person was making an honest attempt to do the job properly. When you do not support your employees and put obstacles in their path instead of removing them, you are asking for a frustrated, angry workforce.

When a follower does a task well and you praise them you are supporting them. When someone makes a mistake and you tell them frankly, and re-direct their behavior you are supporting them. Indeed, when you openly praise people for their efforts you are supporting the entire workplace because you are defining what should be done. Conversely, even though criticism and discipline should be private, the word gets around about the limits of conduct. Therefore, all of your actions are supportive in that they define the values, goals and even the limits of conduct.

Figure 37.1 (Performance Curve)

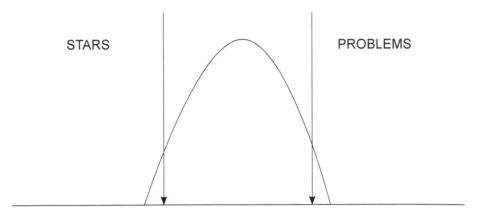

Some of your followers need more support than others. If you asked just about any leader, they would tell you that a small percentage of their followers are stars and a small percentage are problems. Those same leaders spend the lion's share of their time working with those two ends of a very large bell curve. Consider that if you evaluated your employees, ranked them based on performance, etc., you would end up with a normal distribution. On one end you would have the problems and the other end you would have the stars. However you measure your workplace, whether through productivity, morale, creativity or innovation, it will somewhat mirror the distribution in figure 37.1. This means that even large changes in either of the opposite ends of the curve are going to have a relatively minor effect on the whole. So, bang away at the marginal. Keep praising only the stars. And, you will leave the workplace largely unchanged. You will not see an increase, by whatever measurement, until you work with the middle.

According to Professor Thomas J. DeLong of the Harvard Business School, you can think of the marginal performers (or problems) as C players, the stellar performers are A players and the middle as B players. Delong says, "B players are the "heart and soul" of any company. B players are loyal. They are the ones who do their work without fanfare or fuss. They are the keepers of institutional memory during hard times such as a merger or downsizing." If you want to move your workplace, you move the B players. Yes, you should still praise and support the stars, but you should also understand that praising and supporting a star probably has little affect on the middle. Likewise, you have to work with the C players, but truthfully, if you have a problem employee, it is likely your organization has a system for working with them. In subsequent chapters, when we look closer at "Saying No" and "Firing," your options will become clearer.

The largest part of your daily efforts and support should be directed squarely at the B players. If you think about it, your stars are probably internally driven and would be stars with or without you and the marginal would remain marginal, also. Look around your workplace. Who are your stalwarts? The people who show up, day in and day out, and do their job? How can you be supportive of them?

A leader has the responsibility to support people so that they do not end up feeling upset and frustrated. Sometimes, too much attention on either ends of your distribution will frustrate the middle. It is also important to understand that B players, the ones that are consistent, probably enjoy consistency and therefore you should look for ways to be consistently supportive. It doesn't take much to make their jobs easier and less stressful in many ways. Speaking up for them or standing beside them during problematic times are the "big ways" leaders lend their support. There are many minor, day-to-day actions that you can take to make a better workplace.

Bringing donuts occasionally or sometimes letting an employee off early does wonders for morale. Supporting birthday and anniversary celebrations is another positive action. Even something as small as buying fresh flowers for the office every so often can demonstrate your support. While these are all concepts we have touched on in previous chapters, the new twist is to begin to think about concentrating your supportive behaviors on the middle section of your crew.

One of the most important ways you support your staff is by listening to them. Listen to what your workers have to say about their needs because they

WORKSHEET:
HOW WELL DO YOU TREAT OTHERS?

1. I am thoughtful and sensitive when it comes to others.
2. I respect the individuality and opinions of my employees.
3. I listen actively to what they say. I devote my full attention to what we are discussing.
4. I am attentive and responsive to their needs and desires.
5. I am flexible and willing to work together to find solutions.
6. I help them to resolve problems.
7. I share with my employees, both personally and professionally.
8. I am a coach and a cheerleader. I motivate and counsel.
9. I communicate goals, problems, and objectives clearly. I discuss these situations with employees.
10. I give both positive criticism and praise regularly.
11. I am easily accessible to my workers. I spend a large amount of my time interacting with them.
12. I am reliable, and I keep my commitments to others.

** As you answer these questions, you should think about what the people in your life would have answered about you. Do you display these behaviors, and if so, how often? You should have answered "yes" to at least eight of these questions. Otherwise, examine where you could improve.

have a better understanding of them than you do. In your next staff meeting or while walking around the workplace, stop and listen to the middle players. You probably listen to the stars all the time and the marginal tend to make you listen in negative ways. Find out what the middle needs to do their jobs. Work as hard as you can to produce this for them. This includes such things as equipment, training, or information. It may also include funding or approval from the organization to take on a project. Helping with the little things that make their day run more smoothly demonstrates your support.

A leader will also be called upon to give emotional or technical support. Being a good listener or helping to solve a difficult problem lets your employees know that you care and stand behind them. Support can come in many forms, but it always helps employees be more productive. The key here is where to concentrate your efforts. Perhaps it goes without saying, but you only have so much time. You have to use your time wisely for the most impact over the widest area of your workgroup. That is squarely in the middle with your B players.

The best leaders are those most interested in surrounding themselves with assistants and associates smarter than they are — being frank in admitting this — and willing to pay for such talents.

Amos Parrish

CHAPTER THIRTY-EIGHT
King of Diamonds
Building Loyalty

I'm absolutely gonna win it, because I'm ruthless. I sit at the poker table and my job is to destroy people.

James Woods

It is easy to see why no one would be loyal to the poker player. Between players, the mission at most tables is to defeat each other. But, not at all tables. Poker games fall into two categories – friendly and competitive. Competitive is where the game is about the player who wins the most by taking from others. There are probably nearly as many friendly games as competitive games. Poker or cards in general, is a social activity used to bring a group together. Indeed, Raymond and his wife play cards every Saturday night with two other couples. The game has occasionally been poker, but it is usually a version of Rummy referred to as Continental.

The social card game is an expression of loyalty among people. Loyalty is the strength of the commitment you feel, either emotionally or intellectually, to a thing. Because we define loyalty as "strength of commitment" we can use words to measure that strength as somewhere between high and low. As an example, Raymond's card group demonstrates high commitment (or loyalty) to the relationships between the players. Yet, loyalty to the game itself is probably only moderate, at best. The group can and has changed games, but has not changed the composition of the group for several years.

As card players the loyalty is actually more complex. Raymond's card players meet as a group because they have similar backgrounds, beliefs and values. Yet, we are all very different people. What first binds the card playing group together is the strength of our commitment to our common beliefs and values. Second, because we are different people, we are loyal to each other as individuals. Over time, we have come to appreciate and celebrate the unique differences. Thirdly, we are loyal to the activity. There are three players who are very competitive and like playing cards, two players who have a moderate commitment to card games and a sixth player with very little commitment to cards.

Loyalty in organizations is very similar. If you think of cards as the analogy of the task the follower performs, you can see that people have a varying degree of commitment to that task. Some people like what they do; it is all that they ever want to do. These followers have a high degree of commitment to the task. Others, perhaps like the B players from Chapter Thirty-seven, have a moderate connection to the task, but would change tasks if properly motivated. The third follower has little or no connection to the task. They don't particularly like or dislike the task.

Followers are also connected to each other. They have personal friendships and commitments in the workplace. These commitments are stronger than the commitment to the task. The strength of follower commitment to each other is demonstrated in a number of ways. However, the overwhelming demonstration of personal commitment is the feeling that you don't want to let you peers down.

The strongest commitment is to the common beliefs and values. It is common beliefs and values that allow us to disagree and then move past ill-feelings. Without this common belief system it is likely that very petty disagreements would cause social relationships to fail. We value the commonality of beliefs above our personal disagreements and more than the tasks we perform. Indeed, once you get past providing for your basic needs, it is likely the sense of loyalty to people and values are ultimately the most motivating forces.

Before we talk about how to build loyalty, let's look at why a leader should build loyalty. It makes sense that all organizations want their people to be loyal. Managers often fail in this area by expecting employees to automatically give loyalty. This may be true at the onset of one's career, but as some employees gain more tenure, their loyalty has to be earned continually. Organizations that do not inspire loyalty in their employees experience a "revolving door" turnover rate. This makes sense when you realize that loyalty to the task is the weakest. Your star players can probably be stars anywhere. Something has to keep them in your organization. Turnover costs the organization time and money because it is expensive to continually hire and train new people. However, if your followers share common beliefs and values they will develop commitment to each other. Common beliefs and values are the two types of loyalty that attract followers to the organization.

While a lack of loyalty can cause the quality of work and production rates to decline, it is only weakly related to loyalty to task. People produce quality and make extraordinary efforts because of their peers. For instance, according to Dr. C. DiGiovanni, M.D., in *Communication, Confidence, Downtime: Stability of Personal Life, and Unit Cohesion*, "Men perform well and courageously on the battlefield primarily because of their loyalty to the men immediately around them." Just as important, people develop strong commitments to each other because of shared values and beliefs. Loyalty has a direct and strong impact on productivity, both in terms of quantity and quality.

To build loyalty leaders must move forward on all three fronts: organizational values and beliefs; follower commitment to each other; and, task design. To gain loyalty, leaders must make the first move in good faith. You cannot expect people to be loyal to the organization, if the organization (through the leader) is not first loyal to them. This may not necessarily seem fair, but it is just the way it works. The first step is modeling the behavior.

Creating loyalty, especially in a comprehensive manner, is a difficult process. It used to be that loyalty from employees was expected. Unfortunately, that has changed entirely, and today's employee is more likely to be skeptical than loyal. This skepticism is well earned considering the recent history of organizations being insensitive, callous and sometimes criminal in their treatment of employees. If you want loyalty, the first step is to be loyal. This means being honest with employees, treating them fairly, and taking good care of them, especially during difficult times. If this is what occurs in your organization, then you have every right to expect people to be loyal. Loyalty is built on a daily basis. Do not think that you can give a raise once a year and keep people loyal. Money or promotions are not the only things that keep people with an organization. People want respect, support, and a chance to grow every day that they come into work. Loyalty is not a motivational strategy, it is a fundamental principle. You are either devoted to it or not. Trying to substitute a commitment to people with a new program or technology is not demonstrating loyalty.

Trust and credibility are the foundation of loyalty to the leader and, thusly, the organization. For a follower, the leader is the human manifestation of the organization. If the follower trusts and believes the leader, they believe the organization. For people to believe you, your words and actions must be aligned. Furthermore, your words and actions must also be aligned with the overarching beliefs and values of your organization. A leader can't say one thing if the organization is clearly going to do another. This alignment is critical to the first and strongest type of commitment – a commitment to beliefs and values.

Loyalty is also built by creating relationships. At several points in the book we have talked about the importance of developing relationships with your followers. You must work through consistent thought, word and action to develop a relationship. As a leader, you must help followers develop relationships with each other. The power of organization-sponsored events is in the ability to help followers socialize. Playing games and having fun are essential to the relationship building process. Any place your followers gather that is not essential to the task is a place to develop relationships. Think about your followers' lunchroom. Is there a bulletin board devoted to followers "off-duty" activities? Does your workplace have clubs, organizations, social activities or sports games? Your newsletter, bulletin board or staff meetings are opportunities for you to lead your followers into developing relationships.

Since loyalty to the task is often the weakest, you can use task development to strengthen the commitment to the task and the beliefs and values of the organization. Recall that in Chapter Thirty-six we examined the power of developing people. Job enrichment is one way in which you can strengthen the follower's loyalty to the task. If the task is more interesting, they have more control or they can be more creative, it is likely that their commitment to the task (as a measurement of the strength of their loyalty) will increase. At the same time you are enriching the follower's task, you are demonstrating what your organization values: the follower; creativity; innovation; and feedback, to name a few. So, enrichment is a means of increasing the strength of the most powerful loyalty – commitment to organizational values and beliefs.

People are more willing to stick around if they feel valued and respected in their workplace. Employees must believe in and support the integrity of their organization and work or they are not apt to stay long. They must know that they are your most valued assets. To convey this idea, it is not enough to merely tell them. You must convince them of this fact through your actions and attitudes.

Remember that this is an ongoing effort. There is no law that requires employees to be loyal. It is not really something that can be required. Rather, it is something that must be earned, and it is earned over a period of time as management's actions are compared to rhetoric. All the concepts in this book deal with creating a workplace in which workers are encouraged to trust their employers and thus become loyal. Being a good leader inspires loyalty in your employees. If, through your own example, you have created an ethical organization where employees feel empowered, motivated, respected, and cared for, you are probably well on your way to having follower loyalty.

There is one element that is worth its weight in gold and that is loyalty. It will cover a multitude of weaknesses.

Phillip Armour

CHAPTER THIRTY-NINE
Ace of Diamonds
Treat People Differently

Avoid people with gold teeth who want to play cards.

George Carlin

If you know poker, you know people; and if you know people, you got the whole dang world lined up in your sights.

Brett Maverick

Throughout the book we have emphasized the need to be consistent. We have also outlined fairness as a process and not an outcome. So, here we are, near the end telling you that you should treat people differently. It sounds odd to say that you should not treat people the same, so let's explain. Recall in Chapter Twenty we outlined "fairness" as a **process** and not as an outcome. In this chapter, unequal treatment is about **outcome**, not the process.

Everyone in your organization deserves respect and courtesy. This is true even of your "problem" employee, the one you would most like to rid from your organization. Courtesy and respect are about process. This is how you do what you do. In the realm of process, or the how, every one of your followers deserves to be "treated" as if they are gold. Without followers there are no organizations,

---

HOW DO WE ORGANIZE?
You can make a fuller exploration of issues like organizational design and strategic management on the companion website at
www.pokerleadership.com

---

there are no goals realized, and there are certainly no leaders. Your followers make you the leader. Beyond this though, you do not have to treat everyone equally.

As a leader, how you treat followers with respect to outcome is different than process. Leader behavior in relation to outcome should be directly tried to follower performance. In this sense, treatment is, by nature, varied from follower to follower. Perhaps it is easiest to say, process is always equal, outcome is rarely equal. Although this may seem like a somewhat fine point, it is a place where both the leader and follower become entangled with disastrous consequences. Let's look at a few examples of how leaders and followers confuse equality of process from equality of outcome.

Unequal process treatment is unfair. On the other hand, equal outcome treatment (reward) is also unfair. In fact, when you treat a marginal employee unfairly (through misapplication of process) you are damaging your entire workplace. It is a pretty good workplace maxim - If one of your followers knows, all of your followers know. Your actions can begin the journey toward followers treating each other unequally. As an example, many leaders are quicker to publicly chastise marginal employees than good performers. Many leaders give the good performer a break and take them aside. On the other hand, the marginal gets the dressing down on the shop floor. This is an unfair process because both human beings deserve to be treated equally, "as a process." If the leader displays unequal process treatment he or she is modeling behavior for subordinate supervisors and other employees. The message is, if you don't perform you aren't a human being and you don't deserve respect.

The United States Declaration of Independence reads, "We hold these truths to be self-evident, that all men are created equal." We know that isn't true. We aren't all equal. We are all different. In fact, some are better looking, smarter, born into money – there is simply nothing true about that statement if you view it as an outcome. However, if you view the intent as we are created equal under law, we are all born with certain rights and deserve similar "process" treatment, the original intent and practical meaning shines through. All of your followers deserve equality in process, but might not deserve an equal outcome.

This type of treatment may be viewed as a type of motivation. The harder you work, the more consideration you will get when you make a special request. We believe that reward should be tied to merit. We are not being partial to people for our own personal reasons but rather for their work records and demonstrated efforts. If you try to be equal in outcome to all employees your middle to top performers will begin to be less motivated by whatever rewards you issue. After all, if you get the same outcome by being marginal, why be stellar or even above average? The leader who tries to be equal in outcome is as damaging as the leader who is unequal in process.

We are sure there are followers in your organization who are your "go-to" people. These are the people that do the most work, do the best work, work best under pressure, and never seem to call in sick. For these people, the leader should do almost anything. A stellar performer deserves to be treated and rewarded in any way possible. Why? If they are "busting their humps" for you, then you should be doing the same for them. It may take the form of allowing them a flexible schedule, accommodating their college requirements, or it may be helping them to get that special day off. Whatever it is, you should be at their service.

On the other hand, followers who do not perform as well do not deserve to be treated, as an outcome, similar to the stellar. Neither Andrew nor Raymond would "go to the wall" for the people that fall below the standard. Without question, both Andrew and Raymond would help marginal followers, but marginal followers would not be rewarded in the same way that stellar performers would not rewarded.

This is where communication sometimes breaks down between the leader and the follower. First, it is difficult to separate out process from outcome. Unfortunately, no matter how good an actor you think you are, when you are displeased with someone's performance it is somehow communicated. It may be your words, tone of voice, facial expression or some other "tell." But, like the player without a poker face, you are "telling" an employee that they are marginal, not by your treatment with respect to outcome, but by your process treatment.

If your leadership is out of balance with respect to outcome and process, the effect of your entire leadership efforts will be eroded. If your process is unfair, you will be seen by the marginal and the stellar as having treated someone as a piece of equipment rather than a human being. If your outcome is unfair, your followers will never relate performance to reward. This is critical because it is so difficult to do.

One reason that balancing outcome and process is difficult is that as we become harsher in our discipline it is easy to do if we distance ourselves from the person. Often times, people are "fired" long before they are "fired." The process of socially amputating someone from the organization begins early so that the loss will not be as traumatic. Indeed, even as human beings, we begin to subtly distance ourselves from those we know are on the road to being out of the organization, but there are some things a leader can do.

For example, if you see an employee who is working extra hours, helping out when needed, and putting in a great deal of effort, you should be more apt to work with them when they need a day off. On the other hand, if the person shows up late, slacks off most of the day, and gets little work done, you should be less apt to help this person. The point is, your effort is directly related to their performance. Raymond recalled a conversation with a subordinate supervisor who wanted a Sunday off on short notice. When Raymond declined the request the supervisor said, "But, two weeks ago you went below minimums for Manny." Raymond replied, "Stan, that's not quite true. Two weeks ago, I worked Manny's shift for him. I covered it because as we both know he is our watch's top supervisor. We both know that if something needs to be done, Manny will do it." Raymond paused and then said, "Stan, if you can look me in the eye and tell me that your work deserves the same reward as Manny's work, I will work your shift."

When denying a request you should tell the employee why you are not granting or supporting the request. Then discuss what behaviors would result in your support. This is sometimes an enlightening conversation for the employee. Afterwards, they will have a concrete example of the results of their behavior. This can be one of the tough parts of leadership; separating out process from outcome. However, it always demonstrates respect for your followers when you answer them candidly. Your process is fair; your outcomes depend on the follower.

What if someone accuses you of treating people differently? You should confess that while everyone is treated with the same respect, courtesy and process, they earn their rewards. Ultimately, this approach is best for the organization and the followers. It tends to send a strong, clear message as to the type of employee that is desired. The less committed employees may accuse you of favoritism and inconsistency, but that is very much like someone who thinks they are calling your bluff only to find you are holding the better cards.

Andrew and Raymond encourage all leaders to take the same approach. In the short-term this may seem a somewhat controversial leadership tactic and it may not work or be acceptable in every organization. Check with your boss as well as organizational policy on individual procedures. Further, the current culture of your company may not support such an approach. As a leader, if your process treatment is equal then you will have an easier time unequally rewarding outcomes. Furthermore, in the short-term with some, and the long-term with a few, you won't necessarily be the most popular person in town, but then leadership is not supposed to be a popularity contest.

Military and law enforcement executive Keith Bushey has stated that the only legitimate popularity for leaders is through respect. If you earn your people's genuine respect, and as a byproduct of this you happen to become popular, that's not a bad thing. We agree with this philosophy in that popularity per se is not a leadership issue. However, leaders who set out to seek popularity often go in the wrong direction. Perhaps better to think of popularity as something you may or may not attain, but if you do, let it be a natural result of your other efforts instead of a conscious effort on your part to be become popular.

Equality is not fair!

Actor Carroll O' Connor as Archie Bunker

There can never be human happiness in a society that imposes a rule of "equality" which disregards merit and rewards incompetence.

David Lawrence

CLUBS

Then remember one of the axioms of the game of poker: play the hand you are dealt. Don't waste time wishing you had better cards - or better people. Study the ones you have. See how they fit, how they might be rearranged to fit better, and what they can do as a group. If the time comes, you may have to decide whether to discard and draw or keep what you have, but in the meantime, do what you can with what you've got.

Colonel Ben H. Swett

CHAPTER FORTY
Two of Clubs
Accountability

I recently watched a rank novice win $10,000 in an hour-long poker session at the Dunes Hotel Casino in Las Vegas from five men who are considered to be among the twenty best Poker players in Las Vegas. That was chance, a momentary aberration in the probabilities. They are inevitable in any gambling game. If it weren't for them - and the long-odds winning they make possible - gambling would be barren of what makes it gambling. Certainly luck operates, to this limited extent, within the theory of probability. All that theory guarantees is that ultimately each player will have been dealt an approximately equal number of opportunities to win, an approximately equal number of good, bad, and indifferent hands.

John Scarne, legendary gambling author

Poker is a wonderful analogy for accountability. It clearly demonstrates all of the aspects of accountability and responsibility. It gives the leader some weighty clues on how to increase accountability and responsibility and understand the difference between the two. At the poker table, accountability is exemplified because the goals are clearly defined and shared by all players – to win. Each player is competing against the others, but within very specific rules. The rules of the game and table define what a win looks like. It tells the players who has the winning hand. Because it is simple to verify who has the best hand, feedback is immediate. These are the traits of accountability – goals, means to achieve those goals, and feedback on goal attainment.

At the table you are accountable for how you play. But, are you always responsible for the outcome? Responsibility has many of the features of accountability, with the extra dimension of capacity. When you sat at the table, you assumed accountability. You knew the goal, the rules and received the feedback. Recently, Raymond was playing and was dealt a very strong hand. The hand dictated that Raymond should bet and raise. There were very few hands that could beat Raymond's. He played the hand well, exactly as anyone would, and lost to one of the very few better hands. Was he responsible? Raymond was certainly accountable. He knew the goal, the rules and received immediate feedback. But, he was not responsible because as the other players noted, "I'd a played it the same." His capacity for responsibility was diminished because he lacked the tools to win – the best hand. In this particular instance there were intervening variables (an unlikely stronger hand) that prevented Raymond from winning. In the workplace, a follower can do everything right and the result still be an undesired outcome. When something outside the follower's control intervenes and changes the outcome they are accountable, but their responsibility is diminished.

Accountability has to do with knowledge of the goals, the rules and receiving feedback on performance. You can be accountable, yet not responsible. Responsibility has to do with having the capacity, or tools, to achieve the goals, within the rules. Indeed, legally, when someone is charged with a crime, their accountability (the sentence) can be mitigated by their responsibility being diminished. Generally, diminished capacity in the arena of criminal responsibility, focuses on mental tools, or capacity; the ability to know right from wrong, etc.

Wild Card **Accountability and Responsibility: For the leader, follower accountability is a continuous cycle of goals, behaviors and feedback. On the other hand, responsibility involves the degree to which the person completing the task has control over intervening variables.**

Leaders and followers get in trouble over issues of accountability and responsibility when they confuse the two terms. Let's tackle accountability first. Accountability in your organization begins with clearly defined goals. You begin to establish accountability by linking follower behavior with the goals. The linkage between the goal and follower behavior are the rules you establish. These rules include general rules like your workplace schedule, dress code, etc. And, they include specific rules like performance expectations. A critical part of this linkage is the ability of the leader to draw a clear line between the expectations of behavior and organizational goals. Think about your workplace rules. It is likely you will discover several that have no clear link between performance and the goals.

The strength of the link between performance and goals is a measure of the degree of accountability. A rule or expectation with a weak linkage to your organizational goals will result in weak follower accountability. Again, look around your organization, the rules that don't get followed are the rules that are weakly related to your goals. The final step in ensuring accountability is feedback. Feedback is letting your followers know when their performance has or has not met expectations. It is this continuous cycle of stating expectations, follower behavior and leader feedback that increases accountability. Notice that feedback, while it may be negative (the follower didn't do it right, or as with Raymond's table, they did it right, but an unforeseen and unpredictable circumstance intervened) the feedback may not be punitive. Accountability is increased by the continuous cycle of teaching and improvement. While accountability is not punitive, responsibility may be.

When people make mistakes they either argue that they weren't accountable or weren't responsible. These are two different, albeit often confused, arguments. People aren't accountable when the cycle of goals – rules – feedback is broken. People's responsibility is diminished when a factor outside their control diminishes the outcome. Unfortunately, as a society we have confused and in some instances ignored these concepts. Instead of taking personal responsibility, when we have the tools to complete a task, we deflect blame and there is little responsibility focused on one's own conduct. Whenever something goes wrong, it seems it is always someone else's fault. Extreme examples include:

- The burglar who fell through a roof and sued the property owner for failure to properly maintain the roof.
- A man competed in a strongman competition in which he ran a 40-yard dash with a refrigerator strapped to his back. He was injured and sued the manufacturer of the refrigerator for failing to post a sign on it warning people that it was hazardous to run a race with the appliance strapped to their backs.

This trend is not completely new, as evidenced by this story about former New York Yankee Yogi Berra. One afternoon, Yogi swung at three very wide pitches in succession and struck out. He returned to the dugout shaking his head. The other players sat waiting for an outburst of self-blame. Instead, Berra, addressing no one in particular, muttered, "How does a pitcher like that stay in the league?" Berra was both accountable and responsible. He knew the goal, rules and received feedback. Perhaps more importantly, he had the ability to complete the task. Yet, instead of taking responsibility for failing to complete the task he deflected responsibility onto the pitcher.

Some people will never take responsibility for their actions. However, a leader can short-circuit claims of non-responsibility by ensuring that followers are held accountable through a continuous cycle of improvement and by ensuring that followers have the proper tools to complete the task. Just as important, as the leader, you should know when you are focusing on accountability versus responsibility. If you have established accountability through the continuous cycle and your followers have the tools to complete the task, you increase both accountability and responsibility via punitive measures. If someone knows better and there are no intervening circumstances, there must be consequences.

As leaders, we must hold people accountable, but we must begin with ourselves. Whenever a mistake is made that even remotely can be traced to our actions, we must first accept the burden onto our shoulders. This sets an example for everyone else in the organization to do the same. If the leaders do not encourage this through their own behavior, they will likely not see the behavior they desire in others. Lead by your own example.

If you view the continuous cycle of improvement as a chain, with each wheel like link interlocking with the other, you get the idea of leader responsibility. As an example, you may set goals, determine performance expectations and give feedback to a subordinate leader. Part of the subordinate leader's task is to institute this cycle with their followers. If they are not doing this you need to take corrective action. No matter how high up in an organization, the leader is always responsible for ensuring the cycle of accountability.

The most common mistake leaders make in this area is to voice the importance of accountability without holding themselves accountable and responsible at every turn. If this is your action as a leader, we can guarantee that people will notice, and as we have stated in many chapters, they will be inclined to follow your actions, not your words. Ultimately, when it comes to the organization, the leader is accountable for everything. When a problem or crisis arises, the leader is the first person looked to regardless of whether or not he or she is the one personally responsible. No matter who is at fault, the leader will be given (by customers, clients, and employees) the task of acknowledging the situation and solving the problem. Transferring blame will only tarnish your image. What a good leader does is accept accountability, correct the current situation as much as possible, and take preventative measures to ensure that the same mistake does not happen again. Indeed, when an organization experiences massive failure, an in-depth look at the failure will often reveal that the chain of accountability was broken and the leader is indeed responsible for not recognizing the break before the failure.

If you require a certain behavior from yourself, it is easier for you to require it from others. Everyone should be accountable for the actions they take. This is not a blame game at all, and in fact, people should be recognized and rewarded for taking responsibility for something that went awry. The best leaders ask the most important question first: "What is my responsibility?" You see, if the leader failed to institute a cycle that created an environment of accountability, they are responsible for the failure. It could be that as the leader, you really are responsible for some action occurring far down the chain of command.

You create an environment where people can feel comfortable admitting mistakes by seeing mistakes as within the cycle of continuous accountability. When feedback is a common occurrence in an organization, people accept it and do not view it as a hostile reaction. They view accountability as part of the cycle of learning. You increase responsibility by holding people accountable through the cycle and providing them with the tools to their job. Finally, you model the behavior and always hold yourself accountable and responsible.

No individual raindrop ever considers itself responsible for the flood.

Anonymous

It's a sad day when you find out that it's not accident or time or fortune but just yourself that kept things from you.

Lillian Hellman

CHAPTER FORTY-ONE
Three of Clubs
Saying No

Baseball is like a poker game. Nobody wants to quit when he's losing; nobody wants you to quit when you're ahead.

Jackie Robinson

To master poker and make it profitable, you must first master patience and discipline, as a lack of either is a sure disaster regardless of all other talents, or lucky streaks.

Freddie Gasperian

One of the most difficult bosses Andrew worked for was incapable of saying "no," even when the boss wanted to. The boss would go to immense lengths to avoid having to say "no." His first technique was simply to not give an answer until the person or group quit asking. This particular boss's second defense was to set up obstacles so that it would be impossible to accomplish what was desired. This caused people to give up; it became more trouble than it was worth. His final strategy was to actually say "yes" and then work behind the scenes to sabotage the project.

Perhaps, this particular boss had trouble saying "no" because he wanted to be popular, and it is hard to be popular when you are the one saying "no." Or, maybe he just didn't have the fortitude. Whatever this boss's reasons, he found it was easier to employ his evasive strategies which, in effect, resulted in a "no" answer. The "advantage" of this was that he got his desired result without actually having to deny anyone. To add insult to injury, when the issue invariably came up again, he would always be sure to let everyone know that he had not turned down the request when it had come up the first time. Did he really believe that he was fooling anyone? These sort of game players usually end up using their "moves" so often that everyone in the organization eventually knows exactly what is going on. What's more, they end up losing what they craved the most: respect, popularity, and admiration.

There are a few reasons a leader has to learn why and how to say "no." Broadly speaking, there are two categories of people to whom a leader must learn to say "no" to - followers and others. Let's look at others first. There are only 168 hours in a week. It is a fairly good assumption that if you are reading this book you are seeking personal development. People who search for personal development and excellence are the "go to people" in life. You are likely one of them. That means if your boss wants something done quickly, or done right, or even saved, you are the person they turn to. In addition to your boss, you have probably developed a network of peers and others who also turn to you for advice and assistance. Simply put, the better you are, the more people turn to you.

It is difficult to say "no" to people who are relying on you. A good step in saying "no", without actually saying "no", is to set boundaries. As an example, Raymond, in his second career as a university professor has on average 150 students each semester. He has a reputation for giving personal and full attention to students when they ask questions outside of the classroom. But, he sets very strict boundaries. If he answered each question fully he would never get home and if he wasn't approachable he wouldn't be serving his students. Typically, a student will approach him just before or just after class with a somewhat complex or involved question or request. When approached, Raymond says something like, "That is a good question. I really want to devote enough time to fully explore it with you. Come by during office hours so we can discuss it." Or, when a student makes a request, "Send me an email to remind me. If you do that I will get to it as soon as I can." Both of these techniques set boundaries and perhaps more importantly, require the other party to take some affirmative action.

Setting boundaries with your boss is just as important. You might tell your boss something like, "We have a ton on our plate right now, can we get to this in a week or so?" Or, "This looks very important, but with our workload I am not sure we can do it justice." There are many ways to express to your boss that you are willing, yet not able because of time and resource. If you can learn to set boundaries with your own boss, your followers are a piece of cake. As a cautionary note, you should make sure the boundaries are real and legitimate.

Jackie Robinson was right – nobody wants to quit when they're ahead or behind. Whenever Raymond's family gets together there is almost always a card game. Recently, after Thanksgiving dinner, there was no football. There were two separate card games. At Raymond's table, one of his youngest children was finally allowed to play with the adults. The card games involve no gambling! As the game progressed, the conversation turned to the great family players. His daughter asked, "Who is the best card player in the family?" Her grandfather answered that a certain uncle was the all-time best. The natural follow-up question was "Why?" Four of the seven players said simultaneously, "He knows when to quit!"

As a leader you are called upon to stop the throwing of "good money after bad." You have to say "No, we're done." Can you imagine the pressure on an emergency room doctor who has to call off CPR? But, somebody has to say "no." As a leader, when the answer is "no," say so! Be decisive and give a clear and resounding "no". Although people may not initially care for your response, in the long run they will accept it and your followers will respect you for making a decision, even if they don't agree with it. You earned your leadership position because of your judgment, your ability to know when things have gone too far, when it's over and when it's a bad idea.

Setting boundaries and realizing a part of your leadership task is to call off unproductive ventures will help you. Employees would rather hear a firm "no" than an insincere "yes." They want the full support and backing of their leader. This means that saying "no" too abruptly can alienate your followers. Saying "no" is difficult because you are walking a fine line between creating innovation and excellence and making sure the train doesn't run off the tracks. If you realize that many times followers are coming to you with ideas that are not fully formed, you are not saying "no," you may just be guiding the follower to the conclusion of "no."

Both Raymond and Andrew have had followers come to them with ideas they have not fully thought through. As they explain the idea, your job is to listen and ask questions. Based on your experience, you may immediately see the reason the solution won't work. If you abruptly tell your follower, "No. That won't work," they may be discouraged from bringing forward more ideas. Also, you may not have heard out a really good idea that is simply disguised in poor presentation. Try asking questions like, "Have you considered this?" The idea is for you and the follower to probe the idea for weaknesses. More often than not the follower will reach the conclusion that the idea wasn't very good. Sometimes, you will reach the conclusion that a really stellar idea knocked on your door in beggar's clothing.

Setting boundaries, calling off the obviously defunct and exploring ideas with your followers will help you with most situations where you have to say "no". However, there will be the occasional time when you hear an idea, or see that something is going in the wrong direction, and you just have intervene with a "big fat no." A cardinal rule of the "big fat no" involves safety violations. If someone is doing something unsafe, or they may be putting themselves in an unsafe position, you intervene immediately and directly. It is much better to say to a person, "I intervened because I thought you were going to be electrocuted," than having to console the widow.

Explain the reasoning behind your answer if at all possible. Do it in a matter-of-fact way. In order to avoid your decision being seen as weak, your explanation should avoid being apologetic. Saying "no" is often a teaching opportunity. You have the chance to show your followers some aspect of their task they didn't consider. Make sure your followers understand why you are giving them the explanation. When you explain your reasoning, you communicate respect, and it helps the person to accept the decision better. Also, the more employees understand the reasons actions are taken, the greater they develop their depth of organizational understanding. You actually engage in a form of training, helping your employees to be prepared to assume more responsibility when the need arises.

It is a great evil, as well as a misfortune, to be unable to utter a prompt and decided "no."

Charles Simmons

The art of leadership is saying no, not saying yes. It is very easy to say yes.

Tony Blair, British Prime Minister

CHAPTER FORTY-TWO

Four of Clubs
The Imporrtance of Failure

Sometimes you'll miss a bet, sure, but it's OK to miss a bet. Poker is an art form, of course, but sometimes you have to sacrifice art in favor of making a profit.

Mike Caro

The winner is not the player who wins the most pots. The winner is the player who wins the most money.

Anthony Holden, author of Big Deal (1990)

Winston Churchill flunked the sixth grade. Albert Einstein was four years old before he could speak and seven before he could read. When Thomas Edison was a boy, his teachers told him that he was too stupid to learn anything. A newspaper fired Walt Disney because he had "no good ideas." Beethoven's music teacher once said of him that as a composer, he was hopeless. As Grantland Rice, the sportswriter said of poker, "It's not whether you won or lost, but how many bad-beat stories you were able to tell." Winning (or success) is often defined by failure because it is the individual who learns from failure that ultimately goes on to be consistently successful. Sure, you can draw a lucky card, but can you learn from each failure? Can you take failure in stride? These are the hallmarks of those who are consistently successful. General George S. Patton summed it up for leaders, "Success is how high you bounce when you hit bottom."

 Recall from an earlier chapter, a bad beat is when a player has the best hand but is beaten by an unlucky draw.

While the list of "failures" goes on and on, you don't have to fail spectacularly to learn! Failure is perhaps the greatest steppingstone to success. More specifically though, it is how you respond to failure that is the real key. Growth in an organization only comes with stretching and risk taking. When trying something new, mistakes are inevitable. It is up to the leader to create a healthy environment where people are not afraid to fail. Mistakes should be seen as an integral part of the organizational process. They are a normal part of striving for excellence. As a leader, you should look at failure from both your perspective and your follower's perspective. That is, you must give yourself and your followers permission to try and fail.

Personal failures are critical to leader development. Your developmental failures don't have to be in your leadership venue. You can learn the habit of trying, experimenting, failing, debriefing and trying again from most any kind of failure. Therein might lie the key – good failure requires introspection to learn, acceptance of responsibility, and courage to try again. A short time ago, Raymond was asked to teach a graduate course in public policy. He had nearly two years experience teaching undergraduate courses and was excited about teaching in a new arena.

 No one likes to fail. How can you avoid it? Here are some steps you can take to help you achieve success:

- Clearly define your goal(s);
- Write a detailed plan of how to accomplish your goal(s);
- Be decisive; don't procrastinate once you make a plan;
- Be a lifelong learner. You must continue to obtain new knowledge and skills;
- Do not quit because you see failure as a possibility. Have courage in the face of adversity;
- If you make mistakes, acknowledge your responsibility;
- Learn from your errors and do not let failure stop you; and,
- Be open to feedback and criticism.

On the second day of class, Raymond opened his briefcase and was horrified to find his lecture notes were not there. An opening lecture on how the thirteen different criminological theories impact policy development is a big task, especially since the theories are not well-outlined in the primary text. Well, forging ahead, the lecture went downhill fast. Twenty minutes into the second lecture Raymond stopped. He told the class, "I'm bombing. Why I am bombing is my problem to fix, but I am not going to waste your time. I'll see you Tuesday." He then dismissed the class.

These steps should be shared with your employees as well. Encourage them to make goals and to take appropriate risks. Support them in this approach by handling the results appropriately. Move your organization away from bureaucracy and toward entrepreneurial enthusiasm. Explore goals and goal setting on the companion website at www.pokerleadership.com.

It's tough to admit defeat, but it would be stupid to avoid admitting defeat when everyone else can see or sense it. Raymond regrouped by evaluating his mistakes, clarifying his goals and reorganizing the information. At the end of the semester he received the student's evaluation that were substantially higher than his peers. The students evaluated the course very high on the amount they had learned and one student comment was especially rewarding for Raymond. It said, "I was impressed after you returned from that #@#!# second lecture. I thought the class was going to suck, but the way you went forward and presented everything with such passion and logic I wanted to learn it too." When they fail, Raymond and Andrew ask themselves – What is my part? What could I do differently? How can I recover? You should be at least as tolerant with your follower's mistakes and failures as you are with your own. Indeed, when a follower "bombs out," you have a fantastic teaching and motivational moment.

Obviously, some mistakes are easier to tolerate than others. Action should be taken when a mistake is made, but ordinarily, it should be corrective action, not censure. Mistakes present a unique opportunity to teach and develop your staff. Growth and success cannot come without risk taking, and progress does not occur without mistakes.

As leaders, one of the ways Andrew and Raymond approach errors is by judging whether the poor result was a "mistake of the heart" or a "mistake of the head." A mistake of the heart is a situation where an employee intentionally did something that was known to be wrong and tried to get away with it. Mistakes of the heart are times when leaders should act decisively and punitively. A mistake of the head occurs when an employee is working hard to do the right thing, but for some reason, it does not work out that way. Good leaders tend to be very lenient on these types of mistakes. In fact, there have been times when Andrew and Raymond have actually praised one of their people for a mistake because their intentions were so good.

Oddly enough, sometimes the best time to praise someone is when they have failed, particularly if their overall work is good. This is not always easy to do, especially if you are angry or upset about the failure. That said, if you can pull it off, it is a great time to praise someone as it is the time they need it most. How wonderful to know your leader still believes in you even though you may have just recently failed!

If you chastise or punish employees for every mistake, their focus will be on self-preservation, not on striving for excellence. Instead of working to succeed, they will work to avoid failure. These two approaches are vastly different. People working to avoid harsh criticism will do the least amount possible. They will show very little initiative and creativity and will rarely do anything without authorization from the boss. They will shirk from accepting responsibility, look for reasons to assert that it isn't their job and, in general, act like inefficient bureaucrats. Mistakes may be avoided, but it comes at the cost of overall organizational success.

The goal of a leader is not to avoid all possible failures. It is to avoid errors that can be easily foreseen, as well as risks that are not worth the potential costs. Good leaders are willing to take risks in order to improve their operations. If you never try anything new, you cannot possibly hope to improve. Expect that failure is usually the result the first time you try anything. It is how you learn from your failure that counts.

While you often want to step in when you see things going sideways, there are times you want to let mistakes play themselves out. If no one is going to be hurt, the organization isn't going to lose a valued customer or some major resource and if you see your followers making a mistake they can learn from, you may want to let it play itself out. This is a very valuable, yet somewhat risky leadership strategy.

It is especially risky in the area of trust. If a follower has failed, and later learns the leader expected a failure and did nothing to prevent it, or guide the person in a better direction, trust can be breached. Therefore, although this technique can be useful, we recommend it be used most judiciously. That said, if you have a

CONSIDER THIS MAN'S LIFE STORY:

- Failed in business at age 22;
- Ran for legislature - defeated at age 23;
- Again failed in business at age 24;
- Elected to legislature at age 25;
- Had a nervous breakdown at age 27;
- Defeated for Speaker at age 29;
- Defeated for Elector at age 31;
- Defeated for Congress at age 34;
- Elected to Congress at age 37;
- Defeated for Congress at age 39;
- Defeated for Senate at age 46;
- Defeated for Vice President at age 47;
- Defeated for Senate at age 49; and,
- Elected President of the United States at age 51.

This is the life and career record of Abraham Lincoln.

follower with high-potential you may be better off letting them learn from actually making the mistake and failing rather than intervening and telling them they are headed down the wrong direction. This is so because the experience will imprint on them much more than it would merely through your words.

Facilitating learning and development by controlled error is challenging for the leader. It may grey your hair, but it has huge potential for reward. A very long time ago Raymond trained rookie police officers. One day, as he and his new partner were leaving the jail after booking a suspect Raymond noted that his young partner had forgot his sidearm in jail lock-up. Police officers put their firearms in a small safe before entering the jail. Raymond said to his rookie, "Before we go back out, let's practice car stops here in the parking lot." Raymond pulled the police car behind a car in the parking lot, activated the lights and got out as if it were a real traffic stop. The rookie froze at the door of the car. As they looked at each other Raymond asked the obvious, "What's wrong?" The rookie said, "I forgot my gun in the jail safe." Raymond replied, "Well, you might need it. Go ahead and get it." Afterwards, as they were patrolling, the rookie was very silent and finally asked, "Are you going to report me?" "What did you learn?" Raymond asked.

After the rookie had recounted his learning experience Raymond bought him a cup of coffee and talked about searching suspects and firearms. And, about the importance of searching suspects before you put them in the car, even if another officer had already searched them because, as Raymond told him "I've seen veterans make mistakes and we have to watch out for each other." Sometimes, as the leader, your job is to control failure to the point of a teaching moment. In these instances, learning and development is more important than the failure. People learn quite a bit more when they are allowed to fail, allowed to experiment and allowed to grow.

Success is the ability to go from one failure to the next with great enthusiasm.
Winston Churchill

Failure is only the opportunity to begin again more intelligently.
Henry Ford

In great attempts, it is glorious even to fail.
Cassius Longinus

CHAPTER FORTY-THREE

Five of Clubs
Competing Concerns

Try to decide how good your hand is at a given moment. Nothing else matters. Nothing!

Doyle Bunson

The phrase "balancing competing concerns" sums up the career of almost every executive. A leader is constantly confronted with clashing issues. Sometimes these issues are conflicting goals; sometimes they are conflicting people or groups of people. A look at the underlying features of competing concerns may help shed some light on how a leader can best balance, or perhaps manage competing concerns. A fundamental aspect of competing concerns is the concept of scarcity. Scarcity is a classic and central concept in the study of economics. Essentially, we live in a world with unlimited wants and needs, yet limited resources. Often, the critical job of the leader is to choose between the unlimited wants and needs and use the limited resources wisely.

Most of us approach a poker game with limited resources. We bring only so much money to the table. If you bet and/or raise on each turn of the cards, or even each hand, you will lose. In poker, as in leadership, you must apply your resources at the points they will do the most good. For leaders, finding the right place to apply your limited resources may ultimately be a search for leverage points. In poker the currency of resource is the chips, but in leadership the currency is attention. Your resource, as a leader, is the attention or time you give to the competing concerns.

A leverage point is a point in work processes that have a disproportionate amount of effect on processes that follow. For example, think of driving down a desert highway. You come to a sign that says, "Next Gas 2 Miles." Would you stop? It is likely that your decision would depend on other information. What if you had a quarter tank? What if, a mile later, another sign said, "Last gas for 100 miles." If you had a quarter tank and the sign said "Last gas for

100 miles" you would hopefully stop because the gas station is a leverage point. Your decision to fuel now can have significant impact on your future down the highway. Unfortunately, finding leverage points is like playing poker; it is not a science. There are guidelines and rules, but how you play is an art. It is your judgment on the application of a few guidelines.

Recognizing leverage points will help you balance competing concerns. Suppose you are in your office working on a major proposal. You have many pages of documents to review, your recommendations are due tomorrow and your organization is going to make a decision on whether or not to commit to a six-month contract. It is important and you are feeling the pressure. Just then, an employee knocks on the frame of your open door and says, "Can I talk to you for a minute about a personal problem?" This is a leverage point. We all know the employee is going to need more than a minute. We also know that after the employee leaves it is going to take time to focus back on your proposal. What do you do?

Most people will answer "talk to the employee." Even though this is the correct answer, if you don't realize the importance of taking time to listen to the employee, the leverage, you may not focus on the employee and actually give this leverage point the focused attention it deserves. The employee is the leverage point because they have more of a long-term impact on the success of your organization. In this instance, you are choosing between spending time analyzing a six-month commitment or spending time working on your only true resource, and one that you are likely to have in the workplace for decades. Generally speaking, a good guideline is that leverage points involve your followers.

This guideline concerning followers also highlights a concept for all of the guidelines. You must focus your attention. If your attention isn't focused, you're actually dividing trying to further parcel out your scarce resource. You can't do it. You either apply yourself or you don't. Think of the times you were talking to someone and they were not giving you their full attention. Raymond took several steps to help him focus with followers. In each of his offices, his work desk either faces the wall or he has a small coffee table between sets of chairs. When someone comes into the office, the discussion does not take place over the desk. The desk is both a barrier and a distraction. The conversations take place over a coffee table, a lower barrier, without distractions. This type of arrangement often makes the follower more comfortable and signals that you are giving them your full attention. The main point is to focus your resource (your attention) on the leverage point.

 Visit the books companion website at www.pokerleadership.com for an in-depth view of decision making models and theories.

A second guideline involves the decision making process. There are dozens of methods for making decisions. The leaders must take in as much information as possible and make the choice that best accomplishes the organization's mission. A good vision statement, clear goals and quantifiable objectives are vital when attempting to balance different issues and problematic situations. It is like going down that desert highway. Often general information can be key to your decision. Think about the scenario. Did you really need to know or calculate the miles per gallon of your vehicle? Or, was it enough to know you had a quarter tank and a 100 miles of desert to travel with no real way of knowing the next gas station is open? Sometimes, the proper course of action will become clear simply by consulting the corporate vision statement, your goals, and looking at your objectives.

Many conflicts between competing concerns can be resolved at the planning phase. Indeed, a part of planning should be looking for leverage points and competing concerns. A third guideline is to constantly plan and revise those plans. Plans should be ambitious, thorough, flexible, and realistic. Goals should be specific and achievable. Plans and goals must take into account competing concerns, and they must prioritize tasks. Once you know what the top priorities are, situations that jeopardize them can be more effectively assessed. It is also helpful to think of potential obstacles while still in the planning phase. You should analyze what problems may arise while working toward your goal and think about possible solutions to these issues.

In addition to long-term and short-term planning you should have a plan for every day. Some leaders do not use daily planning techniques such as keeping "to do" lists because, invariably, your day unfolds unpredictably despite your best efforts to plan. However, you will accomplish more, see more leverage points and be more effective if you use some method of planning your day. You probably will never work the plan exactly as it was laid out, but you will be better organized and better able to focus on leverage points.

Leaders should require their people to plan properly, as well. When Peter Uberroth was the director of the planning effort for the 1984 Olympics, he had a sign on his desk that read: "Lack of planning on your part, does not constitute a crisis on my part." Planning, like all behaviors. must be modeled. Good leaders rely on planning to help balance competing concerns. They also effectively react to changing conditions and work to identify emerging issues. It is more difficult to make a good decision when a situation takes you by surprise, so good plans always try to include several alternative scenarios.

A final guideline concerns the leader who finds that they are mediating competing concerns between people or groups of people. The leader's job in such a situation is to negotiate between the disputing factions. There may be many different views on one issue and it may seem difficult to maintain cohesion in your organization at these times. The key is to rise to the occasion and serve as an impartial mediator in such disputes. Whether you are hearing a conflict between two people or many, you must bring people together to communicate on the issues, discuss them, and focus on possible solutions.

You should always seek out a mutually acceptable conclusion. Recall from an earlier chapter that fairness is in the **process**, not the **outcome**. Your followers and other stakeholders who depend on you as a mediator are much more likely to see a decision as fair if the process is fair. If you don't appear to be fair in these situations or if you display favoritism, your integrity and reputation will be hurt. People will not want to come to you with disputes.

Effective leaders possess mediation skills, and they can negotiate between conflicting concerns and people, bringing both parties together in rational, cooperative discussions. Often times, what initially seem be competing or mutually exclusive concerns are actually simply two different views. As the leader/negotiator, your primary job in these matters is to help people state their concerns, issues and goals. Then, help both parties understand the exact position of the other. The leader/negotiator often finds that they are in a position that is more like a translator, than mediator. Managing competing concerns is accomplished through attentive focus on people, the decision making process and planning.

A President's hardest task is not to do what is right but to know what is right.
Lyndon Johnson

CHAPTER FORTY-FOUR
Six of Clubs
Innovation

Business shares a lot in common with poker. The goal in both is to make as much money as possible—either over the long or short-term—to win. You are competing against other people with similar objectives, with a finite amount of potential returns available. In order to be successful, you must observe and understand people and situations, devise strategies based on those observations, and use skill to successfully execute the strategy and accomplish your objectives. In gambling, it's called play; in business it's called design.

Upping The Ante: Understanding Business and
Design Through Casino Poker
Dirk Knemeyer

For the leader there are two main thrusts of innovation – innovation in leadership and innovation in workplace and/or product design. Innovation in leadership concerns how you work with your followers. Ray Anthony, in *Innovative Leadership: Spark Plug of Progress*, noted that there are over 500 definitions of leadership. Andrew and Raymond agree with Ray Anthony's assessment that "Although an executive or manager can be a "leader," leadership is more a role and state of being than a position or title. Leadership is not about systems or procedures. It's about people—about motivating, inspiring, directing, and developing them for peak (goal-oriented) performance."

Being an innovative leader is thinking outside of your own box. It is looking for new and unique ways to motivate and help your followers. The first step in being an innovative leader is to look inward and examine how you conduct business. Personal innovation is about learning and growth; it is about experimenting with new leadership techniques and finding out what fits you, your followers and the organization. If you begin to innovate with your style your followers are very likely to take the clue and begin to innovate themselves.

There is a problem, innovation is risky. Developing new ways of looking at problems and trying different solutions means you may fail. Indeed, you should fail. This is where innovation in organizations is very much like playing poker. If you don't play you can't win. And, playing means you assume all of the risks associated with the game. The idea is to learn to play well, to learn when to risk and when to conserve. Poker is different from innovation in that you can choose to play poker. You really can't choose not to innovate. Your competitors are innovating. You, as a leader, are losing follower effort by not innovating. Your organization will lose its edge if it fails to innovate. You have been forced into the game and need to learn.

Innovation means to create something, or to try something, or introduce something for the first time. Generally, people get stuck on the first part of the definition – to create. When we ask you to be an innovative leader we don't mean you should create some new leadership paradigm. In reality, when we talk about innovative leadership we are talking about you trying something or introducing something for the first time. It is the rare person who can create something out of nothing. The person who has a flash of insight or inspiration and comes up with a new idea, a new way or a new product, is a rare individual. If you tell your followers that they must be innovative, be sure you explain that you don't mean you expect them to create entirely original stuff from thin air.

Being innovative as a leader means you are looking outside your workplace. You are taking the first step toward being an innovative leader by reading this book. By reading this book you may see information you have never seen before. It is much more likely you have seen this before, but it is presented here in a very different manner. Our innovation as writers is focusing the information on leadership through a different lens. However, for the most part, we have taken information that has been developed by thousands of academics and practitioners and distilled it through the lens of poker. As we did this we came up with some innovative ideas in that some of the information you have read is not written elsewhere. Innovation can be a creative process, but it is mostly about finding things that are lacking in your workplace and trying them there– for the first time.

By looking inward (examining your own strengths and talents) and looking outward (to information outside your organization) you should be able to see ways to innovate your leadership style. Before you innovate, take another lesson from poker. Sometimes it is best to approach winning incrementally. There are times when you have an unbeatable hand. Or, your back is against the wall and you decide to go "all in." While you may occasionally go "all in" with a new

innovation, you are much better off to try and introduce your innovations in leadership style incrementally. Try a technique, tactic or strategy from this book. What were the results? Did it fit your style, the follower and your organization? Did it work? If not, did you do it right? Is there something else you could do? Be innovative by introducing changes to your style incrementally. Constantly innovatie, evaluate and innovate again!

The power of incremental innovation cannot be over emphasized. It is probably the most overlooked way of innovating. Recently, Raymond decided to upgrade his computer system and implement a small innovation – dual screen monitors. As a writer, he spends a lot of time going back and forth between screens. Indeed, as this passage is being written, an article is open on the other screen for ready reference. Saving one or two seconds, hundreds of times per day, adds up to saving minutes every day. For someone who writes nearly every day, hours are saved and productivity increases. Generally, small innovations aren't costly but they add up over the long run. More importantly, having dual screens has caused Raymond to examine other ways to innovate.

Just as you look inward and outward to innovate your leadership style, you can apply the same technique to your workplace. In *A Whack on the Side of the Head*, Roger Von Oech recounts the story of how the keys on a typewriter came to be ordered in the familiar but inefficient "QWERTY" fashion:

"Back in the 1870's, Sholes and Company, the leading manufacturer of typewriters at the time, received many complaints from users about the typewriter keys sticking together if the operator went too quickly. In response, top management asked its engineers to figure out a way to prevent this from happening. The engineers discussed the problem for awhile until they concluded that the answer was to have a fairly inefficient keyboard configuration. Engineers designed a keyboard so that the weaker fingers would be required to hit some of the more common keys. This approach was used to solve the "problem." Since that solution was reached, typewriter and word processing technology has advanced significantly. There are now typewriters that can go much faster than any human operator can type. The problem is that the "QWERTY" configuration continues to be used even though there are faster configurations available. Once a rule is established, it is very difficult to eliminate it even if the original reason for its generation has gone away."

> **Environmental scanning as it relates to the strategic planning process is discussed more fully on the companion website at www.pokerleadership.com**

Leaders should be innovators and they should always be on the lookout for "QWERTY" situations occurring in their operations. Look inward and ask "Why do we do it this way?" There may be very good reasons but you are likely to find out there really isn't a good reason to do it that way anymore. Look outward; keep abreast of your field. How are your competitors or peers conducting business? What part of their creativity can you introduce (for the first time)in your workplace? Remember – innovation is about introducing for the first time and not necessarily about reinventing the wheel.

Innovation, like change, is difficult to implement. It is better inspired than imposed. Fortunately for leaders, if they have hired good people and created an innovative environment, this will not be a problem. Innovative ideas will continually emanate from followers. It becomes the leader's job to ensure that innovative ideas are not met with resistance. It is your job to coach your followers through the process of looking inward and outward. Teach your followers to ask "why" and then to compare and contrast their way of doing business with others. Demonstrate innovation and your followers will innovate.

> ## SOME CLASSIC, INNOVATION-KILLING PHRASES ARE:
> - **Yes, but we've always done it this way;**
> - **It's not in the budget;**
> - **If it ain't broke, don't fix it; and,**
> - **We already tried that.**

While you must reject some ideas or set guidelines, and many times it will be appropriate to do so, proceed with caution. Your words have more power than you realize; it is easy to kill a new idea in its infancy with a careless, off-handed comment. New ideas are like any newborn form of life. They are weak at first and must be nurtured until they are strong enough to survive on their own. Leaders should treat promising new ideas with respect and, if they are to be discarded, it should be done gently. One never knows – the idea that is not right today may be perfect tomorrow or next week.

You want to create an environment where people are encouraged to come to you with new thoughts or approaches. If you ignore people's feelings, they may not want to offer their thoughts in the future. In treating sincere suggestions carelessly, you may inadvertently drain your office of the creative and innovative thinking that precedes beneficial change. An environment devoid of freethinking is never good for the long-term health of any organization.

When you do successfully implement a follower's innovation insist that they receive credit for the innovation. Your boss should know that your follower came up with the idea. Your follower should know that you credited them. All of your followers should know that you credited the innovative follower to your boss. When innovations fail, shield the innovator. In other words, when it works your boss should hear, "John Smith came up with this idea." When it fails your boss should hear, "I tried this and it didn't work out."

"But what about me?" you may ask. The answer, of course, is that this is leadership not ego gratification, so it is not about you at all. Take heart though, because in the long-run, the approaches we are recommending will, in all likelihood, bring you far greater respect and acclaim than you could ever achieve by taking credit for success and deflecting blame for failure. As leaders, you don't have to be without ego, in fact, a healthy ego is almost part of the job description. The key, though, is to make sure you keep it in check by putting your contributions into the broader context of organizational success and team performance.

Great innovations should not be forced on slender majorities.

Thomas Jefferson

CHAPTER FORTY-FIVE
Seven of Clubs
Consistency

Most likely when we look at our game we aren't doing it because we are winning. We do it when we are losing and we try to figure out why we were winners before and not now. Long term winning in limit texas holdem poker depends on your consistency in making good decisions. Because poker has luck involved you'll have a portion of correct decisions that end up losing. That is normal and not really a problem. The problem with luck is that it can sometimes corrupt or taint your view of what you are doing correctly and incorrectly. It can reinforce bad play that eventually leaves you a consistent loser and you'll have no idea why.

Texas Hold'em: Playing well or getting lucky?

As you read through each of the chapters of this book, consistency is the glue that binds all leader actions. Unfortunately, we often confuse consistency with uniformity. In poker, you can't do the same thing the same way with every hand. Your opponents can develop a good sense of what kind of cards you are holding if you play uniformly. A simple illustration is a player who only bets hard when he or she has a killer hand. Uniformity can tell your opponents too much about your play. On the other hand, consistency is always playing the hand you're dealt to the best of your ability. As your cards change, your tactics and strategies change. Consistency starts with clear organizational goals and sub-unit objectives.

In *Consistency is Critical to Good Leadership*, Lieutenant Bill Morgan, United States Coast Guard, related, "The greatest challenge I experienced as a follower, and as a leader, resulted from working for an inconsistent supervisor. I gave orders to personnel based on my supervisor's instructions, knowing those instructions could be changed unexpectedly and in opposition to the original instructions. Before long, this pattern of inconsistent tasking led my shipmates to question my sanity as well as my leadership ability. At times, I was not allowed to make decisions without my supervisor's approval; then I was berated for not assuming the responsibility and making the decision myself. My supervisor's policies, procedures and expectations changed from one day to the next."

As you can see, Lieutenant Morgan faced a leader who changed policies, procedures and expectations without warning. This type of inconsistency is akin to sitting at a poker table to play one game and after you have been dealt the cards being told that the rules have and will change constantly. While situations change, the rules (as outlined by your organizational policies, procedures and goals) do not. Rules and procedures can be thought of as written manifestations of your organizational norms and values. It isn't that they **are** the norms and values, they are only written examples of what the exercise of discretion looks like when compared against the norms and values.

Consistency reinforces expectations and enhances performance because followers come to know what is rewarded and what will be sanctioned. If workers have a common complaint, it is lack of consistency on the part of management. People want the same action to be taken each and every time the same issue occurs. First and foremost, they want consistency because they perceive it as the fair way of doing things. Nobody likes favoritism or special treatment. They want to see that management imposes an even and fair hand in comparable situations. This means giving out rewards and punishment in a consistent manner.

People also want management's actions to be predictable and consistent. Workers want to know what will happen to them in given circumstances and they want to be able to predict this based on what occurred in the past. The ability to somewhat predict what will happen makes people comfortable in their jobs because it gives them a sense of control. Recall our discussion in Chapter Thirty-four on Expectancy Theory. If you believe in the power of the expectancy theory to motivate followers you must accept that consistency is a large part of the theory. Consistency is the link between the different parts of the expectancy model. Without consistency, there is no motivation.

Leaders need to understand employees' desire for consistency. However, it is a very difficult thing to achieve for a variety of reasons. First, management usually has access to a greater amount of information about the specifics of an individual situation. This is particularly true in confidential personnel matters. Two situations may appear alike to the worker but, in fact, may be drastically different.

This type of misunderstanding most commonly comes into play in disciplinary cases. Two employees, at different times, might engage in the same misconduct. The penalties might be quite different based on such things as the employee's seniority, aggravating/mitigating factors, work history, and past record of discipline. To workers viewing the situation, it might appear that the two situations are similar and that the penalties should be equal. This is where the question of fairness and consistency is often raised.

In addition, times and circumstances do change. No organization is going to do things the same way forever, so there will be changes along the way in what is emphasized and prioritized. When actions taken by management appear in contradiction to established norms consistency with past practice is brought forward as an issue.

The necessity for different actions taken in similar cases is shown in the following story:

When Harry was a young boy in Louisiana, he was always getting into trouble. One morning, while waiting for the school bus, he pushed the outhouse into the bayou and went off to school as if nothing had happened. When he returned, his father was waiting for him. He said, "Son, did you push the outhouse into the bayou?" "Yes, father," said Harry, "like George Washington, I cannot tell a lie." Harry's father took off his belt and said, "All right, son, bend over. I'm going to have to whip you." Harry tried to explain that Mr. Washington had not spanked George when he had admitted to chopping down the cherry tree. "Yes, son," said Harry's father, "but George's father wasn't in the tree."

In Harry's mind, his situation was no different than what had happened to George Washington. Therefore, he felt that he should receive the same penalty. His father explained the not-so-subtle differences between the situations. Although Harry might not have liked this "inconsistency," at least he understood his father's reasoning.

As a leader, you should strive for consistency when handling matters that are precisely the same. If you are going to change what you do, explain to people why extenuating circumstances make the situations unique. When you articulate rational reasons, people will be much more inclined to understand. This in turn creates less friction among management and employees and reduces the perception of inconsistent practices. You may not always be able to explain your decisions because of confidential or sensitive information. However, if you have built a reputation for fairness and consistency, you will likely retain the support of your staff.

The idea of communicating the differences in sanctions also applies to communicating the differences in rewards. When followers see a leader interacting with another follower they often have imperfect information. Followers simply don't know and, in some instances, can't know all of the information that made a leader choose what, and how, to sanction or reward. We have recommended that you have two options: first, you can explain your decision making to the fullest extent possible; second, you must rely on your follower's interpretation of the present based on their past experiences with your judgment. The only way followers are going to rely on your judgment is if they have seen that you were consistent in the past. In essence, through consistency you are developing credibility.

You can build credibility through consistency by telling your followers what you are going to do and then doing it. You don't have to wait until a situation develops wherein you must either sanction or reward. You don't have to wait for a good time to demonstrate consistency. You can and should begin your first day. Furthermore, a good leader builds consistency and credibility by telling, doing and then reminding followers he or she was going to do it.

The final two elements of consistency are probably self-evident. First, you, as the leader, must have a clear understanding of your organizational goals, objectives, rules, policies and procedures to demonstrate your organization's norms and values. Then, you must measure your actions against those norms and values. Through self-evaluation you must determine if you are consistent.

Finally, you must constantly communicate with followers. If you can't tell them the reasoning behind a confidential decision, you can tell them about the organizational norms and values. While you may not always be able to directly address a decision, you can always approach it obliquely. Moreover, constant communication of the norms and values will help your followers understand what is expected. They will know what consistency looks like and if you tell them you are going to do something, you do it, and then remind them that you did it, they will begin to expect you to consistently follow-through. This, in turn, should enhance performance.

It is not best to swap horses while crossing the river.

Abraham Lincoln

CHAPTER FORTY-SIX
Eight of Clubs
Proper Equipment

Last night I stayed up late playing poker with Tarot cards. I got a full house and four people died.

Steven Wright

One of the most fundamental aspects of being a leader is ensuring that your people have appropriate tools to do their jobs. This seems elementary, but it is an area that leaders sometimes forget about. We see the leader's role as similar to that of an offensive lineman in football. You need to block in order to ensure that your people are able to get the football (resources they need). Once the running backs (employees) have obtained the necessary resources, they proceed down the field (doing their jobs). The offensive lineman (the leader) then identifies obstacles and moves them out of the way, so that the running backs can score a touchdown (accomplish the mission).

Leaders need to proactively work to identify what resources and equipment their people need. This seems simple since employees will be more than happy to tell you what they need; all you have to do is ask. There are some leaders who either don't think to ask or don't care to ask. Then, there are some who feel that the returns on investment can be maximized by minimizing expenditures on equipment. The other issue that sometimes comes up is the propensity of people to request caviar when a turkey sandwich would do. A leader must realize a balance between needs and desires.

Proper tools and equipment are important to employees so that they can do their jobs properly, but there is another component to this equation. People want to feel needed and respected. Management shows concern for people when equipment needs are taken care of promptly. People will know that you value their time and efforts because you are actively working to ensure that they can proceed uninterrupted.

There is the issue of cost in justifying equipment. A wise leader looks for cost and return on investment. The constraints of the organization's financial plan are a good place to start. The leader should seek a return that exceeds the cost of capital. In the end, there are many quantitative and qualitative factors.

One method of determining the tools your followers need is through Needs Assessment. Needs Assessment is a type of action research that looks at the difference between "what is" and "what should be." Although a Needs Assessment is a formal, systematic way of discovering our weaknesses and planning for the future, it is something we do informally throughout the day. Making a list for the grocery store is a simple Needs Assessment. What is in the pantry and what you want to cook give you an idea of what you need from the store. An understanding of how to conduct a formal Needs Assessment can be critical for a leader, especially one that intends to seek to use the limited resources of their budget to fulfill unmet needs.

All organizations use some type of Needs Assessment in their planning process. As an example, in the arena of emergency preparedness, a Needs Assessment begins with an analysis of what could happen. An emergency planner would ask themselves, "What are the potential terrorist targets in my jurisdiction?" This is a creative process that calls for us to imagine what terrorists could do. In most organizations, the question you might ask is somewhat more mundane like, "Based on current sales and growth how many employees are we likely to have in 24 months?"

For both the emergency planner and the leader in any organization, there is a fine line to walk. That line is between the "fantastic" imagination and practical imagination. As an example, an emergency planner might ask, "Is it more practical to plan for terrorists detonating a nuclear device in a small town or to plan for an overturned tanker truck containing poisonous gas? Both are possible, but which is more likely?

Through this process the emergency planner begins to identify potential emergencies. Once potential emergencies are identified the planner then begins to assess jurisdiction's current ability to strengthen or protect against the potential emergency. An analysis of current ability leads to an analysis of what is lacking. Planning for a terrorist incident is a dramatic illustration of the process. Generally, for most of us, we are looking at what we think will be happening in the future and comparing it against our current resources.

An additional way of doing this is by looking at your current operations and assessing what you do, how you do it and then looking at potential capital resources that would improve your operations. If your fleet needs a new vehicle, does it need a luxury SUV? Or how do you manage competing resource concerns?

Typically, an emergency planner examines potential targets and through this analysis ranks them according to risk. By risk, we mean a combination of the probability that an event will happen combined with the potential outcome.

Figure 46.1 (Risk Assessment Matrix)

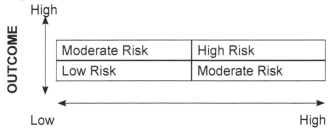

PROBABILITY

One method of ranking risk is through the use of a two by two matrix like the one in figure 46.1. This matrix may give us a helpful way to rank and prioritize our resources and planning. Consider that a potential incident with a high outcome and high probability of occurrence would be ranked over a potential incident with low outcome and low probability. For example, take a moment and classify the detonation of a nuclear device in a small town. It would be a high outcome, yet low probability event and therefore a moderate risk. The chemical tanker explosion might be considered both high outcome and high probability, making it a high risk. Once ranked, locations and/or incidents are evaluated as to their current state and their needs to bring them to a full state of preparedness.

Most managers would rank outcomes similarly. Your outcomes might be a decrease in production or increase in sales, or some other outcome that would change your resource needs considerably. Your question in ranking is "What is the likelihood of this outcome?" "How likely are we to actually increase our sales?" The second question is "What would be the effect of an increase in sales?"

For the emergency planner, once locations have been ranked and analyzed, the preparation of a second matrix may help in establishing agency need priorities.

In Figure 46.2, the locations are listed vertically while the different needs are listed horizontally. Note that not all of the locations need the same resources for improved preparedness. Yet, patterns emerge.

Figure 46.2 (Risk Assessment Chart)

Location	Interoperability	Access Control	Surveillance Cameras	HazMat Suits	Metal Detector
Ajax Chemicals	x		x	x	x
Grade School	x	x			
Power Station	x				
Freight Yard	x			x	

In Figure 46.2, it is clear that improvements in interoperability will impact all four locations. Obtaining hazardous material protection gear will have an impact on preparedness at two locations – the chemical plant and the freight yard. With this type of Needs Assessment, emergency planners can not only make good decisions on community preparedness, but also have significant information to provide funding authorities. This type of Needs Assessment Model works equally well when looking at family, individual, community or business needs. In a time of scarce resources, this type of matrix can assist in making decisions about funding and acquisitions. This means getting the most protection for your efforts.

The leader's job is to look over the horizon and make approximations on what might happen and what will be needed to deal with what may come. Great leaders use their education, training, experience and insight to look as far into the future as possible. In addition to listening to your employees and looking over the horizon, equipment issues can be both morale and risk management issues.

It's not enough that you supply your followers with enough equipment to get the job done. They must also have the equipment necessary to get the job done safely. Window washers could be lowered by hemp rope and wash windows on high-rise buildings. It could be done, but it could not be done safely. The window washers would know it was not safe and would be very unmotivated to go over the side. It is a safe bet that the first time one fell there would be a civil action. Your followers deserve the best protection equipment available. Besides, if you don't get the best equipment, someone will eventually make you wish you had.

Law enforcement officers possess a lot of equipment, including a car, a handgun, handcuffs, a radio, report forms, and other items. All workers have their "tools of the trade." It is a leader's job to ensure that their people are properly equipped. Other than the hardware that your employees require, they also need proper training and on-going education to succeed. Obviously, you will not excel if you lack the knowledge or skills required to do a job. With the rapidity of change, leaders must make sure that their workers are receiving adequate training.

The introduction of new equipment is a change. All change calls for leadership. Even a minor software upgrade can cause leadership problems if you don't plan for the proper training and support. Consider the advent of Anti-lock Braking Systems (ABS). How many of you had to learn that the funny pulsating feeling coming from the brake was the brake working and not the brake failing. During the early days of ABS deployment, some people responded to the pulsing by "pumping the brakes." Unfortunately, "pumping the brakes" on early systems caused them to disengage. Oh, you still had brakes, but you didn't have the ABS which would allow you to brake and steer simultaneously. Simply put, new equipment equals change. Change equals leadership, training and support.

So much of what we call management consists of making it difficult for people to work.

Peter Drucker

CHAPTER FORTY-SEVEN
Nine of Clubs
Micromanaging Away Imagination, Innovation, and Individuality

The poker player learns that sometimes both science and common sense are wrong; that the bumblebee can fly; that, perhaps, one should never trust an expert; that there are more things in heaven and earth than are dreamt of by those with an academic bent.

David Mamet, playwright. "Things I Have Learned Playing Poker on the Hill," in Writing in Restaurants (1986)

Leaders should recognize that workers typically know a great deal more about their jobs than anyone else, including the leader. The leader may have done that job in the past, but that does not mean it is done the same way now. Leaders need to recognize that not everyone does things in the same way. But, when does your leadership trait of "attention to detail" become micromanaging and how much should you know about exactly how your followers accomplish certain tasks? On one hand we have the advice of getting out of your employees way. It is fairly certain that too much "attention to detail" can cause your followers to look over their shoulder, mistrust their own judgment and delay making decisions without input. On the other hand, one of former Secretary of State and retired General Colin Powell's leadership rules is "Check small things." A key leadership trait is the ability to balance these seemingly mutually exclusive demands.

The first clue is knowing the difference between style and substance, and determining the amount of importance to attach to each. Style is how it is done whereas substance is what happens, or the outcome. In some instances, style is as important as substance. For example, a school bus driver is charged with the responsibility of taking children to school. How the driver performs the task (style) is probably more important than if the children arrive on time (substance). We want the driver to conduct this task as safely as possible. In this instance, style is as important as substance.

A very long time ago Raymond worked in sales. One of the store employees was rather strange and had a very distinctive style, yet he was the top producer. His antics drove the floor manager crazy because the floor manager wanted everyone to have a similar look and feel. The floor manager was constantly arguing with the store manager because the store manager's position was that the customers liked the salesperson and he was the top producer. His style, as perceived by the store manager, didn't matter as much as his substance.

For both the bus driver and the salesperson, making a decision on the level of micromanaging necessarily begins with an examination of the importance of style and substance. People have methods that work best for them personally and they need to be able to have some control over how they accomplish a task. Some people's instincts dictate that they plan out how they will accomplish a task step by step and they follow this plan sequentially. Some people do their best work at the last minute under pressure of a deadline. Sometimes, bosses label these people calling people who work at the last minute procrastinators or lazy. However, when bosses do this, they have failed to recognize that each person has an individual, natural style of doing things.

To reach their full potential, employees must be allowed to work within their own natural styles as much as is appropriate to the task. Rather than make your employees adapt to how you do things, you should lead them in regards to how they work. If one person needs specific instructions and a clear plan on how to accomplish a task, you need to supply that. If another person needs space to create a more individual plan, then that should be acceptable, too. You will have much more productive workers if you manage them by their style and not your own.

Note that we are not talking about intervention over matters of substance. That should be fairly straightforward. Substance is determined by the organizational goals and sub-unit objectives. Most of the time, when followers complain about micromanaging they are not talking about issues of substance because goals and objectives are usually clear. Rather, it is style, or the amount of leader imprint on **how** something is accomplished. Another clue to working out the difference between the amount of leader intervention over style is follower readiness.

With seasoned employees, smart leaders give clear direction to their people, telling them what they want done and when they need it accomplished. Any other restrictions should be stated up front. Other than that, capable workers should be allowed to use their own creativity to get the job done. Most people do not appreciate your standing over them while they work critiquing every move or idea. This is a waste of time and an annoyance to your employees. If you do not feel comfortable letting a person do an assigned task without your constant supervision, then perhaps you should not assign that particular task to that person. It is the follower's readiness to accomplish the task that dictates the amount of style intervention. If someone hasn't done something before, they need to be taught how; they need direct style intervention. At the other end of the spectrum, if you have a very tenured employee who is completing a task they have done many times before style intervention is going to be seen as micromanaging.

Don't let your ego convince you that nothing can get done without your input. Do not be arrogant enough to believe that no one can have valuable ideas except you. You really want to avoid the tendency of making people follow your style rather than their own. Keep this in mind when you are managing your employees. Let them work in the style that is right for them. They do not have to do things exactly as you do. Chances may be that the way in which you work is not conducive to maximizing their work potential.

Andrew once had a job where he had to represent his boss at important meetings when the boss was unavailable. This was the type of boss who wanted things said and done exactly the way he would have done them. One time, Andrew told the boss that although Andrew certainly didn't mind going to the meetings, it was harder for Andrew to go than it was for the boss. When the boss asked Andrew why, he told the boss that when the boss went to the meetings, all the boss had to do was say whatever he thought about any issue that came up. However, when Andrew attended the meetings, Andrew had to try and say what he thought the boss would have said.

This is a difficult task because there are a lot of different ways to get the job done correctly. As a leader, you should try and avoid narrowing the path of your people. They do not always need to take the one that you would have traveled. If you allow creativity, you will get creativity. Otherwise, you create oppression and resentment, and this makes it impossible to reach an organization's highest potential.

The question is now – if you can see the difference between style and substance, when should you double check tenured employees? How do we reconcile the need to check small things with our desire to foster an open and creative environment? Powell is right, the devil is in the details and small things must be checked. Even our best employees fall into unhealthy routines, learn unacceptable short-cuts and sacrifice style over substance. You can incorporate attention to detail into an innovative workplace by determining "choke points," conducting audits and training.

"Choke point" is a term we have borrowed from the military. Generally, it refers to a strategic geographically location that narrows, forcing an enemy into a specific path. Look around your organization. There are likely to be a number of "choke points" – places where getting the job done narrows to one or two people or tasks. A failure at this point means a major failure in your organization. These are places you want to check the small details. Look for locations, procedures and policies where a simple, single failure can be catastrophic.

Auditing tasks is another way to check the details. There are two basic types of audits – announced and unannounced. Both have their places in your organization. The purpose of an audit should be determining need in your organization – not finding fault. As an example, in the United States Navy, before taking over command of a ship, a new commanding officer does a complete audit. This tells the new commander what improvements need to be made. Many organizations conduct these types of audit periodically. Moreover, employees know that at, certain points, routines, material, policies and procedures are going to be audited for compliance. In addition to routine audits, periodic unannounced audits are excellent ways of ensuring critical areas of both style and substance are maintained.

Through your analysis of choke points and audits you should continually be looking for training issues. Could you pass the practical portion of your driver's test today? Have you developed personal short-cuts in your driving procedures that might not comply with the department of motor vehicles? The point is we all tend to find short-cuts. It's not necessarily a bad thing, but it is something for which you should look and of which you should discuss with your followers. Indeed, your observations about choke points, audits and training needs should be continually discussed with followers. There is great value in telling a follower that their task is an organization choke point. Let them know that you are following up, not because you are concerned they won't perform, but because the organization requires you to follow up on critical tasks. If their task is critical, or style is as important as substance, let them know. Otherwise, leave them alone and they will surprise you with good results.

Never tell people how to do things. Tell them what to do, and they will surprise you with their ingenuity.

George Patton

CHAPTER FORTY-EIGHT
Ten of Clubs
Active Management

I think that we are all in the right place at the right time almost every day. It's the people who are prepared to be lucky who can take advantage of being there. How do these people position themselves to be lucky? It was Goethe who said, 'Anytime that you take the first step toward trying to achieve something in life, all manner of good things will mysteriously fall into your path to help speed you along your way.' Amen to that!
Phil Hellmuth, 1989 World Series of Poker Champion

Leaders must take an active approach toward management. It is your job to know what is going on in the organization. There are many ways to stay informed and communicate with employees. Both Andrew and Raymond used an approach called "managing by wandering around" (MBWA), a superb management technique put forward by Tom Peters. The essence of this technique is that managers get out of their offices and find out what is happening in the workplace. Managers will obtain more accurate and timely information and use this information to make positive improvements. The key is for managers to follow up on the information they receive.

Retired General and Air Force Chief of Staff Ronald R. Fogleman remarked that "we may never have a perfect vision of what is happening on the battlefield. We'll know the movement, however, not only of the enemy's forces, but of our units with a degree of confidence that has not been possible since the days of Napoleon." General Fogleman explained that "as warfare evolved over the years, commanders have been constrained by their ability to visualize their forces. Napoleon's century was a period of time when the size of the battle was shaped by the ability of commanders to physically see and maintain line of sight to their units." Like the battlefield commander, any leader is constrained in their ability to make sound decisions and influence outcomes by their ability to see what is happening.

The MBWA concept is great, but only if it is applied properly. Many managers were under the impression that if they went out, roamed around, and made small talk, they had effectively done their MBWA for the day. They missed the point. There are several critical components to MBWA. First, it must be done with sincerity. If you are not speaking with employees from a sincere standpoint, it will show and it will backfire on you. If you really do not want to use MBWA, then don't. Insincerity is a waste of time and rarely fools anyone.

Secondly, you must be working to elicit more than surface feedback. Initially, employees will probably provide very superficial information. You have to take the time to get the "good stuff." MBWA is not something to be done once a month on Tuesdays between 3:00 and 4:00 p.m. It is a perpetual, ongoing process. Once it begins, it never ends.

Thirdly, you must be responsive to what you are told. If someone tells you they need a particular piece of equipment, get it for them. If they need some additional training, get it for them. If you sense that they need some recognition, give it to them. Feedback is not worth gathering if you do not do something with that information once you have obtained it. Again, if you are insincere about this process, people recognize it and resent you for it. It is frustrating for you to ask them what they need or what they think then never do anything about it. Make sure that you are putting effort into responding to their input.

There will be times when you cannot do whatever it is your people ask of you and that is acceptable. The key is to get back to the employee in a timely fashion. Tell them that you cannot do what it is they would like and give them the reason why, if possible. People understand that they will not always get what they want, especially if you give a good reason.

Wild Card **KEYS TO ACTIVE MANAGEMENT**
MBWA can be an effective tool when used properly. How you go about gathering information is important. Here are some things to consider as you use an MBWA approach:

- MBWA must be ongoing and routine or it is ineffective;
- You must approach it with a sincere attitude;
- Know which projects employees are currently working on;
- Use probing questions. Yes-and-no answers are not going to help you assess problems in the workplace; and,
- Respond to employee feedback. They will be more forthcoming if they know their views shape your actions.

In addition to MBWA, in today's modern office, the leader has the ability to extend his or her vision further. Recall Fogelman's conclusion; your ability to influence is constrained by your vision. Vision isn't just what you see in person. Vision is also how you get timely, accurate information from sources within your organization. There are a number of technologies that provide leaders with timely, up-to-date, information. The problem is selecting which information or data accurately reflects your business environment. The idea is to use your internal technology to track those items which have the greatest potential of telling you there is a change in the environment.

The change can be either good or bad. A sudden upswing in sales is good, but near real-time information on sales may tell you that because of the sudden surge you have to change production schedules. What would you deduce from an upswing in employee sick time usage? Would you presume the flu has hit your shop or would you peek into the subordinate leader's office and see if there were morale problems brewing? Generally, our 21st Century ability to track multiple sources of data in near real-time is a good thing. Just as with MBWA, if you don't follow-up, go out into the trenches and see what the data actually means, you may miss an important leadership opportunity. Simply put, the data tells you something has changed. You, the leader, must interpret the data for your organization.

The concept of actively interpreting data applies to your conversations with followers. Your ability to institute MBWA is directly related to your ability to interpret what you are being told and what you see. Physical access is the easy part – you can MBWA anytime you want. It is getting your followers to open up and then being able to interpret what they tell you that is difficult. There are three major helpers for increasing your ability to interpret. First, you must be familiar with the follower's jobs. In order to cut through their jargon, slang and short-cut speech, the leader must know what they do. Second, through constant MBWA and follow-through, you must gain the follower's trust. Finally, it is critical that you gain the support and trust of subordinate leaders. Subordinate leaders can be a major impediment to active management. Few want to make their boss look bad. If you are talking to a follower who has a subordinate leader, they are likely to tailor their comments based on their relationship with their primary leader. Short-circuit this; take the subordinate leader along on a few trips. Show everyone that you are interested in what is going on, interested in making improvements, not interested in laying blame or causing dissension. Enlisting and modeling for subordinate leaders is a very powerful active management tool.

Active management is external as well as internal. The further you move up the leadership hierarchy in your business, the more it is expected that you are a boundary spanning agent. Your organization has boundaries. These are the organizational, cultural and physical locations where your firm ends and the real world begins. Sometimes these boundaries are very firm and clear, at other times they are not so clear. No organization is a closed system and your organization is impacted by your environment.

As a boundary spanning agent, the leader scans the external environment for changes that can or should impact his or her organization. Examples of things that can impact your organization are changes in the price of your inputs. Perhaps you notice that fuel costs are increasing. How is that going to affect your organization? On the other hand, the search for new and innovative ideas is an example of something that should impact your organization. Things that can impact your organization are coming no matter what, and you should prepare your organization. Things that should - are probably going to be picked up by your competitors and then the things you missed in the environment will move from the "should impact us" to "can impact us" category!

Open source information about the business, government and even world environment can become critical to your operation. We have grouped together some of the critical digests that you can receive via the Internet on the companion website at www.pokerleadership.com. The website is meant to be a constant work in-progress, so send us your e-sources for possible inclusion.

Among the ways to stay ahead in your industry is to read about what is going on. While trade journals and newspapers are a great source, but they may not provide you with the exact niche you should be looking at. Raymond uses technology to help him stay in tune. He belongs to several "group digests," "listservs" and "blogs" on the Internet. These sources can be general or very specific. But, what they do is provide you a quick, one or two sentence, digest of an article or event. You can quickly scan multiple sources and explore in-depth the most important to you.

Community service and non-governmental organizations are another source of boundary spanning active management. Organizations, like your local chamber of commerce or Rotary Club are an excellent source to get the local "back story." Finally, remain in contact with peers outside your organization. These peers could be people you meet at conferences or from your university, or from your work with a local community service organization. By contact, we mean "loose contact." Loose contacts are people you touch base with every three or four months. You send them an email, make a telephone call, or drop them a note. You will be surprised at the boundary spanning information you will get from loose contacts.

Good management consists of showing average people how to do the work of superior people.

John Rockefeller

CHAPTER FORTY-NINE
Jack of Clubs
Anger

"Tilt" is the term used when a player is upset and their emotions take over. Often, a player on tilt will begin raising with sub par hands in an attempt to win back lost money. Only a poker player with great hubris claims that they never go on tilt. There may be one or two people in the world who are actually capable of never going on tilt, but I have yet to meet any of them. Chances are, what really happens, is that players who claim to never go on tilt actually recognize immediately that they have gone on tilt, and then use relaxation techniques or other measures to regain their composure and allow their brain back into the game.

Oliver Butterick

Leaders can get angry the same as anyone else. However, with the privilege of leadership comes responsibility. One of those responsibilities is to maintain control over your temper. At the card table you pull bad cards and good cards. Some people get angry at the dealer or they get angry at fate, but they are probably really angry at themselves. When card players get angry, they look stupid and they play poorly. On the other hand, sometimes you are playing cards and another player is making your angry. They don't know how to play, they are playing slowly, they are winning when they shouldn't be, or they deal poorly. If you are playing in a really good game they are trying to make you mad because they know when you are angry you will tend to lose.

When you are angry you cannot think clearly. The words you choose will tend to be much more abrasive than when you are calm. Harsh words can have long-term, destructive ramifications, particularly with people who are sensitive by nature. Twenty minutes after you were angry, you may have forgotten what you said. We would be willing to bet that people will take longer to forget. They may never forget at all.

This is not to say that you cannot let your employees know when you are angry. No one expects you to be an emotionless robot. Just be cautious when you feel anger starting to rise and do your best to keep it under control. If you are going to express your anger, do it without raising your voice, pounding your fists, or throwing things. If you just have to spout off, remember: a word off the cuff can end up cutting someone terribly. Finding ways to manage your own stress may keep you calmer in the workplace. You have a greater chance of erupting more often if you let things build up without dealing with them.

Wild Card There are some people who are prone to expressing anger in the workplace and others for whom it is only an occasional occurrence. How do successful leaders avoid problems with anger? Here are some tips:

1. Avoid the "fight" complex. Your body reacts to things going wrong as a threat. You have to intercede and break the pattern so that frustration and anger do not push the violence button. Verbal abuse, tantrums, storming off, and heavy-handed behavior are forms of violence. They have no place in the work environment.

2. When you begin to get angry, remember to take control. Step back and look at the situation from this perspective: what difference will it make in five years?

3. If you begin to get agitated, remember that your adrenaline is flowing. Now is the time for a good brisk walk. Run up five flights of stairs. Work up a sweat. Your body needs to convert the adrenaline or you will have a chemical imbalance that could affect your judgment.

4. As you take your walk, slow down near the end. Pause. Look at the scenery outside. Relax. Remember, whatever the situation, "this too will pass."

5. Meditate and reflect as soon as you are under control and calm. Ask for strength and guidance. Have the assurance that you will make wise choices.

6. Ask yourself "What are you really angry about?" Sometimes people think they know what they're angry about, but it turns out that they have misplaced their anger on the catalyst – the thing that brought your anger into the open. You can't solve a problem until you know exactly what the problem is.

Use these methods, and after a while, you will be able to avoid the "fight" complex entirely. Your heartbeat will remain calm under a trying situation. You will come to realize that the situation does not matter but your reaction to it does. If you can detach yourself far enough to have a long-term perspective, you will be on the way to mastering your emotions. Your confidence will grow because you have achieved self-mastery.

In addition to saying and doing things you might regret, anger has a way of poisoning everything you do. Consider that even, if you have your anger under control, there will be subtle changes in your mannerisms. Changes in your mannerisms (perhaps you're curt, or frown, or gesture with your hands more rapidly, etc.) are a reflection on what is going on inside of you. This means two things. First, everyone knows something is wrong and probably suspects you are angry. Recall in Chapter Fourteen we talked about the importance of your actions and your words working in concert. If there is a disconnect between how you are acting, speaking and the situation, your followers will know it. You will lose credibility. Two, if your mannerisms are an indication that your inward state has changed, so has your decision making ability. In other words, even suppressed anger will manifest itself in poor decision-making.

Dealing with problems as they arise cannot be over emphasized as an anger management technique for both leaders and organizations. How often have you become angry with someone after they did or said something that rekindled a previous problem? Some people tend to add up problems. Recall in a previous chapter we referred to this as "stringing beads." Instead of working through problems as they occur, people ignore something temporarily and add it to the "blast-off list." You've probably experienced this. You said something to someone and they go into orbit for no apparent reason. When they finally land, you find out it wasn't this comment or action, it was that this comment or action was the ignition switch for an already fueled rocket. Leaders can avoid anger in themselves and their organizations by effectively dealing with problems as they occur and not piling straw on camels.

A 1969 episode of Star Trek was entitled "Day of the Dove." You may recall this episode where an alien being takes control of the ship and manages to bring an equal number of Klingons and Star Fleet personnel together into personal battle. As it turns out, the alien entity survives on the emotion of anger. People like these aliens actually exist, and as a leader you have probably encountered them. We are talking about the employees who seem to thrive on strife. The "pot stirrers." Like the witches of MacBeth, they gather around and stir their brew of dissention. Simply said, there are some people trying to make you angry because, when you are angry, the other party has control over you.

When a leader is angry they have given up control. Whatever or whomever made them angry is in the driver's seat. One valuable technique for dissipating your anger is to realize you are not in control. As the leader, you want to be in control, of yourself at least. Regain your control and composure. Exercise your leadership internally; over your ego, over your memory and move forward. Sometimes you can regain mastery of yourself by taking a tactical pause. Recall from an earlier chapter, a tactical pause is walking away from something in order to buy yourself time to think through your actions. Indeed, on some issues you may want a longer or strategic pause. Perhaps, the best advice is to walk it off and think it through before you act.

If you feel that your behavior or thoughts are completely out of your control, you may decide to seek the help of a professional. You could speak to a private therapist or, if your organization provides one, to an employee counselor. If you decide that this is the best route available to you, do not feel that this is a weakness on your part or something of which you should be ashamed. True strength is recognizing and admitting that you have a problem and then taking the necessary steps to correct it. It is just as important for you to recognize when your followers may have an anger control issue. Part of your leadership responsibility is to make sure your followers learn to manage their own anger. If you don't think clearly when you're angry, neither will your followers.

It is easy to fly into a passion – anybody can do that – but to be angry with the right person to the right extent and at the right time and with the right object and in the right way – that is not easy, and it is not everyone who can do it.

Aristotle

When angry, count ten before you speak, if very angry, one hundred.

Thomas Jefferson

CHAPTER FIFTY
Queen of Clubs
Stress

Cards are war, in disguise of a sport

Charles Lamb, "Essays of Elia" (1832)

As a leader, you will have to deal with a great amount of stress. Some of it will be externally imposed and some will be from demands that you impose on yourself. You must first take care of yourself physically and mentally. You cannot effectively lead from the sickbed and you can only psychologically handle so many things at once. According to NASA, "Stress can be defined as a physical and/or emotional reaction that occurs when external demands do not correspond to an individual's capabilities, resources, or needs." As leaders we have some choices. We can increase our capability to handle stress by increasing our physical and emotional state, we can decrease the amount of external and internal demands on ourselves, or both of these approaches can be used in combination. Because we have the ability to control either of the variables (capability or demand) we have the ability to manage our stress.

A certain amount of stress is expected and actually necessary for life. You cannot eliminate all stress from any job and besides, some stress can be beneficial. It motivates us to stay on track and get a job completed. Too much, however, can create problems. A leader must realize that stress can become distress in both the leader and followers. Take care to watch your stress levels. You can help to manage the stress of your employees only after you have ensured your own well-being.

Realize that stress is something that we in part create and control in ourselves. It is an individual reaction to mental or emotional strain of the demands placed on our capabilities. Everyone will have a different stress level and a different reaction to stress because they have different physical and emotional capabilities. Stress, or distress, often derives from frustration and anxiety coupled with fear.

The first defense against stress may be to understand that it is not so much the situation but how you respond to it that creates what we experience as stress.

Sometimes it helps to put the situation or event into perspective. Realize that whatever you are facing may not really be that important. In the big scheme of things, so what? Do not let your mind make more of it than it is. Step back and try to get perspective. Divorce yourself for the situation and look at it from an outsider's point of view. Is the matter at hand worth a heart attack or stroke? Probably not.

Take a break and take a walk. Think about things that are really important: your family; your friends; your life. Imagine a beautiful scene in nature. Relax. Meditate. Ask for spiritual guidance, calmness, and insight. Exercise and relaxation are among the simplest and most powerful techniques for dealing with stress. Exercise not only increases your physical capabilities, but it can also channel the stress into the productivity. As they say on the field of play, "walk it off."

Once you have calmed down, carefully and slowly approach the situation. What are things you can change and things you cannot? Focus only on the things you can change. Don't waste time and emotions on the "would have, could have, should have, if only, or why didn't" factors. It is done; let go of that. You can get all hot and bothered about these things, but you are wasting your time, except for the context of what was to be learned from what happened. Move on.

Make up a list of what you can reasonably expect to do to address the issues that you can change. If there is a time deadline, can you get it changed? If there is information you need, how can you get it? Where can you find help to achieve as many of the objectives as possible? In addition to changing your perspective, you may have to change or adjust priorities. Being able to properly prioritize your work and life will aide you in accomplishing what is important. Realizing that whatever you are unable to accomplish perhaps wasn't that important in the larger scheme of your tasks.

Once you have a list of prioritized action items, work on the list of items one at a time. Check them off. Proceed carefully but as efficiently as possible. If you are not going to make a deadline, let people know ahead of time. Ask for help. Relax, work hard, but remember that whatever the task or deadline, it is likely to be arbitrary. Do not try to be a hero by shouldering all this "pressure" to prove something.

Take time to meditate during your work. It is amazing how inspiration can come from a little time spent thinking about things from a different perspective. We are not talking about you placing yourself in some yoga position and humming out loud. Close your office door, dim your lights and think. One of the biggest recommendations for reducing stress is to control your environment. Reduce the noise and action around you, relax and focus your thoughts. You may choose to focus on some pleasant place, or perhaps to focus on the smallest part of the task you are facing. The point is to focus your mind internally and control the external environment.

Don't unnecessarily stress your followers. Be conscious of the amount of work you give your employees. Check with them continually to see how they are doing in managing their workload. Do not overload subordinates to the point where they are overwhelmed. When employees feel overly taxed, they begin experiencing burn out. This is when stress levels will rise. This is not good for performance and it is not good for the long-term welfare of employees or the organization.

This story illustrates a failure to understand the amount of work someone has to perform:

Mary was married to a male chauvinist. They both worked full-time but he never did anything around the house and certainly not any housework. That, he declared, was women's work. But one evening, Mary arrived home from work to find the children bathed, a load of wash in the washing machine, dinner on the stove, and a beautifully set dining table. She was astonished and asked her husband, Charley, what was going on. He said that he had read an article that suggested working wives would be more romantically inclined if they were not so tired from having to do all the housework and hold down a full-time job. The next day, she couldn't wait to tell her friends at the office. They asked how it worked out. Mary said, "Well, it was a great dinner. Charley even cleaned up, helped the kids with their homework, and folded the laundry." One of her friend's asked, "But what about afterward?" "It didn't work out," Mary said. "Charley was too tired."

Wild Card ARE YOU TOO STRESSED?

It is important to recognize stress-related problems early on before you become overloaded. Take measures to deal with it before the problem gets out of hand. Look for these symptoms:

- You feel tired at work and lack energy;
- You become easily irritated at work;
- You feel like everyone is on your case to get things done;
- You can't seem to get anything done. Your productivity is poor, and vital projects get ignored;
- You can't seem to get started on a project. You procrastinate for no reason;
- Doing a good job is less of a priority for you than it used to be;
- You drag your feet all morning or have trouble getting out of bed because the thought of going to work is torturous;
- Work is becoming increasingly boring, even activities you used to enjoy seem tedious;
- Your attitude toward your job, company, supervisors or coworkers has become increasingly negative;
- Work, its consequences, and feelings toward it are affecting your personal life; and,
- Your sleeping and eating patterns have changed, either increasing or decreasing markedly.

You need to be aware that being stressed out for long periods of time can be symptomatic of clinical depression. If you exhibit these symptoms, you should seek professional assistance from a psychologist or other mental health professional.

Manage workloads carefully. Be sensitive to people's stress levels by observing them and asking them directly how they are doing. Remember that your goal as a leader is not simply to get them to finish the current project; it is to keep them functioning at a high level for many years.

In addition to decreasing the external demands by prioritizing work demands, etc., work on increasing your capabilities to handle stress. Diet, exercise and a wide range of interests will increase your ability to manage stress. Remember, stress is a necessary part of life. Stress is the result of balancing our capabilities with external demands. You control the balance. Don't let it become distress.

People who cannot find time for recreation are obliged sooner or later to find time for illness.

John Wanamaker

CHAPTER FIFTY-ONE
King of Clubs
Firing

The next best thing to gambling and winning is gambling and losing.

Nick "The Greek" Dandalos

It might seem odd to find a chapter on firing in a book on leadership, but when forced to take such an action, it is the ultimate test of a good leader under the most trying of circumstances. One of the most common misconceptions that employees have about firing is that it is enjoyable to take such actions. Show us a person who thinks it is fun to fire an employee, and we will show you someone who probably has never had to do it.

We have been involved in many cases that resulted in firing: some were trainees; probationary employees; tenured employees who were fired for poor performance; and, tenured employees who were fired for engaging in misconduct. Every single one of these cases was a difficult experience for us. Even if the employee deserved it, the act of firing is painful and awkward. Firing someone is a gut-wrenching action and it is one of the least enjoyable duties of leadership.

That being said, sometimes firing has to be done when it is in the best interest of the organization. No one person, no matter how high up, can be allowed to drag everyone else down. Employees are required to carry their own weight and act in accordance with law, policy, and procedure. They are expected to be capable and competent. If not, termination of employment may be the result. There are a few salient leadership issues about firing a follower. The rules regarding cause, documentation and method vary widely depending on local laws and organizational agreements, customs and policy. There is no one set of rules about how, why or when a follower should be fired. The act of terminating employment has huge personal and organizational consequences. The best advice is to be up to par on your local laws and organization's policies.

Although there are no universal laws (save those outlined in the Civil Rights Act) or universal organizational policies, there are two interesting and quite common occurrences. First, leaders wait too long. Sometimes, because termination is unpleasant, leaders delay the inevitable. Once someone has to go, they generally have to go now. Avoiding an unpleasant act is only going to make it worse. A second mistake leaders make is terminating employment in a manner inconsistent with the law or organizational policy. This is one of those occasions when you, as the leader, should seek expert advice. It's not that you should avoid terminating employment; it is that you should protect your organization by making sure that you have done the right thing the right way.

If your position requires that you fire people when necessary, you may hear rumors that you are known by such lovely names as "assassin" and "hatchet man." Sometimes, your popularity will decline because of the actions you had to take. The truth of these situations may be distorted completely by rumor and speculation. It is your job, however, to distance yourself personally from this. You will have responsibilities as a leader that you do not enjoy, but that comes with the territory. Recall that leadership is not a popularity contest; it is a trust between you, the followers and the organization.

An example of this happened to Andrew once when a popular and tenured employee had to be terminated. There was absolutely no question that this employee needed to be fired; it was not even a close call. As it happened, the case wrapped up almost on Christmas Day. Firing someone at Christmas is not Andrew's idea of a good time, whether they deserved it or not. The employee was kept on the payroll for two weeks beyond Christmas out of compassion for his family and the time of the year. A week into the new year, the employee was terminated. Although this happened many years ago, to this day there is still talk about how poor old so-and-so was fired intentionally on Christmas. As we said, it is not a popularity contest and sometimes you will not come out unscathed. This can happen even when you make every effort to be fair and compassionate. This is the responsibility of leadership.

It may be that the term "firing" comes from discharging a weapon – as in firing a gun. Indeed, firing and discharging an employee are often used interchangeably. Firing also means to harden through fire, as in firing clay pots or steel beams. Firing a follower can have this effect on your organization. When you terminate employment, you are sending a message on the outside limits of employee conduct. You are firing the boundaries – making them firmer. It may very well be that by demonstrating the boundaries in such a vivid manner you keep other followers on the correct path. The point is that all discipline, through and including termination, should be done for the good of the organization.

There are a few final points on firing someone. First, if you're going to fire someone, you need to look the person in the eye while doing so. You do not e-mail the person; you do not send a memo; you surely do not call in a consultant to notify the employee. Give the person the respect of a face-to-face meeting. There may be exceptions to this in cases where it is reasonably anticipated that the employee may become violent. We are sensitive to this concern since, being in law enforcement, most of the people we had to fire came to the meeting with a gun strapped to their hip. However, this concern for security must not be used to mask the inadequacy or cowardice of the boss when it is time to fire an individual.

Secondly, if you are positively convinced that someone needs to be fired, do it quickly. As we related, we have seen leaders struggle forever with this issue, even when they knew for a fact that the person had to be fired. If you are sure, do not waste time (Christmas Day excluded, of course).

Thirdly, remember that being let go may be one of the best things that can happen to an employee. As old doors are shut, new ones may open for that person. The leader must respect the fact that the employee is not performing as expected and might even be unhappy. Also, it is more often the case than not that the employee sees it coming. Try to frame it from the employee's perspective. If one is not happy, not doing well, unable or unwilling to complete the work, or cannot adhere to company policy, then it may be in this person's best interest to be separated from the company. Conclude that it is not worth it for them to be unhappy and, therefore, a separation is best. They will then be free to pursue an opportunity that is better suited for them. Express your support and offer to help them, but only if you really mean it.

Also remember that, for many people, getting fired can be one of the most traumatic events of their entire lives. Be as gentle and compassionate as you possibly can under the circumstances. Even if you are upset with the person, present the news in a caring manner. Finally, if you lose sleep over having to fire someone, don't worry. This is normal. We would only tell you to worry if you were able to fire people without losing any sleep. Most likely, this task is going to be stressful and perhaps emotionally disturbing for you. You are human. Do not see this as a weakness.

It is very important that you follow the law and good-business practices before you fire someone. Again, be sure that you have documented the grounds for firing. Be sure that you have a written record of the events surrounding the firing. Never fire someone on the spot out of anger. Have a witness and make a written record of what was said when you fire someone.

Donald Trump's popular television show "The Apprentice", has made "You're fired" a national catch phrase. Of course, all of the contestants are not actual employees, so in point of fact they can't really be fired. However, saying "You are no longer being considered for the position" just doesn't have quite the same impact! Even though the show only pretends to fire people, there appears to still be a great deal of anguish on the part of both the "boss", and the "employees" when one gets "fired".

Back to the real world for a moment, firing is not easy, nor is it supposed to be. It is somewhat of a failure on everyone's part, including the organization. Firing sometimes points out organizational problems because someone hired, trained and supervised the follower. Somewhere along the way, the organization failed in its screening, training and supervision. That said, in some cases it must be done. In all instances it should be handled with complete professionalism and as much genuine compassion as the circumstances allow. Remember, firing doesn't just affect the person being fired. Everyone left behind will be watching what happened and how the person was treated. Many will place themselves in the fired person's position and wonder if they could be next. Keep this in mind, so that after someone is fired you are sensitive to the fact that there may be individuals remaining in the organization whose morale may have dropped as a result of your decision to fire a fellow employee.

Failure is, in a sense, the highway to success, inasmuch as every discovery of what is false leads us to seek earnestly after what is true.

John Keatts

What is defeat? Nothing but education. Nothing but the first step to something better.

Wendell Phillips

CHAPTER FIFTY-TWO
Ace of Clubs
Putting it all Together

POKER, n. A game said to be played with cards for some purpose to this lexicographer unknown.

Ambrose Bierce, "The Devil's Dictionary" (1906)

We started with the concept of leadership primarily as an art. Like most art, leadership has some underpinnings in science. Just as there are theories supporting the use of certain colors and strokes in painting, there are also theories that suggest a course of action for the leader. Walk through an art gallery with someone. What appeals to you, the painting or music that reaches you, may not reach the person you are with. You may see inspiration, they may see confused swirls; you may hear a symphony, they may hear organized noise. Art is both inspired and interpreted. Leadership is thusly so.

There is no one master technique that applies to all followers at all times. You may employ one leadership strategy one day and find that it fails the next, or your efforts to motivate one follower works well while with another they fail. People are very different and respond to different types and methods of stimuli. Added to the confusion of all the different people is the rapidly changing environment. Everything grows, shifts and changes and the people and environment are not going to adapt to you. You must learn and adapt to them.

Of course, just as there was a Rembrandt and a Mozart, there was an Eisenhower and a Jack Welch. There are people who have natural talent. They come along and make it look easy. Then there are the rest of us. We are the studio musicians who work hard, practice and play because we have some talent, but a lot of heart and passion. We make it to the top by hard work, practice and timely mistakes. You may have learned about leadership in this book and others, but you aren't a leader until you're out there in the trenches with your followers.

Leadership is probably more like poker than we have been able to express. The rules are always the same but the hands, games and tables are always different.

Each play requires your experience and your intuition. Your ability to read the situation, rely on your understanding of the theories of play, and your decisive use of the cards. The leadership tools in the preceding chapters are the cards. You have to decide when to play them, when to fold, and when to raise. Leadership is about people, not things. That's why it's difficult. If you build a brick wall (assuming you know how to do this), the bricks stay where you put them. You lay your plumb line, place your brick, apply the mortar and move to the next brick. After a few days, the bricks are there – set in stone. You could never do this with people. As soon as you lay your plumb line someone will knock it over, another will move one end and a third will find fault. As you place the people in a line, they squirm and resist. You would simply never be able to force people to line up and stay lined up. However, you can convince them, you can influence them, and you can get them to line up. Yes, they'll still squirm, resist and move your plumb line, but they will line up for you. To get them to line up you are going to have to figure out which of your leadership tools will be the most influential.

Just as the cards change, the people at the table change. Like your followers, some come and some go. Perhaps more importantly, the players that stay are also growing; they are learning and changing. What works in one hand won't work again. Just as you figure out how to get them to line up they will change or the environment will change. You have to grow with your followers. Stay ahead and lead. If you are a really good leader you are going to find your followers surpassing you. They're going to know the play before you do. This is because one of the fundamental tasks of leadership is to grow the next batch of leaders.

Las Vegas entertainer Wayne Newton started out in show business with Jack Benny as his mentor. Someone once asked Benny if he was concerned that Newton would "steal the show" from him. Benny replied that if Newton wasn't capable of stealing the show he wouldn't have hired him in the first place. So it should be with leadership as well.

At the end of the day, how can one sum up the essence of leadership? We're not sure it can be done, but we'll try: Leadership is about being fair, ethical, and kind. It's about knowing where you want to go, and leading by example. It's about being honest and trustworthy, caring and competent. It's about showing every day that you have your follower's best interests at heart as you balance the need for overall organizational success. Most simply put, it is about the people.

Every victory and every mistake in your organization is an opportunity for you to groom the next generation of leaders. Here, we return to both the art and poker metaphor. Both master artists and poker players had master teachers. Someone taught you because leadership, like art and poker, is an apprenticeship. It is a life-long journey. More than passing on your skills to the next generation, you should be identifying those followers with the most potential for leadership. Pick an apprentice – be a mentor.

REFERENCES

Anderson, Leith, How to Win at Parish Poker. January 1, 1986, ChristianityToday.com.

Anthony, Ray. Innovative Leadership: Spark Plug of Progress. Innovative Leader, 7(3), 1998.

Associates, The Department of Behavioral Sciences and Leadership at the United States Military Academy. Leadership in Organizations. Garden City Park, NY: Avery Publishing, 1988.

Bennis, Warren G. Managing People is Like Herding Cats. Cambridge: Perseus Pub., 2000.

Blanchard, Kenneth H. and Spencer Johnson. The One Minute Manager. La Jolla, CA: Blanchard-Johnson Publishers, 1982.

Brown, R. (n.d.). Design Jobs that motivate and develop people. Retrieved November 14, 2005, from http://www.media-associates.co.nz/fjobdesign.html.

Butterick, Oliver. Jedi Mind Ricks. BABBLOG. Retrieved March 19, 2006 at http://www.babblog.com/Nov_04/111004_OB_Poker.htm.

Childress, John R. and Larry E. Senn. The Secret of a Winning Culture: Building High-Performance Teams. Los Angeles: Leadership Press, 1999.

Cooke, Roy. Integrity — Part II: Sooner or Later? That's the $64,000 Question! Card Player Magazine, 18(8): 2005.

Cooke, Roy. Telegraphing your Thoughts. Card Player Magazine. 17(15) Retrieved November 1, 2005 at http://www.cardplayer.com/poker_magazine/archives/showarticle.php?a_id=14113&m_id=65540.

References

Covey, Stephen R. Principle-Centered Leadership. New York: Summit Books, 1991.

DiGiovanni, C. Stability of Personal Life, and Unit Cohesion, United States Marine Corps, Infantry Officers Course, Retrieved January 15, 2006 at http://www.mcu.usmc.mil/TbsNew/Pages/Officer%20Courses/Infantry%20 Officer%20Course/Human%20Factors/Pages/page5.htm.

Effective Stress Management. NASA. Retrieved March 19, 2006 at http:// ohp.nasa.gov/cope/welcome.htm.

Fogleman, Roland. Information Operations: The Fifth Dimension of Warfare. Remarks as delivered by Gen. Ronald R. Fogleman, Air Force chief of staff, to the Armed Forces Communications-Electronics Association, Washington, April 25, 1995.

Gifford, Jack J. Invoking Force of Will to Move the Force [Electronic Version]. United States Command Studies Institute, Studies in Battle Command. Retrieved January 1, 2006 at http://www-cgsc.army.mil/carl/resources/csi/battles/ battles.asp. Communication, Confidence, Downtime,

Hawn, C. (2004). The B in Business Stands for Bluff. Fast Company, 80, p. 38.

Hersey, Paul and Kenneth H. Blanchard. Management of Organizational Behavior: Utilizing Human Resources. Englewood Cliffs, NJ: Prentice-Hall, 1982.

Katzenbach, J.R. & Smith, D.K. The Wisdom of Teams: Creating the High-performance Organization. New York, NY: 2003.

Kaufman, Herbert. Time, Chance and Organizations. Chatham , NJ: Chatham House Publishers, 1991. Henry, Nicholas. Public Administration and Public Affairs. Upper Saddle River, NJ: 2001.

Kouzes, James M. and Barry Z. Posner. The Leadership Challenge: How to Get Extraordinary Things Done in Organizations. San Francisco: Jossey-Bass, 1987.

Loynes, Chris. "Expedition Leadership." Planners Handbook and Directory 1993-1994. London, Eng.: Expedition Advisory Centre, Royal Geographical Society.

McComas, Rich. 101 Famous Poker Quotes. Retrieved November 1, 2005 at http://www.holdemsecrets.com/quotes.htm.

Moore, Mark H. Creating Public Value: Strategic Management in Government. Cambridge, MA: Harvard University Press, 2001.

Morgan, Bill. Consistency is Critical to Good Leadership, Leadership Essay, United States Coast Guard. Retrieved March 1, 2006 at http://www.uscg.mil/LEADERSHIP/news/summer03/essay.htm.

Phillips, Donald T. Lincoln on Leadership: Executive Strategies for Tough Times. New York: Warner Books, 1992.

Powell, Colin. My American Journey. Ballantine Books, New York, NY.

Robbins, Stephen P. Organizational Behavior. Upper Saddle River, NJ: Prentice Hall, 1998.

Sashkin, Marshall and Kenneth J. Kiser. Putting Total Quality Management to Work: What TQM Means, How to Use It, and How to Sustain It over the Long Run. San Francisco: Berrett-Koehler, 1993.

Swift, Ken, Rounders: The Intersection of Law and Poker . Picturing Justice: The Online Journal of Law and Culture. Retrieved December 1, 2005 at http://www.usfca.edu/pj/rounders_swift.htm.

Tannenbaum, Robert and Warren H. Schmidt. "How to Choose a Leadership Pattern." *Harvard Business Review.* Boston: Harvard Business School, March/April 1958.

Townsend, Robert. Further Up the Organization. New York: Knopf, 1984.

Twain, Mark. The Prince and the Pauper. New York, NY: Tor Book: 1988.

Urwin, George J.W. Discipline, Camaraderie, and Luck: A Tale of POW Survival. Twenty-Fifth George Bancroft Memorial Lecture, United States Naval Academy, Annapolis, Maryland, October 18, 2004. Retrieved December 20, 2005 at http://www.temple.edu/cenfad/strategic-visions/SV-Spring2005/features-urwin.html.

Wheeler, Michael. True or False? Lie Detection at the Bargaining Table, Negotiation, 1(1): 2003.

Whittington, Beau. Why Soldiers Fight. Army News Service, Aug. 27, 2003.

Williams, Walter E. Fairness: Results Versus Process [Electronic version]. The Freeman: Ideas on Liberty, 38(10): 1988.

Wolford, Henry. Delegation Strategies: Playing the Hand you're Dealt. Chiropractic Economics, October 2001, retrieved December 20, 2005 at http://www.chiroeco.com/article/2001/2001.php3?article=1001f2&menu=1001.

Wouk, Herman. The Caine Mutiny. New York, NY: Back Bay Books, 1992.

Von Oech, Roger. A Whack on the Side of the Head: How to Unlock Your Mind for Innovation. Menlo Park, CA: Creative Think, 1983.

Von Clauswitz, Carl. On War. Princeton, NJ, Princeton University Press: 1989.

Made in the USA
Charleston, SC
20 September 2011